CLASS STRUGGLE IN CLASSLESS POLAND

CLASS STRUGGLE IN CLASSLESS POLAND

Stanislaw Starski

SOUTH END PRESS
BOSTON

943.8
S

Library of Congress Catalog Card Number: 82-80691

ISBN 0-89608-139-7 paper
ISBN 0-89608-140-0 cloth

Design, typesetting and paste-up done by the South End Press Collective

Cover by Wojciech Wolynski

SOUTH END PRESS
302 Columbus Avenue
Boston MA 02116

CONTENTS

Publisher's Preface

Stanislaw Starski first got in touch with us about two years ago. He had read some of our books and wished to receive others. We wrote letters back and forth and on one occasion even met. When the Polish workers' struggle intensified, we asked Starski if he would be interested in writing a book describing and analyzing the events for a Western audience. He replied affirmatively and the project that led to this book was under way.

In October 1981, with much of the manuscript complete— Starski sent us regular installments, the book being simultaneously journalistic and analytic, maturing with changing circumstances— two of us were again able to meet and interview Starski and others in Solidarity and to visit Warsaw, Poznan, and Gdansk.

It was agreed that upon arriving back in the states with still another installment of the manuscript, we should prepare the finished book as soon as possible. We would continue to edit to make the finished work more readable in the West, while also trying to preserve its Polish idioms. At that time we felt that the last installment, received from Starski during our October trip to Poland, would be the conclusion to the book. In early December we decided at a South End Press meeting that events had again changed significantly enough to warrant still another chapter. We wrote Starski requesting that he address the question "Which Way

Poland?" and he replied in a letter sent just two days before the December martial law crackdown was announced. He wrote, "Yes, I am quite willing, I will tour Poland, do many interviews, and get thirty to forty typewritten pages to you by early January."

Not having heard from Starski as of January 20th 1982, we decided not to delay publication any longer. We can only hope that Starski is well and that he will not only have the pleasure of seeing his book in print but will also be able to write a sequel about events since martial law was declared, events which we hope will lead to the ultimate resurrection of Solidarity and transformation of Polish society.

In the absence of Starski's concluding chapter, we decided to add our own brief postscript addressing some of the issues raised by the crackdown, and describing some possible outcomes of the current repression. We are not attempting to put words into Starski's mouth, nor do we claim that our postscript represents his views exactly though we have tried to make it consistent with the rest of the volume and with ideas he has expressed in person. In this sense, it is our effort to conclude Starski's book rather than to comprehensively present our own views on the issues. When and if Starski can provide us with a concluding chapter of his own or a supplementary volume covering the period after martial law was decreed, we will certainly make these available. Until that time, however, we hope he will appreciate our postscript in the spirit of solidarity in which it has been written.

Class Struggle in Classless Poland is a volume written in the crucible of unfolding events. The author has of necessity not even had an opportunity to examine his publisher's editorial alterations to the finished volume. Each chapter was written and then dispatched to us. There was to be no fine-tuning as the author's own perspective changed with unfolding events. Western readers must keep in mind that, while they assess the book and its arguments at one point in time, it was actually written over many months in a different and rapidly changing context. *Class Struggle in Classless Poland* is not a careful, after-the-fact scholarly analysis, but, as Starski himself says, a "committed study," something unfortunately far more rare.

Why Support Solidarity?

The Polish revolutionary upheavals addressed by this book are of world historic importance, yet there is considerable confusion about exactly why this is so. People with different motives equally proclaim the importance of the Polish events and equally pronounce their solidarity with the Polish resistance movement. We would like to take this opportunity to explain why we at South End Press feel the events are important—why we feel solidarity—and how our motives and those of many other Western analysts differ.

Perhaps it will be clearest if we begin by describing some ways that others conceive the importance of the events. On the night of December 23rd, President Reagan appealed to the country to support the Polish workers and expressed his own horror at their plight. On the surface his words were moving and noble; they seemed sincere. Was it the truth or only one more effective performance?

Among the people who feel the Polish events are profoundly important, there are, first, those we might lump in the "Reagan camp." Certainly the President himself fits here, as do Alexander Haig, many other politicians like Patrick Moynihan, and many ranking members of society, whether industrialists, journalists, or members of our "academic elite." No doubt, there are also many other people who identify with Reagan's pronouncements, but whether all these people really belong to this camp is in considerable doubt. For what distinguishes the Reagan camp is its members' power and their rank hypocrisy, traits that are not shared so palpably by "regular folk."

Proclaiming solidarity with the Polish people on grounds of horror over injustice in any form, these men do little to let the American public know the real motives of the Polish workers. Their "support" is insincere, incomplete, and ill-motivated. For example, the industrialist who bemoans the plight of Polish steelworkers thinks nothing of firing U.S. workers, of forcing those he retains to accept reduced wages and benefits, and at the same time redoubling his efforts to pressure the government to restrict unemployment insurance and welfare payments. He is prepared to call in the police, arrest union officials and bust unions if the workers resist. Imagine his apoplexy if "his" workers were to occupy "his" plant, refusing to leave until everyone fired was rehired, as workers have done in Poland.

The "unbiased, objective" journalist who writes glowingly of the "fires of freedom" in Gdansk, neglects to relay the whole truth about the PATCO workers in the U.S., has no time to notice the denial of labor and human rights throughout Latin America, and even extols the virtues of political thugs who engage in the most repressive conceivable policies, so long as those policies are labelled in our "national interest." Like the industrialist, this friend of freedom and truth sees the world through cloudy glasses. Reality is what serves one's interest, what complies with one's beliefs and desires, what one wants to be true. Realities that are other than the industrialist or journalist likes are not seen, or obscured, or simply distorted. We might add that Western bankers have been a bit more honest in their perceptions and appraisals. One need only read the pages of *Business Week* and similar organs to learn of their equanimity over the Polish events. They are pleased to see that these rowdy workers are to be disciplined and brought back into line so that Western loans can be properly secured.

The industrialist concerned for the Polish workers and the journalist basking in the light of his "honest, hard hitting reports on Poland" are like the technocrats and reporters in Czechoslavakia who brag of their concern for PATCO workers or migrant workers in New Mexico, but who are oblivious to the truth about Poland or their own country. Hypocrites.

Free enterprise does not equal freedom. The same president who lights a candle for Polish workers, snuffs out the Christmas cheer of thousands of U.S. workers by redistributing their wealth into the hands of "defense" industrialists and other "needy" souls. The same president who bemoans Soviet support for Polish martial law militarily supports the perpetual crackdown in Chile, Salvador, Guatemala, South Africa, South Korea, and other bastions of "free world" values. Reagan's consternation over the plight of Polish workers is only a facade covering his glee at the opportunity to use international crimes of "the East" to promote a nationalistic fervor that might mask the crimes he is committing and intends to continue to commit and to enlarge in the West. His noble sentiments for Poles run no deeper than his fear of Khaddafy— both are simpleminded manifestations of his need to divert the U.S. public's attention from his efforts to rob from the poor and give to the rich here in the U.S. and to impose multinational horrors on the people of Latin America and throughout the so-called free world.

Reagan's camp is not distinguished by its intelligence or humanity but by its cynicism and corruption of human feeling. That many people are confused by its expressions of "good will" is a testimony to the power of our media to distort reality. Hopefully this will be at least partially undercut by this first hand presentation of the history of the Polish events and of the Polish people's desires.

A second camp of people who find the Polish movement very important are those who are horrified by injustice wherever they perceive it, but have no real ideological commitments. Their concern for the Polish people is sincere but limited to a desire that no more blood be shed. It does not extend to a deep understanding of the systemic reasons for the Polish events, nor do these individuals see the events as a source of inspiration and lessons for other people throughout the Eastern or the Western alliance of nations. Hopefully this volume will not only promote such understanding, but also give evidence of the need for political and social commitment if indeed we are to ever reach a time when "no more blood need be shed."

It must be added, regrettably, that there is also a group, both in the United States and in Western Europe, who feel that Solidarity is indeed an anti-socialist movement, one disruptive of the stability of the East and deserving of repression, either at the hands of the Polish authorities or, if necessary, their Soviet allies. This group takes the illogic of the popular slogan "my enemy's enemy is my friend" to its ultimate irrationality. As they are opposed to capitalism in all its forms and as they hope for "socialism" (in some form or another), they feel allegiance to the heritage that extends back to the Russian revolution. Their vision is no less clouded than that of the Reagan camp. Where the latter cannot perceive the crimes of the West, the former simply cannot accept the possibility of crimes—unpardonable crimes—in the East. As the Reaganites reorder their perceptions to preserve the myth that the West has a just, equitable, and humane social system, so these people readjust their perceptions to preserve the myth that the East is socialist. They deny that there is "class struggle in classless Poland," instead cynically arguing that there is only confusion sowed by Western agents. It is almost an exact reversal of the time-honored mythology that all strikes, civil rights movements, and other struggles for change in the West must be products of manipulation by outside agents, preferably in service to Moscow. While it is necessary to understand how this inversion can come about, it is wrong to give in to it. It is a disservice not only to the Poles who are seeking extrication from both international and national servitude, but also to all people who would fight for social change in the modern world not out of fealty to others, but out of respect for human potentials. Hopefully the detailed accounts in this volume, the transcriptions of speeches by Polish leaders, and the clarification of the aims and methods of Solidarity will go a long way to reducing the membership of this camp.

A final group feels solidarity with the Polish workers' movement not only out of empathy for people enduring acts of repressive violence, but also out of solidarity with the movement's aims and methods. Most members of this last group also call themselves "socialists" yet simultaneously decry the systems of the Eastern Bloc countries as dictatorial and in no way desirable models. This camp—and South End Press is a part of it—wishes the Polish movement success both for the well being of the Polish people and in the hope that their success might initiate a process of true socialist transformation in the East, simultaneously providing some models and lessons for us in the West. While we do not live in the same kind of system as the Poles, neither do we have the freedom and self-management over our lives that the Polish workers are fighting for.

The rage which members of this last camp feel over injustices in Poland is not much different than the rage we feel over injustices occurring in other parts of the world where people are also denied their human rights, their well-being, and their lives, often in even more repressive and debilitating circumstances than those in Poland. As great as our outrage at the killing of miners in Poland or the denial of Poles' means of communication, or the imposition of curfews or increases in hunger in Poland, we are also outraged at the yearly massacre of tens of thousands of people throughout Latin America, the starvation there and in many other parts of the world, and the general degradation and denial of rights that occur in many of the fascistic dictatorships that compose the so-called free-world.

At the same time, the hope which members of this camp feel about the Polish events is somewhat different than the hope we feel regarding liberation movements in many other countries equally savaged by injustices. To this group, the Polish workers' movement has visibly embodied *real* socialist values—a desire for self-management and participatory democracy, a growth of real human solidarity, the burgeoning of institutional forms that decentralize power and enhance social participation—to a degree that few other movements have. It has revealed the inadequacies of societies that call themselves "socialist"—the so-called classless societies in which class struggle persists—yet it has done so not to foster a sense of helplessness about a better world and not to extol the virtues of a system that is equally bankrupt and hypocritical as it masquerades under the label "free," but to try to create a new system that could truly bring to life the values people have long cherished as social and humane.

Our hope in publishing this book is that it will have a meaning and impact that affects at least some of the followers of all four camps mentioned above. First, hopefully the book will provide a rich source of analysis that can clarify what exactly has happened in Poland and what lessons can be learned regarding processes of social transformation and their aims.

Second, the reader who has always felt empathy for those who suffer injustice but has never taken political sides is asked to take the leap to a positive stance; he or she will hopefully learn to ask, "what needs to be changed to alter the circumstanes that give rise to injustice in the first place?" Taking this question seriously is what has made Solidarity such an important historical force.

Third, if this book is to be read by citizens of the West in a productive manner, its lessons must be applied not only to a world we can have almost no impact on—the world of the Poles, Czechs, and Russians—but also to our own lives and societies. The spirit of the Polish movement and the values it seeks to make real must be compared to the spirit of our own lives in the West and to the values that characterize our factories and shopping malls, our defense department, drug dispensaries, and supply sider think tanks. And we must then begin to think about, to judge, and to act on our own circumstances and potentials in our own ways, much as members of Solidarity have thought about, judged, and begun to act on their circumstances in their own ways.

Finally, regarding the Reagan camp. Hopefully those people who have been deceived into thinking that Reagan, Haig, et al. really care about the well-being of people in Poland will be assisted by this book in realizing that it just isn't so. Their "feelings" of solidarity with the Polish people have literally nothing to do with the actual aims these people espouse nor even the pains they endure, but are instead purely opportunistic. If Reagan's rhetoric about Poland were real, if it were backed by humane concern, he would be on the TV every day also decryng the atrocities of members of the so-called free world, including the U.S., and presumably acting to terminate them. But no, his human concern, his words of empathy, solidarity, and even of praise for the virtues of social justice and popular struggle surface only when they can serve as a tool in his own efforts to create an international climate of fear and hostility suited to his inhumane designs for U.S. machinations in Latin America, the Mideast, Southern Africa and other parts of the world. Hopefully readers of this book will see analogies not between Reagan and Walesa, where there are none, but between Reagan and Brezhnev; between the Polish miners in Silesia and U.S. miners in Appalachia; between Poles as a nation trying to extricate themselves from Soviet domination and Salvadorians as a nation trying to extricate themselves from U.S. domination. Then Starski's volume not only will have served to increase our understanding of events in the East, but also to sensitize us to the reality of our own circumstances in the West.

Foreword

The world response to the Polish Summer of 1980 was mixed
and slightly confused. Though commentators recognized that a
strong, organized, political movement had won a major victory for
Polish working people, and though they also understood that the
political struggle was won via political forms, formulae, and organizations, very few saw the profoundly socialist, egalitarian and marxist nature of Solidarity.

No wonder. "Existing socialism" has for many years monopolized marxist and socialist imagery, thus rendering many ideological catchphrases suspect and ambiguous. Observers could not
help being amazed by the force of religious and nationalist feelings
and by the generally mild character of the whole process.

1

This book has been written to explain why Poles have remained determined to change their political, economic, and social system while simultaneously respecting the force of external restraints imposed on their domestic political processes: Poland's vast economic dependence on Western capitalist states and its equally vast dependence on the military and ideological system of the Eastern "socialist" states.

This book has been written by an eyewitness and active participant in the struggle at the local and regional level. Ever since August 1980, I have participated in the work of Solidarity. But I was not at all unique in this. On the contrary, what happened to me after August 1980 was very typical for a member of my generation and life experience. In all branches of Solidarity and in all walks of life I have met similar people with whom camraderie and communication are spontaneous—together we knew what was to be done, and, needless to say, we shared the energy and commitment necessary to do it.

However, no one in this generation of Polish activists has been free of doubt and fear. Graduating around 1968 and growing up in increasingly absurd circumstances, we knew all too well that there would be no easy victories, no swift and happy march forward, but we felt there was no other choice but to try. We were sentenced by circumstances to political activity, to genuine political thinking, to striving for a more just, truthful, and socialist society. When the Gdansk shipyard workers produced the banner "Proletarians of all factories unite" (instead of "all countries"—which in our part of Europe implies only brotherly tanks representing the Voice of Historical Materialism) we understood that a new struggle was being waged and that we were a part of it.

This foreword should therefore inform readers that this is a committed study. The author feels no remorse—and hopes that neither will the reader.

PART ONE

A HISTORY OF
CLASSLESSNESS IN POLAND

Chapter One

Historical Statism
In Postwar Poland

After 1945 the making of a new type of state in Poland met with relatively tame responses from most sectors of Polish society. The reasons for the relative lack of discussion and struggle over reconstruction in Poland were twofold.

On the one hand, there was the experience of WWII. This started with a new partition of Poland due to the Ribbentrop-Molotov pact and ended with Poland in the allied camp but at the mercy of Stalin, who treated Poland very much in the same manner as allied forces treated defeated Germany. This subservience, coupled with the mass destruction and systematic genocide that had taken place during the war, left most sectors of our society too debilitated to be actively concerned about Poland's postwar destiny.

Secondly, the making of a new Polish state occurred in stages. The mixture of gradual state-ization and monopolization of political initiatives by a new ruling elite coupled with a systematic but very carefully controlled and graded use of terror made it hard to recognize that something more was occurring than just the post-war reconstruction of a wrecked country.

The experience of WWII had another aspect which should be mentioned as we talk of social reconstruction. The independent Polish state, resurrected in 1918, had been greeted with immense joy and satisfaction by all strata of Polish society, which for 150 years had been divided among three different foreign powers. Marshall Pilsudski, who was the principal architect of this resurrection, used to say: "I have left the streetcar called "socialism" at the stop called "independence." He referred to his activities in the Polish Socialist Party (PPS), where he energetically opposed those factions which emphasized the struggle for proletarian internationalism while neglecting the importance of national independence. In the present context, it is important to remember this conflict within the socialist labor movement of the early years of the present century when, for example, Rosa Luxemburg emphatically denied the right of Polish workers to fight for a state of their own. What was only a mistake at the time of Bernstein became a conscious and malicious policy of Stalin's Russia. The conflict between materialism and "existing socialism" stretches back to the turn of the century, but it became entrenched in the thirties, when Stalin's International officially condemned the Communist Party of Poland (KPP) on trumped up charges, murdered the majority of its cadres in Soviet camps, and then used the Party's crippled condition as an excuse for the joint Nazi/Soviet dismantling of Poland in 1939.

Thus it shouldn't be surprising that the Polish resistance, which was surpassed in scale and sophistication only by the Yugoslavian, was predominantly nationalistic. The Home Army, led by a London emigre government and supported by Peasant Batallions, accounted for almost all anti-Nazi activities in occupied Poland. Communists played even a secondary role only in the last stages of the war, when the arrival of the Red Army became certain.

The tragedy of the Polish resistance fighters culminated in the Warsaw uprising of August 1, 1944. With Soviet forces waiting on another bank of the Vistula river, the Home Army undertook the final effort to sweep Warsaw clean of the occupying German troops. However, this provided Stalin with an excellent opportunity; by delaying his attack he allowed the Germans to destroy both the Polish capital city and the pride of the Polish intelligentsia, (the insurgents within Warsaw included the country's most promising mathematicians, poets, essayists, engineers and lawyers) thereby greatly undermining the position of the Home Army in the postwar political situation. The Germans recognized Stalin's tactic and systematically destroyed Warsaw, reducing it to ashes. The Soviet Army waited patiently, refusing British access to airports from which practical aid could have been supplied. The Polish units accompanying Soviet troops, even though composed of communists who had not been shot in the thirties and staffed by Soviet officers, almost mutinied. Indeed, General Berling ordered a first attack against German forces on another river bank. But the attempt was intercepted half-way through and Berling became a non-entity, reduced to silence for the next thirty-five years until the first public mention of his name in the late seventies. Thus the last act of the Ribbentrop and Molotov scenario was completed in early September 1944. Warsaw practically ceased to exist. The state that emerged later was able to reconstruct the capital as it liked, populating it with inhabitants selected from all over the devastated country, without fear of resistance from a skilled, organized, and established fighting community.

To sum up: in contrast to the elation accompanying the creation of an independent Polish state in 1918, the appearance of the Polish state in 1944 and 1945 was not greeted by popular enthusiasm. Of course there was satisfaction because of the defeat of Hitler, who had run Poland in a merciless manner, killing 6 million Polish citizens, two thirds of whom were Polish Jews. But at the same time the behavior of Soviet troops clearly indicated Stalin's intention to purge the future Polish state of all independent and genuinely Polish social forces. After the Germans were pushed back, thousands of Home Army soldiers, who had aided Soviet and allied troops in liberating Polish territories, were either shot or sent to concentration camps in Siberia—some of them after having spent years in German camps. Thus the result of WWII was a society profoundly demoralized and little able to produce a coherent alternative to the communist elite supported by Soviet troops.

The last factor insuring a relatively mild passage toward the Stalinist post-1945 period was that the new elite only brought the new state into existence in a very gradual and systematic manner. In 1944 the Lublin provisional government, composed of communists who came to Poland with the Soviet troops, issued a popular manifesto, the so called "July Manifesto." They were led by Boleslaw Bierut, who headed the "Soviet-based" fraction of Polish communists, as opposed to the fraction of which Gomulka and Moczar

were typical examples, and which consisted of clandestine remnants of the native regional communist party organizations. There
was a certain confusion as to the division of power between these
two fractions—in some towns party activists witnessed two "first
secretaries" acting simultaneously, one from the domestic underground and one who came with the Soviet troops. However, this
uncertainty did not last long. Clearly, in Stalin's eyes the communists brought by Bierut directly from Moscow were more reliable.
The decisive moment came in the late forties, when Tito emerged
as a ruler independent of Stalin's orders. Domestic leaders were
quickly repressed. Gomulka, for example, went to a prison which he
accidently shared with Cardinal Wyszynski, enabling Gumulka to
emerge as a national hero in 1956.

In any case, the manifesto promised land to peasants and
factories to the workers. It promised democracy to everybody and
literacy to all social strata. It promised that the new state would
have a political system decided upon by a majority of the society. Yet
at the same time the communists, aided by Soviet occupation forces
and secret police, started the policy of undermining existing political parties, especially those of the peasants and socialists, and of
taking over the coordination of all political activities of the society.
A public referendum, the outcome of which is supposed to have
been "helped" by the security forces responsible for the democratic
execution of due process, convinced everyone that there was,
indeed, only one ruling party.

Even before the 1949 breakthrough in the rate of centralization of social, political and economic decision-making, when the
socialist party was forceably "united" with the communist party to
form the "Polish United Workers Party," it was already clear that
the new political elite would act in ways other than had been
promised in the "July Manifesto." It was not only interested in
nationalization, understood as state-ization (the premise being that
society as a whole would own the means of production and thus that
the people's state, as the legitimate representative of the whole
society, would supervise it), but was also interested in a large-scale
social construction to ensure that society would assume the form
required by marxist theory.

This point merits attention. The only possible legitimation of
the ruling elite after WWII was the claim that it was furthering the
application of marxist revolutionary theory to push society from a

capitalist phase of development into a socialist one. But it is clear that no such revolution was in sight, as the only tradition of militant struggle in Poland always took independence as its first priority. There was also, of course, a vivid tradition of more general social struggle, but in Poland it was represented by a socialist movement favoring cooperatives and non-revolutionary measures, very much like Western social democracy, not by the Communist party, which had never been too popular due to its indecisive, non-nationalist, pro-Soviet stance.

Therefore a solution had to be found which would enable the communists to have a strong national political state in a generally indifferent or hostile society. The solution was ingenious. State-ization was conducted on a large scale, but since it was called "nationalization," it was tolerated by a society which prized a national state for historical reasons. Yet at the same time as it met these legitimate nationalist urges, the state-ization in question allowed a huge restructuring of the whole society in a manner concentrating power in the hands of the state decision makers.

Consider the industrialization of the country. It was undoubt-edly a popular idea. Poland was not as industrialized as most West European countries and a considerable effort in this direction undertaken in the thirties, albeit very successful, was still incom-plete when the war broke out. Indeed, it was clearly perceived that one of the reasons for losing the war in 1939 (though this loss had not been as rapid and unavoidable as many tried to present it— Poland actually defended itself longer than France and caused far greater losses among the Germans) was the lack of an industry capable of providing the army with sufficient technical equipment.

However, industry requires both capital and labor power. Since Soviet Russia was actually draining postwar Poland of its capital and since international (Marshall Plan) aid was refused on political grounds, the only domestic source of capital was the land. Peasants had to pay a double price—they provided the necessary agricultural labor power to furnish a sufficient amount of surplus product and to finance a program of industrial investment. This proved a very effective solution. Industrialization began and pro-gressed at an astonishing rate. Heavy industry and particularly mining, which had been perceived as basic, thrived and they were easily centralized. At the same time a number of other advantages of enforced industrialization became clear. The draining of the village labor pool was presented as a transition toward a new urban life style offering good education, clean healthy housing, and limited labor hours as opposed to round-the-clock farming activities. In light of this success, it was also possible to start selecting from the millions of city newcomers thousands of future coordinators, functionaries, and agents of the state, which was thereby able to grow in its power and in its control over increasingly numerous areas of social life.

The peasants paid for this: compulsory state deliveries were not abolished until the early seventies and their price was very low, clearly indicating that the peasant was paying for the industrialization of the country in more ways than one.

Another advantage was a pacified working class, not totally satisfied with its living standards or the dominant ideology, but at least manipulable, given its memory of the relatively greater hardships of overpopulated village plots before WWII. Since this working class was new, it took years before it was able to overcome either the internal obstacles to organizing articulate social actions or the external obstacles constructed by the emerging state.

Had state-ization followed this course for a longer period, it might have had a greater degree of lasting success. However, the international situation changed rapidly. It deteriorated after Churchill's Fulton Speech, and in 1949 Stalin decided that extra precautions would have to be taken to avoid undesirable developments in his area of influence. This meant that the pace of centralization had to be increased, more money had to go for armaments, and the consumer sector had to yield to heavy industry which could in turn become a direct supplier of the war industry.

It also meant that whenever the process of centralization was not rapid or efficient enough, terror was employed. Whatever short term institutional gains might have resulted from this policy which was followed by all East European countries under the Soviet influence, these were definitely offset by the unexpected revelation to the populace of the degree to which their society had become controlled by the state.

Take the example of Polish agriculture: the tradition of peasant cooperatives, especially vital in western Poland, might have resulted, in the long run, in some kind of a socialized, non-individual farming policy. However, the precipitous enforced establishment of state farms, a form despised by the peasant, especially in view of the disastrous experience with "kholhoz" in Russia, effectively ruined any immediate chance of a socialized agriculture. Peasants did everything they could to defend themselves, and the state farms left after 1957 are still economically much less profitable than individual and cooperative farming, in spite of the hidden subsidies they receive.

Or take marxism, for another example. Polish marxism had a very interesting tradition; it produced Rosa Luxemburg and also the anarcho-syndicalist variant of Abramowski. It entered Polish universities and intellectual life anew after 1945 in a fruitful and interesting struggle with existing philosophies—phenomenology, the positivism of the Warsaw-Lvov school, thomism, etc. Then came the period of accelerating centralization. It was no longer really important whether marxism was competitive or not. What was needed by the leaders was legitimation of the new state. They required a state ideology with a high degree of coherence and simplicity and an absolute theoretical monopoly. Had marxism been left as one of many possible philosophical options, it might have stood a good chance of becoming enriched and of winning a superior position. Many young and gifted philosophers, for example, Kolakowski, Schaff, and Fritzhand, saw the promising aspects of it and used it as a generational weapon against the grand positivist and phenomenological masters like Ajdukiewicz and Ingarden. But instead, the brutal primitivization of marxism into an ideology to justify police abuses in an authoritarian state and to cover for the coordinating political elite, turned those who might have been the stoutest and most creative adherents of a free marxism into the most astute critics of the mechanical marxism of the state. In 1956 Kolakowski was already writing in "Po Prostu" about the "social functions of marxism" and composing his "Religious Consciousness and Ecclesiastic Bonds," a religious-historical study which can be viewed as a criticism of a marxism turned into a dogma for a new church—the communist party. Schaff was writing *Marxism and the Human Individual* and paving the way for an existentialist outburst of new ideology-free intellectual pursuits.

To sum up: Polish society underwent a very profound process of state-ization in the period between 1944-1950. These first five years witnessed a gradual, systematic, and generally successful introduction of large scale industrialization, as well as the employment of increasing numbers of state functionaries in all walks of life. The process had been ideologically presented as a historical chance at upward mobility for the toiling masses and had been accepted as such by these city newcomers. However, after 1949 enforced "stalinization," i.e. intensified industrialization by police means, revealed the ominous shape of the slowly emerging social Leviathan and made society aware of the dangers of excessive state control of all aspects of social life. Yet, however aware society might have become in this period, it was for the most part unable or unwilling to actively protest on a mass scale. Social pathology— especially alcoholism—and a now stagnating or declining real income were indications that Poland was facing problems which could not be solved within the emerging political structure. Yet, for the time being, there was to be little popular reaction.

It should be added that Poland never became a country comparable to Stalin's Russia. Wyszynski was in prison, but the churches were functioning normally, and even the secret police frequented Sunday services (not to mention army officers, party officials, and functionaries). Gomulka was imprisoned, but he was not shot. No Rajek trial occured in Poland. There was enough terror to make everybody aware of the grave dangers awaiting an individual or social group that resisted state rulers, but there was not enough to beat people into a total submission that would last for years.

So, the new Polish state was a formidable structure. The economy was centralized and worked almost totally at the whim of bureaucratic decision-makers. Political participation was restricted to top party and state circles, while a huge propaganda machine and an equally huge secret police ensured the appearance of consent and supplied a total monopoly of political initiative to the ruling elite. In all walks of life, with the notable exception of the church, social groups depended on the political elite. The population was enjoying the first postwar years of a relative amelioration of living conditions. Everything was under control. The international situation was conveniently frozen into a Cold War which effectively insulated the East from possible foreign influences. Stability had apparently arrived in Poland. The State faced no real opposition. Or so it seemed.

Chapter Two

The Making of the
Class of State Owners

The fact that Marshall Pilsudski got off the streetcar called "socialism" at the stop called "independence" (though not decisively so—he returned to power in 1926 as a result of the so-called "May Takeover") meant parliament had to decide who was to run the country on behalf of whom—with socialist, peasant, social democratic, national democratic and Christian parties as the participants in the struggle.

The process of the making of the top political decision-makers was quite distinct from the process of actual reconstruction of the state administration (with the subsequent attempt to remove the differences between the areas which formerly belonged to three partitions, i.e. to three different foreign state administrations). This distinction became slightly blurred once Pilsudski took over in 1926 and after his death (1935-39), because then a strange kind of legitimacy reigned, namely, of belonging to a "legion" of the first Pilsudski troops formed under the Austrians with the idea of struggling for an independent Poland at the expense of all three partitioning powers. It turned out that the dreamer Pilsudski was right—WWI ended with a defeat of all three Polish foes—though they were not all in a single camp. The immense popularity of the independence won by Pilsudski was subsequently used for political purposes by a semi-lobby of politicians who either stemmed directly from the former Pilsudski officer corps or could use its legitimacy for their own purposes.

The end of WWII was seen by some Polish communists as a very good opportunity to repeat the same game. They returned with the Polish army which was created in the Soviet Union out of Poles who had been incorporated into the Soviet citizenry as a result of the Molotov-Ribbentrop pact. They tried to cast the Soviet-built Polish army officer corps as saviors of the nation from the trauma of Nazi occupation. This did not work. Or it worked only partially—two of post-war Poland's prime ministers came from the elite division of this army, the first Kosciuszko Infantry Division, namely Jaroszewicz and Babiuch (1970-1979, 1979-1980), but none of the first secretaries of the ruling party. There were two reasons the scheme did not work. For one thing, Stalin did not trust the army enough to avoid staffing the Polish army with Soviet officers (only sent home in 1956) and did not want the army to produce the ruling stratum. Then, the regaining of independence in 1945 was too closely linked to the mass prosecution of the Home Army (AK) and especially the joint Russo-German destruction of Warsaw in 1944. It would be difficult to conjure an attractive image for the Polish army which accompanied Soviet troops.

Thus the construction had to be different and for the first time in the history of the Polish state the making of a new administration became strongly coordinated with the making of a new ruling class. The process should be analyzed: the birth of the Polish ruling class after 1945 was in many respects analogous to the birth of ruling classes elsewhere, especially in Soviet-occupied Eastern and Middle Europe. However, it has also had its peculiarities which merit attention. The regularity revealed in the process was manifest in a systematic concentration of control and coordination in a single body—the communist party, which exercised monopolistic rule especially with respect to the staffing of all state functions.

This staffing was facilitated by the fact that both Germans and Soviets strove to incapacitate the Polish resistance by exterminating primarily those social strata and professional groups which are indispensable to the running of a modern state. Huge gaps in the supply of individuals who could have run the daily routine jobs in public administration provided an ample opportunity to organize systematic staffing according to the new principle of absolute loyalty to the monopolistic party system. The staffing process also had a very appealing underpinning. The individuals who acquired elevated new posts owed them to the new decision-makers. This staffing therefore coincided nicely with an ideology of upward mobility and illustrated the propaganda theses with examples of "low-born" but respected decision-makers.

There was always a very careful orchestrating between the actual proceedings and the ideological onslaught on society; the prime targets of the communists soon after Poland was free of the German armies (but not of the Soviet ones, which was not irrelevant in matters of political realities to be taken into consideration by the people who had to decide whom to elect and by politicians who had to formulate new options) were, of course, the army, the police, and especially the secret police and special militarized police units who would fight any guerrilla activity. The swift manipulation of these and the corruption or terrorization of the peasant and socialist parties were increasingly justified by the claim that the ruling communist party incarnated the objective interests of the working class in particular and of the whole nation in general.

This merits attention: the interests of the working class would not be enough to justify the party's authority, as the whole period of occupation was dominated primarily by the more general issue of independence, thus repeating briefly the 150 years long history of partitions. For legitimacy the party had to take a stand with respect to this issue. The propaganda solution was to present the communists of Poland as the sole inheritors of all "progressive" traditions of national struggles for independence, and to present all historical tendencies and parties in Poland as either imperfect attempts at the communist-like social reconstruction or as wrong and blind. This Orwellian re-writing of history contributed to a handful of schoolbook myths about Polish history, but has never been too convincing.

However, there was a greater problem for the legitimacy specialists of the new class which was coming into being. The new Polish state had to be presented as part and parcel of a huge international and supranational historical process, as an element in a great international proletarian movement. Moscow was to be considered not so much the capital city of a neighboring country as a capital of world transformation, the Mecca of Marxist crusaders, the Rome of the communist movement. In view of Tito's independence and the very anti-Polish policies of the Soviet Union throughout its history, this was a hard view to put across. To this end a hypocritical propaganda was almost worthless.

Yet the problem remained that in order to rule one had to command an army of prospective functionaries, a kind of labor pool for state cadres—but this was almost non-existent, since the army was not used for this end and local or Soviet-trained communists were not very numerous. An ingenious solution was found. The Polish ruling class originally arose as a result of the cooption of various groups of prospective members—first, of previous fellow travelers, who were not necessarily communist party members, but who had credibility as authentic supporters of the communist movement in independent Poland. And second, of those who wanted power, state power, and who would remain loyal once given the opportunity to cling to power. It mattered little what the moral level, former political adherence or actual party affiliations of the recruits were. As a matter of fact, many party members remember that they had to persuade those members of other parties who saw through the situation and wanted to change sides that they should remain in their respective parties and act clandestinely on behalf of the communists.

This group was comprised of people from other, that is, non-communist political parties. Thus the Prime Minister in 1949, Cyrankiewiez, was a representative of the left wing of the socialist party, symbolically signifying that there was a non-communist on top governmental levels. But this was not quite true. Cyrankiewiez was the one who headed the socialist party and united it with the communist party, thus automatically becoming a member of the new communist party.

Generally speaking then, the making of the new ruling class, due to joint production of a state administrative body, of cadres of actual and potential state functionaries, and to a shaping of the political elite which was very narrow and concentrated in the communist party inner-circles, happened mainly through coopta-tion in the period 1945-1949.

From outside the elite there was an appearance of variety, because some members of the peasant or socialist parties were holding posts, though the parties themselves were kept in check by the communists. It was only an appearance, because only the political elite decided how many show-cases of non-communist functionaries there should be and who would be eligible. Approval of the communists was necessary to fill even the most insignificant post.

This process of staffing was systematic and far-reaching. Some of the early volunteers to the citizen's militia (the official name of the police) had been offered a chance to acquire higher education after a few years in the ranks, and had been gently guided towards various walks of life where they remained loyal to the same superiors they obeyed in the police units. An irony of fate brought some of them to professor's rank and top university posts and they surfaced in the late sixties or later, especially due to the vacancies opened after 1968.

But the major activity of the new ruling class emerging slowly from the ashes of occupied and prewar Poland was to start a giant industrial investment program. This program had many important features: for one thing, it was a necessity if the country was to be reconstructed without any broad international aid; no such aid existed, since the Soviet Union had definitely forbidden Poland to make use of the Marshall plan—adding its own damage to war destruction. Second, it provided a huge chance for the rural population to migrate to the towns thus becoming absolute subjects of the masters of the means of production. The forging of the new working class was to take place under new masters and victims of the upward mobility propaganda so vital for legitimacy.

Third, it meant that the state means of production would constantly grow, and since the state was controlled, it meant that an absolute control exercised over the whole society in the name of this very society also grew.

For most of the members of the ruling elite, except for a handful of old communists, the construction of a socialist society was only a matter of propaganda and legitimacy. It was more or less clear from the very outset (especially in view of horrifying examples from the Soviet Union) that what was being constructed was neither a typical capitalist society nor a truely socialist one revealing the features envisioned by the classics, eg. classlessness. But the mixture of domestic policies, ideological manipulation, and constant pressure from the outside produced a very compact and dogmatic rhetoric in which what was being done in Poland and the eastern bloc was by definition "socialist" and therefore contributed to the construction of "socialism" in the world.

The making of the new ruling class in postwar Poland can be compared to the making of another new social class—the Polish economically rejuvenated gentry in the 16th century. What happened then was that the politically monopolistic gentry (which comprised 12-20% of the whole society and was very differentiated socially) undertook a vast and overwhelmingly successful economic initiative similar to that undertaken simultaneously by the third estate and the town dwellers in Western Europe. The gentry succeeded in turning the political rules of the economic game in the feudal society to their advantage. They developed a manorial-serf economy obtaining cheap, unpaid labor from all peasants on their estates. Huge economic prosperity followed the superior political organization of the gentry, but the peasants were thrown back for two centuries and did not play a significant political role till the end of the 18th century.

The important points are first, that the political power exercised by the gentry was a starting condition to introduce a new economic order and that the bifurcation between Western and Eastern Europe took place, thus inhibiting the growth of capitalism in the areas east of the Elbe, and stimulating its growth to the west.

Both of these outcomes are revealing. The first suggests that it is possible to construct a new form of socio-economic order by manipulating political power exercised through mastery of the state. The second demonstrates that there is no necessity for some part of the world to become capitalist or socialist, state socialist or something else.

Thus the analogy could be utilized to make the following tentative formulations:

a) After World War II a systematic effort was undertaken to reconstruct the economic and social order of Poland by a group of people who coopted and harnessed enough support to wield the weapon of political power understood as ownership of the state. The effort has been successful and the result is definitely not capitalist—it is state socialist, which has many names (including Bahro's "actually existing socialism," which will be commented on below) but which boils down to the utilization of state ownership in reconstructing the socio-economic order and effectively controlling all social activities.

b) The bifurcation between Western and Eastern Europe resulted not only from an external division of spheres of influence, but primarily from the fact that in each sphere different ruling classes had exercised a monopoly of political initiative. In the case of Eastern Europe the most palpable result was the re-subjection of citizens to a state which acquired a much more important role than was the case in previous societies, especially capitalist ones. The bifurcation was given ideological glamor by skillful exploitation of marxism as state ideology, religion, and doctrine, not to be believed but to be disseminated and made sacrosanct in Eastern Europe.

Before a further explanation of the developmental mechanisms of this class (and of the opposite class of state subjects) is given, let us briefly comment critically upon a popular explanation offered by Bahro in his *Alternative* in which a theory of "actually existing socialism" is developed.

The first point to be criticized is Bahro's stress on the need for an organized state-party apparatus of functionaries as the only truely active political force which could exercise enough influence to conduct a planned and controlled social transformation. I disagree—it is not the only social force and it is luckily no longer the only organized social force. But the fact that for a considerable time it was the only organized political force is not sufficient reason to expect any political change to come from it.

It is a clear instance of utopian thinking to expect that a communist body will eventually become clever and good enough to start a positive, socialist revolution or evolution in its domains. Could one expect the very same from the capitalists as the only politically organized body in the time of Marx? Hardly so—and if anybody did, then history failed to confirm the hope.

The term "actually existing socialism" is also wrong, it prolongs the confusion which is connected to the monopolization of marxism by state socialist societies. If one wants to stick to the name of socialism, then state socialism is not the socialism envisioned by Marx, and the ruling class in state socialist societies has no will to make the two come closer to each other. If one wants to stick to really existing social systems, then the name socialism should better be dropped. State socialism is the name of a state which has "state-ized" social life—and nothing more. It exists actually as witnessed by its subjects and by Bahro too. But it certainly does not develop by the energy of its ruling class alone.

Bahro has also erred, I think, in hoping that a new social structure can be brought about by the abolishing of "vertical" social dependencies, hierarchial posts, and job differences introduced by the social division of labor and the subsequent network of dependencies, hierarchies, and relationships. I do not think that the development of a "horizontal" social structure is inevitable or that it will mean the end of the inequalities brought about by vertical relations. The utopian thinking of Bahro comes to the fore with the idea that a development of productive forces will by itself produce enough "organizational margin of freedom" to experiment with other, more horizontal social divisions of labor. I disagree totally— it is, in my opinion, not possible to expect productive forces to create a new social structure. They are not an independent factor, and they do not determine the degree of freedom exercised by an individual (although without their development such freedom would probably be harder to think of). Quite to the contrary one might think of instances of a considerable growth of productive forces due to the curbing of "loose" freedoms, and subsequent increased productivity further inhibiting the growth of such freedom. Think of the tremendous increase in the productivity of German war industry, of all war industries as a matter of fact...

To put it in a nutshell: Bahro's "alternative" is an alternative within the political system of state socialism which in my view has already turned out to be no alternative at all, as in the Poland of 1956. A positive change in the ruling class only means a cosmetic change even if there is a subjective feeling of relief, but it does not open any new possibilities of social organization. The new alternative can only emerge from a new "ideology of socialization" which has to be fully worked out but which is practically exemplified by Poland's workers in the late seventies and most notably and symbolically in 1980. Theirs is the only real alternative to a "state-ization" of social life, and what any standard marxist handbook may have to say about it is irrelevant and should not be troubled with.

Coming back to our new ruling class and the ways in which it came to power, there is another theory, most notably expressed in the "Intellectuals on the Road to Class Power" by Konrad and Szelenyi and in various essays by Gouldner (who, however, did not make a strong point of it), which claims that the growth of state power is a result of making the intellegentsia into a new ruling class, who use the marxian revolution not in order to free workers from the capitalist yoke, but to impose a yoke of their own—the yoke of a "coordinating, administering, functionary" class, the class of the state apparatus, of state officialdom.

This theory has more appeal to me, although I still consider it wrong. It is possible, for instance, that the history of the bourgeois revolution repeated itself; that the intelligentsia aped the bourgeoisie and kept the fruits of the working masses' struggles to themselves, while issuing universalist appeals and utilizing some universal ideology. But there is a decisive factor which is linked to the fate of the intelligentsia under state socialism—and it is by no means true that belonging to the intelligentsia is enough to secure a powerful and wealthy social position. It is possible that the intelligentsia can become the prevailing social group within the ruling class. However, this is not due to the fact that somehow the intelligentsia is predetermined to rule, but instead, due to the fact that the cooptation process refers mainly to the professionals and controllers who are bought off by the ruling political elite, and due to the fact that the members of the ruling class itself necessarily acquire various airs and graces and education by virtue of their power.

It is much harder to discuss arguments like the ones put forward by Gouldner, who claims that professionals (ie. the intelligentsia in the Eastern European meaning of the term) cheat society by getting their education in a socialized, collective manner due to participation in our educational institutions, while they make profit out of their education "on their own," by making society pay for their services. They share the benefits of social wealth by acquiring knowledge which is social capital but they fail to disseminate this knowledge in a social manner and moreover appropriate all benefits from the exercise of their profession to themselves. This is a very profound and correct observation. I have no immediate argument against it. It may very well be true that there is an incongruity here between the mode of accumulation of social knowledge and the mode of its distribution. But I fail to see the connection between this "reprivatization" of the fruits of the intelligentsia's labor and their dominating position in the state, especially in view of the total irrelevance of important groups of professionals in state socialist societies from the point of view of decision making. No doctors, no lawyers, no teachers—to mention a few—take part in the decision making process, unless they also happen to be members of the state ruling class, membership in which would have nothing to do with the mode of appropriation of the fruits of their education.

The Polish ruling class originally came into being due to cooptation. This process of cooptation did not last long; it was practically over by 1949. It became clear, for instance, in 1956, that all those worker activists whose popular authority potentially exceeded the authority of the party cadres were skillfully eliminated from the social scene. A Polish journalist visited a famous Warsaw worker activist of 1956 who lives presently as a fisherman on the Polish coast. He told a common story of a car, vodka and women, of skillful manipulation which made him lose his job, move from Warsaw and fade into obscurity, while the party officials who formerly cheered him became omnipotent bosses again.

Cooptation was replaced by a brand new kind of production—an autonomous production of the ruling class, a reproduction of sorts. The reproduction was not dynastic—some manifest instances of family relations appeared in the seventies, but they were more linked to ostentatious consumption, conspicuous consumption, one is inclined to say, than to anything else. The new production took place mostly in the party ranks, where promising young people were fished out of the youth unions, the lower party echelons, and the ranks of the professionals. The Polish Students' Union was an interesting instance—Olszowski, a hardliner of 1980, used to be a student leader, and so were many others, although they usually had second-rate positions as "advisers" and "professional secretaries" to more important party functionaries.

After the great leap forward of 1968, the old ruling class ethos could no longer hold. Gomulka disliked too blatant forms of conspicuous consumption (ostensibly abolished after 1956, but reinstated almost immediately), but Gierek had to yield to demands for increased consumption. The new ruling class became over-zealous in the seventies—not only in a visible way (the amount of luxury cars, house furniture, housing itself, country clubs, etc.), but in a legal sense as well.

In autumn of 1973 a bill was passed through the Polish parliament and quietly went into effect. Nobody was aware of it at the time even though it was routinely published in the proceedings of the parliament and dutifully posted in all major offices, in libraries, and in "Monitor Polski" and "Dziennik Ustaw"—both having published all acts passed by the Polish parliament and government. The act is called "On pensions granted to individuals who render particularly important services to the state." The bill defines such individuals, and as it happens particularly vital and important services to the state can be made only by those who rank topmost in all walks of life. A rigid hierarchy was introduced which measured services rendered in terms of the post achieved and the length of time it was held—very elaborate criteria were used to divide all state, party and special (science, army, police) posts into separate groups, and in each of the groups the amount paid, the amount added and the amount of goods to be acquired while in office and then kept for the family and successors were meticulously determined.

This bill was a plain outrage but it was also a clear indication that the ruling class was closed and aimed at a constant amelioration of its position, and at a rigid determination of demarcation lines. A masterpiece of honesty in state socialist countries, the bill is a most important indication of 1980 to come. This single bill closed the whole epoch of the making of the ruling class. Once the bill was passed, once it became the letter of law in People's Poland, it became quite clear that the ruling class would not truely honor any social alliances except for a passing courtesy to some auxillary social group. I think the bill should be printed in all histories of 20th century Europe to indicate the degree of self-consciousness on the part of the ruling class in state socialist societies. There was no doubt about the total cynicism and absolute lack of legitimacy of those rules and rulers.

Such obvious cynicism does not itself mean the ruling class is vulnerable to any effective criticism. As Michael Szkolny wrote in the *London Review of Books*, March 1981: "Where the belief and propaganda of a ruling class differ significantly, that class becomes the victim of a cynicism which penetrates throughout society. It is generally assumed that a contradiction of this type between propaganda and belief represents an ideological dysfunction. The opinion derives from the tacit assumption that the function of propaganda is to convince the recipient of its truth. Such an assumption is, however, a priori, unjustified. If the ideology of the ruling class serves to protect the existing order, then the only necessary function of the propaganda is to induce a set of beliefs in the ruled which in no way threatens that order. Propaganda does not have to be believed in order to be effective."

But the fact that the propaganda was a repetition of old cliches that the ruling class no longer cared for became very important when this class sought legitimacy. As long as there was no alternative to a state-organized framework in sight, the hypocrisy of the ruling class was not important. However, when real or imagined alternatives appeared, the ruling class's position became untenable.

This was not due to the fact that the ruling class itself did not care for the ideological basis of its legitimacy, instead relying on the daily workings of the state, especially on the rigid control exercised by censorship and the police, and by economic management and social pacification—like the provisioning of state-owned trade unions. There was also another factor—the making of the new working class. But this making of a class of state subjects was a much longer and much more painful process because of its size and internal differences. The only early warning signal might have been a very brief span of time between the students' March 1968 and the workers' December 1980. This was not recognized, however, and so 1980 came as a surprise.

I shall discuss the making of the antagonistic class opposing the ruling class in Poland when I discuss the aftermath of August 1980 in Poland. The most important feature of the appearance of this class was the total loss of orientation on the part of the ruling class, which was unable to locate the enemy, being used to a selected small group which could be made a scapegoat. The ruling class could not understand that it was outnumbered, outvoted and outmanouvered. Hence, the aftermath of August 1980 has so far proved to be positive for the socialized society in Poland.

Chapter Three

Landmarks In The
Anti-Statist Movement

1956 or the Aftermath of Stalinism

The year 1956 stands out because of the major social upheavals which shook the state socialist countries: the Hungarian uprising and the Polish Poznan riots. Yet it was not the beginning of the so called political "thaw" marking the end of the Stalinist "deep freeze." East Berlin workers had already rioted in 1953, giving Brecht the opportunity to ask the party elite: "The nation lost the confidence of the government. Shouldn't the government dissolve the nation and elect a new one?" Stalin had died that same year, and the 20th congress of the Soviet Communist Party and Khruschev's secret speech also predate 1956.

Poland, for example, had witnessed serious changes in the arts and sciences long before 1956. Adam Wazyk's "Poem for Adults" was a typical product of disillusionment with the methods of decision-making and with the results of early state socialist accumulation. A small bi-weekly put out by students and young intelligentsia, "Po Prostu" ("Straightforward" or "Plain Talk") gained momentum in this early period and slowly became the mouthpiece of the intelligentsia who wished to get rid of the regimentation of the Stalinist regime. However, this process—and I want to stress this fact in view of almost total ignorance of the period's actual meaning—was a result of some changes in the political activities of the ruling class itself. Basically, a new generation of potential members of the ruling class as well as some members who were already in power saw their main chance for advance in a process of transformation to a more liberal state socialist system. What they wanted was to regroup within the ruling class, using a popular ideology both to oust the previous "crew" of centralized state decision-makers and to win some legitimation for their own activities. And indeed, in Poland their activity was crowned with success as the upheavals of 1956 finally initiated major changes in the structure of the ruling class and in the political awareness of working people. The working class voted only once—in June 1956 in Poznan—and this vote was skillfully used and exploited by the new elite, but it was never allowed to mature and develop into the voice of a partner in leadership.

The Poznan riots broke out as a result of the unfulfilled demands of city communication workers and the workers of Cegielski factory, the largest in Poznan, whose products ranged from ship engines and railroad and powercars to other metal products. The workers' demonstration, mishandled by the local party bosses, marched to Kochanowski Street to free political prisoners from the secret police. A worker was shot. Others dipped a Polish flag in his blood and a few days of riots ensued. The workers succeeded in freeing the prisoners and also destroyed the expensive equipment of a special radio station which beamed "noise" to interfere with the programs of "Radio Free Europe" and other Western broadcasting agencies. The army was called in while police abandoned the city and fled to the outskirts. The government response was typical; at first, all newspapers carried the same story blaming socially marginal outcasts and bums; then Western spies and sabotage experts were blamed; and finally the prime minister, Cyrankiewicz, spoke of "cutting off the hand which is aimed against socialism."

Political trials followed and it turned out that the lawyers were, for the first time in many years, allowed to provide a fair defense. The cause of the Poznan workers had become the cause of the "reformist" top party officials and young party cadre who had brought Gomulka to power. The first secretary of the party (Ochab, an interregnum leader in any case) resigned of his own accord.

None of the concessions Gomulka subsequently granted to the working class lasted and none made essential changes. Workers' councils were quickly centralized on the national level and reduced to decoration, while popular workers' leaders were either slowly corrupted or removed from the political scene. The intelligentsia could listen freely to jazz and discuss existentialism, but the above mentioned Po Prostu was closed down in the summer of 1957 and the ensuing demonstration by students defending their paper was brutally repressed by the police. Thus the "thaw" lasted approximately one year.

None of the economic reforms was completely carried through and none helped to significantly raise the standard of living—although there were gains as less money went into armaments and less was lost on state farms. The only important change was the dissolution of the vast majority of state farms, but a policy of small steps toward further exploitation of individual peasant farmers was quickly resumed.

In spite of these qualifications, 1956 was a very important year. It provided, first of all, an excellent lesson for the ruling elite, who learned both in domestic policy and in international politics. In the latter area it discovered, thanks to the courage of Imre Nagy, Prime Minister of Hungary, that it is unwise to reject the Warsaw pact if one does not want to have the other members intervene. But it also learned that a degree of independence is allowed, especially in the composition of the ruling body. Gomulka was never supported by Moscow; Kruschev flew to Warsaw to take part in a decisive meeting of the Political Bureau, but the Polish military commander of the city did not allow the plane to land.

But far more important was the domestic lesson: it is possible to exploit difficulties in the economic sphere in order to use social discontent to advantage in power struggles within the ruling political elite. This lesson was well understood by the party, as 1968 was to prove, but other social groups were slower to learn. For one thing, the working class was divided. Peasants had been delighted to see state farms dissolved, but there was no organized movement to go a step further and demand that older agricultural policies would not be tried again. Workers had strong functioning workers' councils, and it was not immediately clear that the whole structure of these councils was to be reduced to total insignificance in the future. The intelligentsia had more freedom from censorship than before 1956, although censorship was not abolished in spite of the fact that in 1957 censors paraded on May 1st with a large banner which said "Please abolish our office," and a large influx of both West European literature and of domestic products long banned, caused a widespread feeling of relief.

It is hard to blame people for not pressing for more liberties at once, because for most coming up for political air after years of suffocating stagnation and ruthless propaganda meant a real shock that had to be digested. The enormous popularity of Gomulka, and the success he had in stopping obligatory coal shipments to the

Soviet Union and in bringing 700,000 Polish citizens back from detention in Russia, contributed to a lack of vigilance in following minute changes in party politics even though these already indicated the end of the liberalization period. I find it symbolic that one of Warsaw's publishing houses started a very interesting series of humanist essays—having published, among others, Bertrand Russell, Herbert Marcuse and Bronislaw Malinowski—but had to postpone Karl Popper's *The Open Society and its Enemies* as the period of relative freedom in the ideological sphere ended.

There are many theoretical explanations of what happened in Eastern Europe and the Soviet Union around 1956. The most plausible refer to the necessity on the part of the ruling class to change its tactics because excessive "accumulation" stopped working. There were repeated rebellions in concentration camps, and there was a growing discontent which could have hampered the functioning of the system in the future. Stalinism had been a very negative development in state socialist countries. But stalinism after Stalin's death became the best means of self-rescue for the political elites and ruling classes of state socialist countries. The pattern of ideological manipulation is clear and reminds one of primitive magical rites: the solemn sacrifice of the former ruler is accompanied by a suitable sacrrifice of his accomplices, who are limited in type and number. This rite is rather more picturesque than meaningful. Then follows a period of general relaxation of policy in all branches of social life, and finally a consolidation of the system in the hands of a rejuvenated ruling class.

What matters is that there is complete control of all political change and a total political orchestration of change in all other aspects of life. If something unexpected happens it must be brought under control and exploited, as were both Hungary and Poznan. Although the Poznan rising is a landmark in the history of class struggle in postwar Poland, never in the whole period of the thaw was the state as such in danger. The army remained loyal although the police were routed in Poznan, and no political issues had been fought over. Nonetheless, for the first time social classes which had become quite entrenched in the stalinist period behaved in a class-determined manner.

There was another very important demographic factor which contributed to the relative mildness of the transition to post-stalinism. Most of the adults who participated in 1956 were people who had vivid memories of the terrors of hitlerism and stalinism.

They had experienced mass terror and they clearly hoped not to experience it again. Thus, much could be done to constrict this society with not too subtle hints. The newly constructed urban society longed for stabilization. Most people had small children and welcomed Gomulka's promises of stability.

There was also no immediate cooperation between social strata and groups. Workers organized workers' councils, intellectuals organized "clubs of intelligentsia." They acted separately not because they wanted to limit themselves, but because the prevailing consciousness was still the monopoly of the ruling class and did not allow awareness of the basic dependence of everyone on a sole employer, the state.

Whatever our final judgement of 1956 may be, it is worth mentioning that much theoretical and political work was done in the brief period of breathtaking freedom, and that it was not unusual to see young students throughout the late sixties and early seventies sitting for hours in university reading-rooms and city archives studying all printed matter published between 1955 and 1957. I did it myself and I owe much to this self-education launched simply out of curiosity about my dim memories of being five years old, sitting on a window sill, happy to see so many tanks in the streets and wondering why our radio was full of military commands. The lessons of the working class were painfully and slowly learned. But learned they were.

1968 or Romantic Intellectuals

After the rapid decline of the social hopes linked to 1956, the determined action of the new party elite to secure domination of all parts of the state machinery pushed the country into a political coma.

This did not mean nobody thought about political matters anymore; but it did mean that there was an absolute monopoly not only of political decision-making on the part of the Gomulka group, but also of deciding what was and what was not political. Gomulka cherished two dogmas which were the ideological pillars of his policies. First, economic self-sufficiency at a low but bearable level, a policy fueled by his distrust of Moscow—for example, he dismantled the railroad tracks from industrial Silesia to Russia and limited Polish participation in Soviet-led investment projects which were supposedly for the benefit of all socialist countries. Second, political reliance on the threat of the "German danger" to pacify possible reformist movements.

Contrary to appearances his "reign" was not a bleak period. Society, if not affluent, was fairly egalitarian and not at a starvation level. Modest progress was achieved in the material sphere, while enormous progress was made in education and in a cultural growth both of creative centers and of a receptive, sophisticated public. However, although it seemed that his was a perfect stabilization, destabilizing processes which had seemed innocent, easily subdued and controlled, were already at work. For one thing, the church had tried a modest political step in 1966 when a conference of Polish bishops addressed German bishops with an open letter: "We forgive and we ask forgiveness." Gomulka was furious. His delicate balance of a modestly independent economic policy and blatantly anti-German propaganda was countered by this early attempt to normalize relations with the Federal Republic of Germany, an attempt which preceded his own by four years. In late 1970 Brandt visited Warsaw, kneeled in front of the monument of the Warsaw ghetto, and signed the documents which formally meant legal recognition of post-war geopolitical realities in Europe, including an acknowledgement of Poland's western border, the lack of which Gomulka's propaganda had never tired of stressing.

Then, there were always intellectuals who gave him problems. Gomulka was one of the last state-socialist politicians who still had the time and will to comment on single literary and scholarly cases of opposition in public—to castigate, to admonish, to convince and to evaluate. There were writers who protested censorship and bans on Polish emigre literature; there was a parliamentary group of Christian representatives, "Znak" ("Sign")—also the name of a prestigious monthly read mainly by top intellectuals and opinion-leaders—which was dissolved for failing to comply with the rest of the parliament. There were Kuron and Modzelewski in the late sixties, who tried to draw conclusions from the unbroken development of secret anti-mob police units, from the constant censorship and monitoring of citizens' activities, and from the growing economic inefficiency and political stagnation. Their "Open Letter to Comrade First Secretary" was read by intellectuals but not by the addressee, who dismissed it with prison terms. Kuron and Modzelewski proposed a return to the principles of workers' democracy. They had analyzed the appearance of what they called the CPB— "central political bureaucracy"—and the adverse effects the CPB had on the social, economic, and political development of People's Poland. Their letter was a reminder that 1956 had awakened broad social hopes but that ensuing changes had been limited to a re-grouping manoeuver within the ruling elite.

I met Kuron and Modzelewski in the early seventies, a few weeks after they emerged from prison (they had been freed early in 1968 only to be locked up again after March of the same year), in the Warsaw apartment of Modzelewski, next to Warsaw's ugliest and most central building, the notorious Palace of Culture, Stalin's gift to his Polish brethren. Kuron asked a few of us to join him and Modzelewski for tea and conversation. He was full of political schemes, linking, organizing, speaking up, reaching people who were just leaving prison or army barracks, having served their terms for March 1968. Modzelewski was quiet, tired, careful—I remember that he asked me to put my sheepskin coat on top of the telephone "just in case"—and much more theoretically inclined. What had happened between their open letter and our meeting?

The era of stagnation and political stability was drawing to an end. Students had become, for lack of other outlets of free expression, the spokespeople of ambitious intellectuals, young workers and farmers, and all the people who could not understand why society had to stagnate while they were subjected to tedious speeches on the same topics every successive May 1st, New Year's Eve, or Anniversary of the Glorious October Revolution.

One may say that what happened in the sixties in Poland was in many ways reminiscent of the process which took place in the Poland of the 17th/18th centuries, when refeudalization resulted from leaving the nobility with a monopoly of political activity. Similarly, leaving a monopoly to the CPB resulted in depriving all other social groups of any right to express hopes, articulate designs, or struggle for the actual creation of any palpable alternatives to the established ways of running society. The only group even partially exempt from pressure were the students. For the years spent at the university were the only period when the state was more or less in the background and some actual, unmonitored social bonds could be formed, allowing earnest attempts to look for better social, political, artistic, intellectual, and moral alternatives.

One should also mention the fact that there is a rough parallel between the rise of SDS in the U.S. from the Port Huron statement to the front pages of the New York Times and the TV news, and the rise of the Polish student protest from the "Open letter" to mass actions involving street fights with the police, sit-ins, and mass political education. The parallel results from the fact that both young Americans and young Poles grew up in societies which were basically structured during the Cold War period and very insignificantly and insufficiently modified in the mid-fifties. McCarthy and Stalin were gone, but the political monopoly of the ruling class was almost complete. Still, the rhetoric of the Cold War could no longer appeal to the young in the late sixties. Quite the contrary.

It is, of course, debatable whether the outbreak of hostilities between students and police was provoked by the secret police in order to start a campaign which was supposed to bring a new wing of the elite to power and influence, or just utilized to the same purpose once it happened spontaneously. I do not think the question is essential. No matter what the actual situation was, the facts are that Kazimierz Dejmek, a famous theater director, staged "Dziady" by Adam Mickiewicz. The drama itself takes place in a Poland which has just been partitioned, and the spiritual sufferings of young plotters against the Russan Tsar could easily be interpreted in light of the satellization of Poland under Soviet policies since 1939. Indeed, this is exactly what happened. The audiences read the intentions of the author and director and broke into a patriotic enthusiasm. Pure aesthetic pleasure resulting from the excellent performance mixed freely with a fresh awareness that there is more to responsible political behavior than a socialist state is inclined to allow.

The performance was cancelled very quickly, supposedly after the intervention of the Soviet ambassador in Poland. (It is customary for Soviet ambassadors to take an interest in Polish books, theater performances, films, and the like, so that national censorship will be backed by an international vigilance. Or such is the general view which may very well be spread by central politicians themselves when they want to blame the Russians for their own unpopular decisions.) The students saw this cancellation, very correctly, as an attempt to censor a most precious work of national literature. Imagine that one day a censored edition of the "Declaration of Independence" appeared and all previous editions were confiscated. The response was immediate. Students protested, mainly in Warsaw, but also in Poznan, Krakow, Wroclaw, and Lodz, with Warsaw definitely leading the action, sending special couriers around spreading leaflets, occupying both the University and Polytechnic School. The general population, although very much misinformed by the media, started supplying students with food, and there began a very slow, seemingly insignificant response to the students' open protest.

Of course, the other side had more to say. It turned out the action was well prepared in advance. Top party people rallied for Gomulka and gave wild speeches openly threatening their political opponents. Gierek actively claimed that his region firmly supported the top politicians and that "Silesian water will break the bones of those who want to disturb our march towards socialism." Not since the early stalinist period had Poland heard such threats from party bosses from all regions, while secret and anti-mob police broke the bones of protesting students and the lives and careers of those they managed to detain. It appeared that lists of people who had to be removed from party, state, and university posts had been prepared in advance. Universities had to pay for being the main sites of open unrest and lack of loyalty to the regime. Retaliation was swift and assumed proportions threatening to the continuity of Polish scholarly effort, especially in the humanities.

One of the most shameful chapters in post-war Polish history was the skillful manipulation of anti-Semitic themes in the course of the propaganda onslaught against the students in the mass media. Since a couple of student leaders had Jewish-sounding names the propaganda machine quickly realized that there was a chance to present the protesters as: a) children of the most brutal stalinist henchmen, many of whom had actually been Jewish as the percentage of Polish Jews in the prewar Polish Communist Party was high, and some of these Jews had in fact assumed important state and police posts if they were lucky enough to live through Stalin's anti-Polish policy; and b) collaborators of an international imperialist-zionist plot which threatened the stability of the Polish socialist state.

Both these mystifications are perfectly understandable given the feelings of a power elite insecure with respect to their legitimacy and also with respect to international relations, where it was reduced to following the orders of Big Brother. Thus scapegoating and aggressive propaganda masked the actual take-over and emergence of Mieczyslaw Moczar, the former general of security forces and an alleged "nationalist" as a "strong man" and possible successor to Gomulka.

Though these regroupings of the elite became known later, the 1968 Romantic outburst of students and intellectuals provided an opportunity for the rulers to do something else as well. There were many positions, especially in culture, media, science and university education, which had become vacant once people who were linked to striking students, to Jewish origins, or to anything that could be taken for liberal thinking, had been eliminated. A competition to fill these places ensued, and the rulers won new supporters in middle managerial levels, among the people who owed their sudden upward mobility to the unscrupulous exploitation of an ugly opportunity.

Needless to say, the level of expertise suffered. Almost all important philosophers and sociologists from Warsaw University were forced to leave the country. In fact, the whole Department of Philosophy and Sociology, which had been the heart of political activity, was dismantled. Leszek Kolakowski, Bronislaw Baczko, and the sociologists Maria Hirszowicz and Zygmunt Bauman were forced to leave. In a sense, this was a belated continuation of police actions against the editors of "Po Prostu." There seemed to be no hope left—incompetent party halfwits were everywhere, students were reduced to docility, the media was happily blubbering about the working class's alleged hostile response to the "hooligans."

The legend of workers' hostility to the students in 1968 is false. It stemmed from Gomulka's use of the so-called "Voluntary Reserve of Citizens' Militia," a paramilitary organization which supported the regular police and was recruited from reliable party people in all walks of life just in case there was a need to terrorize the opposition without intervention of uniformed police. These hired "volunteers" came disguised as workers, supposedly outraged that the students dared to riot while they worked so hard.

On the other hand, workers did not openly support the students. Still, most of the propaganda shows on national TV which presented mass meetings during which workers read "spontaneous" invectives against students, Jews, and hooligans, had to be provided with their soundtracks in the studio. Usually the workers on these shows looked very bored and hostile to the speakers, and it was not infrequent that they drowned the speaker's voice by clattering with hammers and other tools against their machines.

But by late 1968 it seemed that Gomulka had succeeded totally. Students were subdued, intellectuals broken, newcomers to political decision-making and mid-level coordinating positions grateful and overzealous, order and peace restored, and prisons and special punitive army units full of previous rebels. How Pyrrhic this victory of "law and order" was to prove became obvious pretty soon. The most significant outcome of the mass reshuffling of the lower and middle echelons of coordinators was a definite block erected in the way of the career expectations of virtually all of the younger generation. The lessons learned under police truncheons also had their effect; almost the whole of the younger generation became united in a critical attitude toward the regime. Sociologists warned that there was no real social bond any longer; the young answered all questions posed by sociologists and journalists in the obligatory communist rhetoric, but their behavior demonstrated quite clearly that they felt profound disbelief and disillusionment. Their life aims became restricted to their family and circle of friends.

The Making of a Generation

Meanwhile, there was a growing movement of student cultural activists and creative artists of all sorts, who flocked to student theaters and clubs where a relative freedom reigned in spite of repressions. A whole new wave of poets, graphic artists, (especially poster makers, posters being a very typical Polish medium) novelists, critics, and photographers slowly emerged at the forefront of the new generation. Decisively divorced from all mass media and from most of the possibilities of mass dissemination of their work, they nevertheless managed to build footholds by means of a network of student art and theater festivals, and by skillfully using the party slogan of "committed art" to come closer to a mass audience.

The years 1968 to 1970 and later are very important for the emergence of this new generation of Poles. Most, like myself, were born around 1950. Most had experienced March 1968 as a "generation-making" experience, and were brought up free of the immediate terror of either Hitler's occupation or Stalin's satellization. Most had nothing to win in a country ruled by a stagnant, elderly elite in a blatantly authoritarian manner. Most distrusted official history handbooks and set out on the painful task of reconstructing the true history of 20th century Poland.

Two processes with respect to culture were born in this period of 1968 and its aftermath. One was a definite reinforcing of the Romantic tradition, heavily represented in the Polish literature of the period, which viewed independent artists and writers as the nation's conscience and as the only legitimate representatives of public opinion. The more debased and pro-state the mass media became, the more desirable it seemed to disregard them completely and to turn towards independent, student sponsored creative pursuits like community theater groups.

The second process consisted of a strange "election" which seems to happen spontaneously every five or six years. It is as if a particular form of artistic creativity emerges as the most vital mode of expression of public opinion, only to be slowly limited and then extinguished by the state, and then swiftly replaced by the next "elected" form. Political student theater was born in the late sixties. A wave of excellent political performances—"In One Breath" by "Theater of the Eighth Day" from Poznan, "Polish Dreambook" and "Exodus" by STU from Krakow, "In Sunny Rhythm" by the Kalambur Theater from Wroclaw and two successive performances by "77" Theater from Lodz, "Circle" and "Tryptich"—swept the country. Gifted people founded new theaters or entered the ranks of existing ones. By the mid-seventies the state, fully aware of the political role of the new student theater, moved successfully to systematically undermine its existence. For a year or two nothing happened, until a new Polish cinema emerged with Wajda's "Man of Marble" to show that art finds its way around, even if its dominant mode of expression changes.

In March 1968 nothing changed in the class structure of Polish society—not even with respect to the class awareness of the participants in the struggle. No new class consciousness was born. Instead, the meaning of 1968 for subsequent developments in Poland can only be understood in terms of the growth of a quasi-class consciousness. "Quasi" because there was no class consciousness in the traditional meaning of the term. Instead of class a new concept organized a sense of group identity—the generation.

The status of the concept of a "generation" is unclear. In the traditional German humanities of the early 20th century Dilthey spoke of a "Generationserlebness" or generational experience. He claimed that since a generation does not cover only those who are born around a similar date but those who share the period's values, it is the experience which decisively shapes the outlook and attitudes of the people of the period. This "generational" experience was definitely a factor in 1968. In terms of the scope of police repressions March 1968 was no world record—the number of people who were punished, beaten up, locked up, or thrown out of work was not overwhelming, though not insignificant, either, considering that the victims were usually either students or scholars and scientists. But the shock of substantial open violence unleashed by the government caused the legitimacy of the ruling elite to undergo a profound crisis. Nobody believed the official interpretations of events any more. There was no reason to follow a logic or description based on a demonstration of naked violence.

Also important was the fact that the full impact of the ruling elite's political wrath fell upon a brand new generation—born and brought up after the war and thus deprived of the psychosocial aftereffects of mass terror. That a sudden unleashing of police state power could occur was a very educational experience from which this generation never recovered. It was educational especially in view of the fact that it was primarily directed—as far as direct clashes with the police went—against institutions of higher education. Students felt the impact, and the experience of this impact shaped the Polish national culture in years to come.

How profound the shock had been and how well the interplay of political forces was understood by the students was best revealed in the student theater which flourished after 1968, surpassing the best achievements of this form of political and artistic expression of 1956. In late March 1968 one of the directors of a student theater spoke to me of his vision of a new play to be collectively rehearsed, shaped, and presented by his group which worked in a "collective-communal" way, utilizing some of the techniques developed by Grotowski and Brook and such visionaries as Artaud. The theme and title were to be *Blood Donors*. The action was supposed to take place in an ambiguous space which would be a mixture of an interior of a passenger airplane (highjacking had just become popular) and of a public clinic where blood is being donated. The situation would be slightly surreal—it was to be left far from clear whether the characters are waiting patiently to complete their voluntary sacrifice, or bleeding because of wounds inflicted on them by the thugs or "noble cause" warriors who have highjacked them. The interior was to be white, with blood slowly rising and producing the red and white of the Polish flag, until the blood rose even higher and everything became solid red—bloody *and* ideologically correct.

When two years later the workers' rebellion in coastal cities was bloodily suppressed by the police, new performances did not have to be changed though they had opened before the event; overnight they became even more politically meaningful.

The new group of young poets, writers, critics, sociologists, philosophers and columnists, graphic artists and poster-makers, assembled in Krakow and tried to make a student bi-weekly into a new platform of their generation's point of view. The group was very successful in artistic and critical terms—virtually every important piece of poetry, criticism, prose and sociological reflection stemmed from people who were somehow connected to this attempt. However, their goal, an independent cultural periodical, "Young Culture," never materialized. They were kept under constant surveillance and not allowed a step beyond the lines enforced by the ever vigilant authorities and censors. Not everything was suppressed: a critical study of Polish literature called "The Unpresented World" announced with its very title the basic feeling, that the authentic spiritual, intellectual, moral, and ideological life of society was monstrously distorted and even destroyed by the political watchdogs. But it was also at that time that party writers published their pamphlets against Milosz, calling him a spy and imperialist collaborator, charges that were denied by the students of 1980, when Milosz got the Nobel prize and major university centers in Poland collected his works for public display.

But in 1968 there was no class to rally around, and the nation was the only reference point, including as it did the political enemy, so that the generation as a reference group, as an "Ersatzklasse," was stressed, and it was around their generation that the young intellectuals rallied. This movement was accompanied by a parallel development among the elite, many of whose members remembered reaching the top as a result of an earlier upheaval, and decided to stick together, knowing that older cadre had nothing to win by siding with them. A generational retrenchment thus occurred in both groups. Meanwhile this generational ideology played a vital role in the development of all Polish youth, not only the students. Young workers and clerks, in fact all young people no matter what their position, felt the same basic uneasiness. No advance, no actual meaningful participation, except in a youth counterculture on the rise, could attract them. These young people were also better educated and better travelled due to sales of Polish technology and the influx of Western technology, and they quickly recognized political and economic realities.

"Generation" as a class substitute was a mixed blessing, but it was ingenious too. It promised immunity from political prosecution —Marx had nothing to say about generations, and a biological explanation of the "Sturm und Drang" period could easily be presented as an alibi—while at the same time it allowed for a development of ideological constructions and personal relationships of a very emotional, close, and public-minded type.

It can be said that although March 1968 did not produce outright class awareness, it produced a forerunner, a mid-construction which helped shape subsequent symbolic discoveries in the course of the seventies. It was not the first time in the history of Europe that a generation was a platform to organize and develop political ideology, (some extreme rightist groups grew out of Polish and German student associations between the two world wars) but it was the first time in the history of the state socialist society that a generation eventually proved to be a vehicle of class consciousness. This did not take long; only two years later the generational bond could be interpreted so as to grow along with a new prototypical class bond between the masses of state subjects.

1970 or the Positivism of Workers

1970 was much more erratic on both sides than 1968. It is often thought that while 1968 was a fanciful but suicidal diversion caused by Romantic intellectuals, 1970 was a proper response of the working class at large, positive and bearing fruit. This is partly true; it bore fruit, although more in a negative than positive manner. As Walesa said during the August 1980 negotiations: "You won in 1970, it was fifty-fifty in 1976, and now we have to win." Neither of the sides in the December 1970 riots on the sea coast moved toward new solutions. It was, in a sense, a re-enactment of 1956. The workers wanted to be co-decision-makers, and they felt aggressive enough not to go to work, and also to demonstrate in front of party buildings. The state felt, at the beginning, confident enough to fire and kill and to instigate mass terror. For example, "dum dum" bullets were fired from helicopters indiscriminately into the crowd and hospital ambulances full of hidden policemen suddenly opened fire while driving by. Later they felt equally confident that a Gomulka-like re-enactment of 1956 would succeed with Gierek coming to the top and asking the workers in a dramatic gesture "Will you help us?" to which they expected half-theatrical, half-resigned approval.

What was the 1970 December riot about? Food prices, especially meat prices, were to rise. It was decided by early December that prices would go up and that at the same time material incentives for more productive labor would be introduced in order to compensate for the rise—but the latter only in those cases where an enlarged labor effort followed. The manipulative, arbitrary and authoritarian nature of this price rise was obvious. Nobody doubted that food was heavily subsidized, though inefficiently—the immediate reason for the rise, an increase in fodder imports, was caused by excessive financing of large state run farms at the expense of middle-sized peasant farms—but nobody could be fooled about a possible compensation nor about the true meaning of "material incentives." Clearly, living standards were to be lowered, while at the same time individual bonuses for a slight rise in private standards were being offered only if an unconditional increase of labor effort was forthcoming. The rulers instituted changes that were definitely necessary if the rate of economic growth was to continue but it did so at the expense of the workers and with a blatantly "managerial" disregard of even the slightest appearance of democracy.

This was far more important than the food prices themselves. The striking workers in the shipyards expressed it clearly; they knew that they made more money than most of the working class (except for Silesian miners) and that they could easily withstand the increased costs. But the majority could not. Moreover, there was the question of how one was treated in this supposed "workers' state". That is why nobody cared to demonstrate in front of the state offices or secret police headquarters; in both Gdansk and Szczecin the demonstrations took place in front of the local committee of the communist party. This has always been the type of building set on fire by Polish workers (in spite of the fact that the word "worker" appears in the name of the party occupying the premises). Indeed, both the Szczecin and Gdansk offices of the party were set on fire, and party officials, undisputed monarchs a few days earlier, found themselves waving in terror for the rescue helicopters to fish them from the roofs of besieged constructions. It never occurred to those humble servants of the working class to go out and negotiate. The first lesson that they drew from December 1970 was that every committee building in every city must be provided with a reinforced helicopter landing on the roof. Another was the need for an exorbitant pay raise for the secret police and special anti-mob police, and a very considerable growth in size and equipment of those units as well.

But let us consider the events first. The original response to the workers' protest had been the same as at Poznan in 1956 and Warsaw in 1968. The police and army were quickly called to the sea coast, while all mass media initially kept silent and only notified the rest of the country after a few days that hooligans had incited very unruly mob behavior and caused some damage to public buildings. To have mentioned the committee of the working class party was to risk recognition of the truth, while using the phrase "public utility building" hopefully insured that no one would know what the TV newsmen were talking about. No mention was originally made of a few hundred killed and wounded as a result of a trap set by Kociolek, then first secretary of the local party committee and a vice-prime minister. He promised workers that they could return to the shipyards in safety and asked them to do so. People agreed and arrived the next morning in huge numbers to enter their shipyard. Mounted machine guns belonging to special police units started "defending" the shipyards from the workers. Hundreds fell, and the period of rioting followed. The official count of those killed was ridiculously low—the data circulated later by independent under-ground sources were usually based on health service and eyewitness accounts. By comparing official notices and by computing the known cases of treatment and deaths one could assume that not 50 to 100 people had been killed, but 200 to 300, with the number of wounded surpassing this considerably.

The local party committee building was set on fire by stuffing its rich carpets into the cellar windows and burning them—while heavy trucks with bricks or concrete blocks were used to break police lines and barricades. Halfway through the riots it was decided that Gomulka and Cyrankiewicz (the prime minister who wanted to "cut hands off" in Poznan and produced a very similar speech in 1970 when the first news of the Gdansk and Szczecin riots reached the media) had to go. Gierek assumed power and went to his Canossa and asked the workers in the shipyards whether they would support him. Reluctantly, they agreed, in return for the promise that the genocide practiced by the police would be revealed and the guilty ones held responsible, and that a regular institution of consulting workers about top party decisions in the large industrial plants would be introduced. But the reports on the police actions never materialized and the chairman of the commission, Jan Szydlak, never a symbol of intelligence or wit, was dropped by Gierek in the mid-seventies, in the course of one of his reconstructions of his power base within the party elite.

Let me stress again: strike, riot, heavy loss of life and severe damage to public buildings led to what outcome? Only a change of personnel in the top executive body, symbolized by a change of both the top party and state officials (first secretary from Gomulka to Gierek and prime minister from Cyrankiewics to Jaroszewicz), vague promises of "consultation" only to the crews of the largest plants which would eventually be able to strike, and equally vague promises that the guilty would be punished.

That is not all; women working in the textile industry in the Lodz area clearly perceived that the top party people played down the original cause of the riots, the new prices, and that these prices were still in effect. They struck a number of times for repeal of the price decision, and succeeded. Old prices were reintroduced. In 1971, a hasty ritual of renewal followed, and life continued as usual.

But not quite. The change in the ruling class was significant in spite of the basic continuity of all institutions and the disadvantages of a centralized economic policy. For there was a definite change in cultural life, a slow and uncertain withdrawal from the 1968 anti-Polish, anti-intellectual policies. And, most important, there was a growing awareness in the working class that politically 1970 was a complete defeat, that nothing was secured. Systematic if delayed action of the party, secret police, and economic managers to purge the activists of 1970 from the shipyards left no doubt as to the impossibility of making advances in such a context. The first signs of an awareness that institutional changes were necessary were cautiously voiced.

The seventies, which began with the December 1970 massacre, were a new period in many respects. There were continuities—the secret police became stronger, more complex and sophisticated, and more heavily financed (the budget of the ministry of the interior was a couple of times larger than the budget of the ministries of culture, education, and science-technology taken together). The Russians exercised increasing influence over political institutions and continued the policies of sovietizing and russifying Polish society, for instance designing new handbooks to eliminate or make harmless Romantic poetry, designing a new constitution which had "love for the Soviet Union" written into it, and prohibiting the

Poles from exhibiting a "Panorama of Raclawice" since the battle of Raclawice in 1794 was a highlight of Polish peasant success in fighting the Russian tsarist army. The "colonialization" of the Polish economy continued and was abused and exploited in the interest of Soviet domestic investments in Siberia and Asia. Finally, the ruling class was definitely the same ruling class it had been since 1945. But there were also changes. The secret police grew more sophisticated and less given to immediate brutality, and the Russians exercised pressure but shifted their interest to economic and military subjection and left some cultural and political questions to the discretion of the domestic ruling class.

The latter also went through a generational change. The older generation of ruling class members stemmed either from the exiled Polish communists who had lived through the period of the Stalinist purges in Russia or from the communist or communist-sympathizing pre-war Polish socialists who stayed in the country and took part in the broad resistance movement. However much their responses to all post-war Polish problems depended on the trauma of the struggle for power in the forties and on their memory of how outnumbered they were by followers of other, non-communist parties, they still knew something about social reality and social processes as they had been before the great state-ization of society took place. The new generation of politicians, while more educated, (though not excessively so, as political power was a convenient instrument in securing diplomas and university degrees for a number of top party bosses whose intellectual abilities remained limited) had been brought up totally within the party-controlled and state-ized society, within the exclusive channels for upward-bound young candidates for the decision-making posts. A typical way to work one's way up was to become a very committed regional or branch organizer (the socialist youth league was good for this, as was the Polish Students Association, or the Woman's League) and then to assume some modest post within the local party committee, to take part in vital party courses and schools, and to serve a period in the party school in Russia, where a rough equivalent of Soviet "public relations" and "managerial techniques" training was coupled with a subtle explanation that a successful party career in Poland depends very much on Soviet views and support.

It meant that this generation was totally incapable of thinking about social development outside of the bonds of state socialist organization. What was to be regarded as anti-socialist was decided by those people who were brought up totally under the protective screen of an inner party breeding farm for functionaries. Tricks of the trade were learned with admiration: a Poznan secretary of the voivodship committee of the ruling party, one of the few princes who waited in the court of the regional first secretary anxious to perform a great leap forward, staged a birthday party for a Soviet ambassador to Poland. He skillfully prolonged the party until midnight came and then discharged his surprise project. A gypsy music group entered the premises and everbody sang "happy birthday." A few months later the secrerary in question became a head of one of the Central committee executive offices, a nice piece of evidence that it pays to cultivate personal liaisons.

The Gomulka victory in 1968 was no setback for this new generation—their steady march forward was secure and they were quick to use every opportunity to confirm their loyalty. The major political upheaval helped; otherwise they would have had to wait patiently until their elders either dropped from the top posts or died off. Instead, the sudden acceleration of political change provided them with a chance they did not overlook. "Polityda," a weekly which replaced "Po Prostu" in 1957 (it was headed by the ambitious Mieczyslaw Rakowski, who cultivated intellectuals and provided an educated go-between for relations with the West) had managed to observe this major re-grouping within the ruling class. In a small note printed in a column on a second page, among brief notes on current events, it observed that almost all the new people whom Gierek's rise brought to power were former ZMP (Union of Polish Youth) members. ZMP was a Stalinist youth organization which systematically terrorized Polish youth and aimed at its total subordination and control in a para-military manner. In 1956, under immense pressure from the Polish young people who wanted to get rid of militarized control of their daily life, ZMP was disbanded and its ridiculous policies condemned, especially its close collaboration with the secret police. For hundreds of thousands of young people this meant a profound liberation from surveillance over their daily lives. But for some hundreds of power-craving well-established functionaries who felt they were bred for a better future of state power it was a disaster. In all their memoirs (and some were actually published by party and state publishing agencies) they stress that the disbanding of ZMP was a painful, inexplicable experience for them. Painful it certainly was; they had to look for another vehicle in order to arrive in the ruling class. But inexplicable it was not; the dissolution was only evidence that although the ruling party was still in power, it had to cut back its own institutions under popular pressure.

The coming of new people to power and Gierek's new policies meant that an appearance of genuine progress had been created. An ambitious economic policy was launched with large scale foreign credits making available some consumer goods previously unattainable. Even here, however, it soon became clear that the selection of consumer goods was not made from the point of view of the public interest. For instance, a Fiat license was bought and mass production of small, cheap cars started, giving about two million more cars in the seventies. But nobody seriously thought about the alternatives like cheaper and less polluting mass transportation. The private automobile appealed to a status-consciousness which was exploited instead of opposed. As a result mass transport inevitably lagged behnd and what had previously been shaky but reliable train, bus, and tramway service became a hell in rush hours, while the lack of proper highways and a relatively sparse network of service stations also meant less comfort for car owners.

Some other purchases (Western brands of cigarettes, alcohols, furniture, and cars) clearly indicated that consumption for the ruling and managerial strata was being taken care of, but at the expense of the average worker. The latter could neither allow themselves the luxury of buying the items in question (a standard cheap package of cigarettes cost 6 zlotys in the late seventies, while "Marlboro" cost 40) or simply had no chance of doing so, as these items could only be purchased outside of the major distribution networks. The prime minister's son, Andrzej Jaroszewicz, ostensibly a rally-car driver, became by the late seventies the head of a special firm which sold Japanese cars to the privileged who did not have to pay in Western currency nor purchase the cars at black market prices.

The seventies thus began with mixed projects which appealed to society by promising to raise living standards and provide better consumer goods, but which at the same time clearly indicated that no change was to be expected in the manner in which society developed. Gierek promised liberalism and encouraged technical managers to side with the party bosses by granting bonuses. But this was the utter limit; bonuses could be had, but no real participation, even at this top managerial level.

People became increasingly frustrated, but their frustration was channeled slowly, especially by the later events of 1976 and 1980. All that immediately followed the 1970 riots and 1971 textile workers' strikes was the emergence of a technocratic-party alliance or a number of such alliances in various branches of the economy. The reason for this occurrence is clear. Managers were rewarded for competence but allowed no final decision-making power. Party secretaries were allowed to make decisions but were incompetent. Both groups understood what they wanted. As a result both achieved stunning successes in advancing their own personal consumption and equally stunning disasters in the economy as a whole. The technocrats provided an economic base for the private use of state enterprises; for example, a few hundred thousand private houses of exquisite design were constructed in the seventies, while public housing collapsed beyond repair. Technocrats learned that increased investments and high-cost projects, which required increased labor, raw materials, and technical supplies for their units and regions, contributed to their upward mobility and increased their possibilities for conspicuous consumption. Party secretaries learned that their regional rule became an opportunity to strike bargains and to make alliances with state managers and other secretaries, with upward mobility and top posts in mind. It is, for instance, no coincidence that Gierek's "power base" in Silesia was considered a model. First came a sound power base premissed on control of a strong industry, even if this required wrecking agriculture as was done in the Lublin area and planned, luckily too late, for Poznan. Only later came the struggle for political power.

Gierek's model of political organization promoted such regional political and economic groupings, thereby providing another chance for the ruling class to reinforce private consumption at the expense of the labor force. Central control had to be less strict than under Gomulka if the above-mentioned strong regional units were to function. This chance was not overlooked either.

Incidentally, the fact that Olszowski and Grabski are presently the hawks of the central committee of the party does not mean that they differ from other members of this body in their views on social life. It only means that they still try to follow the policy of regional party-technocratic alliances, and refuse to acknowledge the political representation of the labor force. They would probably welcome a return to the 1971 situation, and they would try to keep the alliances without at the same time wasting too much on personal consumption. The proud refusal to buy some new brand of car or cigarette for the ruling class could then be propagandized as a reason to refuse amelioration of political and social conditions for the labor force, while gradually bonuses for "good work" would be incentive enough to maintain an orderly working class firmly under control.

It follows from the above that 1970 was a very limited victory (if a victory it was) for the working class. It had certainly been used by one fraction—or generation—of the ruling class against another, and it certainly paid well for those who used it. The gains of the workers were less impressive in comparison, but gains they were: a) Gierek refrained from large-scale terror and even from a thorough dismantling and oppression of opposition groups; b) workers materially profited during the early seventies when more goods were on the market and there was a chance for better living standards, especially for those in the larger industrial complexes and in dangerous or difficult work, c) students and intellectuals clearly benefited from an increased ability to travel and to associate, even if associations were still discouraged and travel possibilities used as an additional means of control.

Poland thus entered the mid-seventies with some actual improvements in living standards, huge for the new members of the ruling class, and a limited but promising liberalization of public opinion.

At the same time 1970 was a threshold. Not because it marked a major awakening of the working class, but because it showed that all previous experiences of the struggle were to be seriously questioned as far as effectiveness went. One major lesson was that neither intellectuals nor students nor workers nor any other sector of state employees could win a major political victory on its own.

The second major lesson was that no regrouping within the ruling class promised much in the way of real concessions. A ruler may go, a new ruler with more credibility may arrive, personnel may be changed, and policies of control may be relaxed, but none of these developments will engender serious changes in the social situation. None promises that socialism will become something more meaningful for the broad masses of working people.

Another lesson was that cooperation with the political elite is good for personal enrichment (which had already been known though by a smaller crowd of technically expert professionals) but does not lead to any rationalization of policy. The distinction between "expert" and "red" became meaningless, especially in view of a whole stratum of professionals, who paraded their party loyalty when "red" was the order of the day, only to become stout and objective professionals and experts whenever technocratic slogans filled the air.

These lessons were to be learned and relearned in the seventies and there was also a growing awareness that state socialism had produced a very complex work force—a differentiated labor force with the state as the sole employer in all walks of life. The class nature of this awareness became clear ten years later.

1976 or the Alliance of the Classless

In June 1976 some adverse effects of the great investment leap forward, accomplished with the help of Western credits, were already obvious. Wage increases coupled with a still insufficient supply of attractive durable goods meant that most surplus money went into current consumption, especially food. Food markets could not hold up, especially in view of moderate or even bad harvests and generally unreliable food production due to the state's quiet yet stubborn attempts to subdue private farmers and make them join the state run sector of agricultural production. Though the policy of limiting the private farmer's productive capacities was successful, the policy of increasing the productivity of state farms was not, and thus food production lagged behind social needs.

So a quick decision had to be made, justifiable from an economic point of view, but executed in a very authoritarian fashion and certainly very painfully for most of the working population: to raise the price of food very considerably. Compensation was offered, but it covered primarily those members of either the ruling class or auxiliary strata of their "co-managers," who were well-off already. The prime minister made his speech and suggested price increases, parliament of course approved it, and two days later the same parliament equally unanimously accepted the withdrawal of the same project by the same prime minister.

What made the prime minister withdraw his definitely sound economic project, and made the delegates to the token parliament make fools of themselves? The political map of postwar Poland had acquired two new sites: Ursus, the huge tractor producing facility just west of Warsaw, and Radom in central Poland, primarily the site of the "Walter" works, where sophisticated metal products and telephones are produced. The workers concentrated in these areas rightly perceived the rise in prices as an attempt to curb their food purchases and voiced their discontent. The ensuing demonstrations were partly organized, partly spontaneous.

In the case of Ursus the protesting workers not only went on strike but also dismantled the railroad on a vital east-west route so that trains from Warsaw to Poznan and Berlin had to be sent through Lodz, which doubled or tripled the time for the journey. Propagandists spoke of hooligans and other "socially marginal" groups, but the move was a very effective one. Ursus is located on both sides of this railroad and the workers have easy access to the tracks. The route is vital from the point of view of Soviet military interests in East Germany and thus decisions on the government level had to be made very quickly. But since clearing the railroad would require a declaration of war on the workers and probably bloodshed, these decisions were not easy, even had other workers not responded so promptly. All major industrial plants had solidarity strikes—brief, local, without outward demonstrations, but to the point and decisive in convincing the government that any armed intervention would mean a general strike in all major industrialized centers.

I remember a worker who voiced his opinions in a streetcar: "I don't care myself, I have enough, and I make enough money not to feel the burden of this rise. But we strike on behalf of those who cannot pay for it, those who have not." It was a June evening, the worker was young and a little tipsy, the streetcar was full, and everybody listened attentively. I had a strange feeling that something was happening that went beyond a struggle for cheaper meat and bread.

The focus shifted from Ursus and other industrial centers to Radom. There the protesting workers were supplemented by women. Housewives went to the building of the regional committee of the ruling party and waved empty shopping bags demanding the withdrawal of the food decision. The economic secretary of the party was stripped naked and run through the streets of Radom. The women demanded somebody to speak to and when nobody appeared they went to look for party functionaries in their homes. They did not find them, but they did see the houses and what they saw inside was another lesson. Nothing was stolen and nothing was touched. The angry crowd of women just marched, rank and file, through the rooms and halls of the luxurious houses of the party officals. Silently, watching every carpet, every mosaic, every antique piece of furniture, every elegant kitchen and bathroom appliance, every golden ornament and electronic gadget. The scene must have been profoundly solemn, and very educational: the women marching silently, as if through a museum, through the private apartments of the local party bosses. The party people and their families stood there in terror, but nothing happened to them nor to their property. Something else happened—people who were being told they should consume less visited those who had made that decision. I can imagine no better lesson of class difference than this one. The women did not achieve what they wanted then, however, as no one took them seriously.

But soon all hell broke loose. It was decided that food prices should be withdrawn, but the unruly Radom workers should be punished, and likewise the Ursus instigators. Special detachments of secret police masquerading as demonstrators were sent to Radom and started smashing shop windows, stealing TV sets, and attempting to assault police and party officials. Not surprisingly TV crews were there and public opinion was formed concerning the hooligan activities of the Radom workers. The police started brutal repressions. So on the one hand people throughout the country had been pacified by the withdrawal of the price rise (I remember riding in a taxi on the evening of the day the withdrawal was announced—the driver was tossing candies through his window when he stopped at the lights; the mood was festive and united almost all social classes) while on the other hand Radom and Ursus had to pay the price.

Radom was the prime target. All public expenditures had been cut; in order to punish the population no improvements were made after 1976 in city services, no new investments to help the local economy. But more astonishing was the police brutality. It was, psychologically speaking, understandable; the police force was overpaid but underused and was anxious to please. It did its job; people were beaten up and imprisoned. All those who had played any part in organizing the workers' protest were swiftly removed from their jobs and interrogated. These interrogations surpassed in brutality anything that Poland had seen since 1970. Police tortured workers by forcing them to run between rows of drunken truncheon-waving functionaries. The name of this particular torture was the "health path" as this was the time when jogging became fashionable and people started charting "health paths" through city parks and suburban woods. Such procedures added, in the late seventies, to the many deaths investigated by oppositional groups.

It became obvious that while generally the police were kept in check they could always be unleashed. It became obvious that people could be killed by the police; the Krakow student, Pyjas, became a great "cause celebre," with his burial becoming a demonstraton. It was also obvious that the police were beyond legal control, a new independent political force, at the disposal of the ruling class but outside the legal framework of society. In other words, battles could be lost or won, but the ruling class reserved for itself the right to start indiscriminate terror whenever it chose. That was the message even without actual mass terror, which Gierek did not like in view of his love for international contacts and his self-image as a liberal pragmatist.

The solution selected by the ruling class was no doubt thought to be best. However, it misfired. People had not forgotten Radom just because food was no longer expensive. Intellectuals did not sit back, workers did not leave their Radom colleagues. 1976 happened twenty years after 1956, and the lessons of those years did not escape the supposedly classless people.

To put it in a nutshell: in 1976 the ruling class still had the political initiative. Responses of the working masses were based on a kind of defensive stimulus-response process. But the ruling class did not have complete freedom either in exercising its political initiative. The limited terror and unlimited withdrawal of the price increases to avoid mass protests drew the attention of all working people to the fact that their economic grievances were part and parcel of their more serious grievances against the way society was organized and run. It also demonstrated the secondary nature of economic as opposed to political decisions. In a society which is state-ized to such an extent, political power is the conditio sine qua non of any other kind of power, including economic.

KOR and the Polish Movement

1976 is a historic date for another reason. It was the year in which the Committee for Workers' Defense (KOR) was founded. It was a very concrete and limited step in the direction of the political organization of society. A group of intellectuals decided the workers in Radom needed political, legal, and economic support in view of the systematic repression which threatened their ability to earn their living and support their families. Money was collected, special publications issued, foreign correspondents notified, lawyers selected, and abuses of police power investigated and reported.

The people who started KOR were not politicians, although most of them had political ideas. They were writers, scholars, scientists, priests, lawyers, actors, students, poets, and graphic artists. That is, they were mostly professionals who were concerned with abuses of police power against workers who had justly protested the arbitrary food prices decided on by the authorities. The people who formed KOR were not taken seriously by the ruling class, and so they were harassed enough to feel repression but not enough to make the world think that Poland was a police state. Moreover, as the sole representatives of public opinion, KOR soon became an overworked agency. It was supported by the church and especially by those church agencies which were responsible for educational tasks and could barely move for fear of state repression (for example, the Dominicans, whose musical and literary efforts were considerable, especially in academic circles) and by students.

The development of KOR coincided with the slow birth of an independent trade union movement, a much more difficult process. One of its pioneers, Kazimierz Switon, was frequently beaten up by police when leaving church on Sunday, then convicted on charges of assaulting policemen; all this in public view, with armed policemen practically reducing the man to a pulp and then announcing that he had been convicted of "hooliganism." Such events could only help the development of independent trade union thinking, although it was also clear that mass growth of this movement was still in the distant future as not everybody was willing to be reduced to pulp and to go to prison for "assaulting a functionary of law and order."

The existence of KOR meant primarily that the fate of those workers whom the police chose to prosecute was not quite so gloomy. They were well defended, their cases were constantly re-examined, lies and discrepancies in police reports were noticed and made use of. Their families were helped—an astonishing amount of money poured into KOR funds, and it was all scrupulously used for the benefit of those who suffered in 1976, primarily those who had been fired and had to be taken care of. The trade union idea was stimulated to a large extent by this very practical activity of collecting money and distributing it among those whom the state persecuted for their views. It was a very important development. KOR funds for political prisoners and the politically jobless provided the first shelter for workers and the first real organized sustained resistance to the overwhelming power of the state.

The ruling class tried to do some old fashioned muckraking, but society felt the worth of KOR and refused to yield to pressure. In one case, a founding member of KOR, Dr. Stanislaw Baranczak (of the Department of Polish Studies, Poznan University, a well known poet, critic, and translator of e.e. cummings, Dylan Thomas and the British metaphysical poets) was accused of bribing a state official and speedily dismissed from his post and given a suspended sentence. Exquisite references for Baranczak made no impression on the judge, though he was impressed by the honesty of the poor bribed state official who testified against Baranczak. As it happened, this official had been caught by police in the course of an affair which involved his considerable corruption. Having been promised impunity, he willingly collaborated in trapping Baranczak, who had had to get his permission to buy or lease a flat in one of the small satellite towns around Poznan. He asked Baranczak for "money for the libraries." Baranczak agreed and sure enough the police agents appeared and listened to what they deemed a convincing story of bribery. The suspended sentence was also no accident; it meant that in case of a changed political situation the sentence could be pronounced baseless. At the same time, during the period of its duration, Baranczak was on probation and could easily be refused a passport or employment in academic circles.

This kind of repression, although extremely base and vicious, was also a demonstration of a limit imposed on state agencies in exercising total power. No direct threat to life, no indiscriminate mass terror was in sight. Constant supervision and control, yes, but no constant terror. The ruling class of the late Gierek period, between 1976 and 1980, tried to both eat the cake (exercise police control over society) and have it (protect its image in world public opinion from the damage usually caused by news of political persecution). The effort was immense and the will was certainly there, but eating the cake and having it too is of course impossible. Luckily, the ruling class knew little of this impossibility, and the whole situation developed to the best advantage of the working class.

The term "luckily" is not used without reason. But it was not sheer luck that determined the behavior of the ruling class in the late seventies. This behavior was also influenced by economic pressures and the impossibility of instituting any rational economic policy while the leaders depended on the increasing support of their creditors, and this, in turn, necessitated reinforcement of the "liberal" image. But the historical constellation of factors which made the Hungarians and Czechs go down in blood and dust before the caterpillars of armored divisions had, in this particular period, worked to the opposite effect in Poland. This was, indeed, a coincidence, and a drop of luck—that in the late seventies the decomposition of the Polish ruling class prevented it from promptly staging a new political ritual, a new nationwide ceremony, allowing it instead only to defend its positions. This defense meant that the military, the media, and the Soviets were firmly kept in check. No good-bye to the Warsaw pact, no Polish Dubcek to ride the wave of reform, but a solid body of functionaries clinging to their positions, revealing the ruling class in its naked will to power.

On the other hand there was the immense social solidarity forged in the late seventies to be used to such astonishing success in 1980. It was the solidarity of a social class which had recognized its own possibilities and made its first moves—enough to snatch and maintain some political initiative but not enough to overrun state institutions and oust the ruling class. This was also, under the circumstances, a lucky outcome.

The late seventies were a period of at least two other important processes. First, there was a very vital student movement and a general feeling that social self-defense against the police and the party state had to become organized. This coincided with some initiatives of KOR, and thus the "Flying University" was born to allow the nation's top intellectuals to lecture despite police harrassment and hired-thug attacks, primarily about the country's actual social and economic structure, the history of people's Poland and the roots of WWII. The lecture rooms were limited, but the underground publications, printed under the brilliant supervision of Miroslaw Chojecke, and distributed by a large network, were attainable in many academic circles. The Nowa underground publishing house managed to publish over 150 titles in a number of copies which would make a medium sized official publishing house envious. Regular underground periodicals appeared and vital works of authors forbidden by state censorship were read, reread, and passed on to the next reader.

Apart from all these developments, 1980 arrived after the most important organizational experience of the working class: the experience of constructing and conducting a nation-wide activity while the ruling class remained neutral and mostly refrained from doing anything. It was as if the ruling class reluctantly allowed some event to occur, withdrew and let the working class run it, then came back and resumed its normal functions.

Yet in the interim the working class, the class of state employees, had already learned its possibilities. Moreover, it had learned that the coordination of social life is possible without any intervention from the supposedly indispensible ruling class, and that this obviously opens up many new possibilities. In a word, the visit of the Pope took place. Religiously speaking, I am unmoved by it. It is nice that the Pope is Polish, for one likes one's own culture and one's own nation, but I definitely do not think that this visit had spiritual meaning as a dress rehearsal, as I read in one of the "Solidarity" publications. Yet it *was* a dress rehearsal, not of a new religious way of organizing life in modern society, but of a new way of getting along without cooperation and coordination on the part of the ruling class. This was decisive. A very successful public event took place, and it awakened the memory of self-reliance for almost all its participants. People ceased to expect things from the state and the ruling class, and realized they could equally well execute things themselves. Self-reliance in matters of organization and coordination was a factor which seemed slight and insignificant at the time of the visit, and it was drowned in exclamations about Poland's greatness (mostly from the ruling class, which liked the idea of the Pope's visit as a kind of entertainment for the masses, who were already getting a little bit hungry and tired of meat lines) and catholicism's victory (from the church itself).

Yet it mattered more than was usually supposed. The experience of self-reliance and of the unreliability of the ruling class coincided with an exceptionally frosty winter. Coal was unavailable, everything came to a halt, and it became even clearer that the state was not coordinated rationally. Material discomfort was widespread and inflation soared while meat shops became practically empty except for a couple of hours per day when huge lines assembled till the last item was bought out. The stage was set for 1980.

Chapter Four

August 1980
Plain Facts On Gdansk

The stage was set for Gdansk. The ruling class was too strong to be directly deprived of influence, but it was also too weak to introduce any reforms which could facilitate its way out of a complex social situation, and especially a way out of a growing public awareness that a shower of foreign credits was improving living standards for the ruling class and its clients, but doing little to ease the fate of common people.

The first sign of new developments came in late July 1980, when Lublin railroad workers fixed to the rails the wheels of a train bound for the Soviet Union and filled with Polish export food, especially meat products. The synchronization of these railroad activities was excellent and support by the local population was overwhelming. The Polish media decided to tell the story, a peaceful solution was found, and a compromise was reached, yet neither side was satisfied.

What follows is a chronicle of the events of August 1980 in the Gdansk shipyards. On Thursday, August 14, leaflets appeared in the streetcars and subway trains which transport people to the shipyards in Gdansk. Leaflets and a special issue of "Robotnik" ("Worker"—a clandestine organ of the independent trade unions published with the aid and support of KOR) demanded the reinstating of Anna Walentynowicz, a heavy-crane operator, who had been removed from her job in section W-2 of the shipyards. The leaflets brought the following news:

"To the workers of the Gdansk shipyards. We address you as colleagues of Anna Walentynowicz. She has worked in the shipyards since 1950. She has been a welder for 16 years, then a heavy crane operator in W-2. She has been awarded a bronze, silver and golden Cross of Merit. She has always been an excellent worker and she has always responded bravely whenever injustice and wrongdoing appeared. This prompted her to aid the trade unions which would be independent of the employer. From that time on she has been persecuted: for a few months she was sent to another factory, she was disciplined for disseminating "Robotnik," and removed to another section. Although these repressions were unpleasant, they were not extreme. In the last few days management has given up even those appearances of legality.

Here is what happened.

On April 17, 1980, the regional commission for labor matters reinstated A. Walentynowicz at her previous post of heavy crane operator on W-2. A. Walentynowicz thus started working there. After an hour of work the foreman Z. Falczynski and the head of prefabrication in W-2, A. Guminski, switched the crane off, making it impossible for her to work. Then her wardrobe was pried open and another worker was ordered to use it. On July 30, she was stopped at the gate and upon orders of the commander of guards, Turowiecki, kept there for 1.5 hours. The manager of the personnel section, T. Zurowski, pretended that nothing had happened and demanded further work. From that day until August 5, A. Walentynowicz spent her working hours in the cloak room of W-2, since she was refused permission to enter the main hall and start working; sometimes she was locked there. Every day she demanded in vain that the commission's verdict be obeyed. On August 4 she began to talk to the general manager and suggested that she begin working on a different spot. During this conversation the recruitment manager Szczypinski said that she had to visit the commission again since a new document awaited her. This document turned out to be a declaration by the head of the commission, Judge Gorecki, who claimed that she had obtained the previous verdict by a mistake. Four days later, when staying at home due to illness, Walentynowicz received a disciplinary dismissal from her job (signed on August 7, 1980) 'because of a grave crime against the duties of a worker.' The dismissal was signed by a manager taking care of personnel matters named Slaby. It has to be remembered that Walentynowicz only had 5 months to go before retirement. The course of events showed that the management of the shipyards did not care for public opinion or law. The latter was broken and bent to management's will with the help of bought people. Walentynowicz became an enemy because she set a "wrong example" to the others. She became an enemy because she defended others and could organize her colleagues. For the authorities always try to isolate those who could become leaders. After the strikes of 1976, a sufficient reason to receive a dismissal was that one had authority among one's peers in the shipyards. If there is nobody with authority, there will be no defense against increased norms, carelessness with labor safety, or compulsory overtime. It is in our interest to defend these people. Therefore we appeal to you to defend A. Walentynowicz. If you do not, many of you may face a similar situation. And we remind the management that such decisions in view of a wave of strikes which continues in the country are unreasonable to say the least.

Signed: Founding Committee of Independent Trade Unions and editors of *Robotnik*: Bogdan Borusewicz, Joanna-Duda-Gwiazda, Andrezej Gwiazda, Jan Karandziej, Maryla Plonska, Alina Pienkowska, Lech Walesa."

The poster which appeared in the shipyards also included demands for a pay increase and a special inflation adjustment.

The document was the first link between 1976 and the 1980 unrest which was spreading, along with the slow tactical price rises the government was introducing, without, however, organizing a single price jump so as to avoid provoking any open clashes with the workers.

The document was read, so were the posters, but the attitudes of a majority of the workers were still indecisive. Thus on August 14 the groups of workers who decided to march towards the management building were not very numerous and lacked any clear blueprint for action. However, the sheer number of workers who gradually joined the marching groups contributed to the feeling of unity and to the first weak and hesitant hope that maybe something could be won. Around 8 a.m. an improvised meeting was about to begin—the national anthem was sung and a minute of silence to commemorate colleagues killed by the police in December 1970 was observed. An excavator which happened to stand close by became an improvised rostrum—management and the strike's organizers improvised their speeches. For a couple of minutes it seemed that management, which had already realized the scale of possible developments, would control the situation. Intervention on behalf of Walentynowicz was hastily promised, attempts to increase salaries were announced.

This was the moment when Walesa appeared. He started by introducing himself: "I worked ten years in the shipyards and I still feel like a worker here, because people trust me. For four years I have been jobless." This was true. He was removed from his job (a secondary electrotechnician's education had prepared him for electric jobs in the shipyards) as a result of his activities with independent trade unions. He was dismissed from his work and often harassed by a well known police method. The law in Poland says that one cannot be kept by the police longer than 48 hours before one receives an official complaint and explanation for police activity signed by the prosecutor's office. Thus the police often keep people who work against the authorities for 47 hours and then release them, especially if this prevents them from attending meetings or staging speeches. Walesa was often harassed in this manner—but what was meant to warn and tire him out, turned out to be a good school of political activity. As he confirmed in a conversation with Oriana Fallaci, on being released after 48 hours he was without money, so in order to use city transportation to get home he had to borrow and beg for change on stations and at stops. This demanded some introduction—and some of his political speeches were created on the spur of the moment, as he approached strangers and explained where he came from and why he was imprisoned. He never had to wait. He not only got money to get home—he got involved in heated discussions, explaining his reasons for fighting for free independent trade unions,

Walesa had never been a political leader. However, rumor has it that his ability to command attention and to win authority easily in very mixed and complex situations had been recognized fairly early. As a regular soldier drafted for two years into the army he was quickly recognized by his superiors to have commander's abilities. It is to the credit of the psychologists in the Polish army that his military "secret opinion" pinned to his personal file says that "he is a very gifted commander and has tremendous potential for winning cooperation from his colleagues and subordinates. He is gifted enough to command large military units, perhaps even the largest, on the top level." As a result of this finding Walesa was promised a military career and attendance at an officer's school with bright prospects. Walesa refused.

It is hard to assess the validity of this story. It was circulating in early 1981 as a result of a leak from the Polish military who were helping in the filming of "Man of Iron" by Wajda, which is a sequel to "Man of Marble" and which includes scenes from the 1970 uprising in Gdansk. I have never questioned Wajda himself, nor his informants (who were not named) but the story was popular among Wajda's assistants during the making of "Man of Iron," though it should be viewed with some scepticism. If I venture to recall it here, it is because it is at least plausible and it is picturesque enough to merit attention, while not destroying any myths nor wronging anyone if it subsequently turns out to be a fabrication.

Be that as it may, it is a historical fact that Walesa's last words spoken from the top of the excavator during the improvised meeting on August 14, 1980 in the Gdansk shipyard were: "We organize herewith an occupational strike."

The history of Poland and the history of world socialism, especially state socialism, has never been the same since these words were spoken. The sit-in technique, an occupation as such, was nothing new. Generations of European workers had tried it with and without success. However, in the Polish context of 1980 it was a rational choice of the only alternative which would not compel a direct clash with the supreme police force of the hypertropic state. The workers stayed at home in the factories.

The correctness of this decision was confirmed by General Jaruzelski during the famous sitting of the Central Committee of the Polish Communist Party, some 7-10 days later, when Olszowski demanded a military takeover in the country and suppression of worker unrest. Jaruzelski replied that there were over 500 factories on strike at the moment and that the army would have to storm five hundred fortified castles—and that no Polish officers would easily command "fire" in front of the Polish workers in those castles.

It should be stressed once again: the timing of Walesa's speech was a historical phenomenon. The experience of the Polish workers since 1945 had matured: a stout stand had been taken, a factory occupied, and decent negotiations were demanded. The Gdansk occupational strike was a blow to the legitimacy of the ruling class (which supposedly represented workers' best interests) and provided solid ground for prolonged negotiation with the state. The state may exercise a monopoly of coercion and legalized violence but it cannot run the factories. In spite of attempts to militarize some branches of the economy and in spite of the argument voiced by one of the less vigilant representatives of the ruling class in Silesia in a conversation with the miners later on—"You do not want to work Saturdays? Then I will import myself Yugoslavian miners..."—in Eastern Europe no real alternative to native labor exists.

As a result of the first meeting a Strikers' Committee was founded: the new list of demands included a reinstatement of Anna Walentynowicz and Lech Walesa as shipyard employees, along with other former members of the Striker's Committee of December 1970, a guarantee of non-repressive treatment of all striking workers, a pay raise of 2,000 zlotys per month, and a rise in family allowances to the level already enjoyed by functionaries of the police and secret police.

The first brief negotiations with management resulted in agreement on the first three demands. This, in the view of striking workers, was not enough. More activities were organized—a workers' guard was created and responsibility for orderly life in the striking shipyard was assumed by the workers themselves. The guards saw to it, for instance, that no strangers entered the area and no alcohol was distributed (the police tried provocation—for example, crates of vodka appeared close to the shipyard entrance out of nowhere) but to no avail.

The occupational strike in the Gdansk shipyards went on.

On August 15 further factories joined the strike: among them the Gdynia shipyards, Gdansk Repair Shipyards, and city communications centers and factories which cooperated with the shipbuilding industry. The ruling class also responded in classical fashion. Poland suffers an acute shortage of telephone networking but there does exist fairly modern automatic communication among all major centers—however, at 12:00 this network was cut off. The Coast was surrounded by a silent "cordon sanitaire." No telexes could be sent out.

Meanwhile management continued talking to the workers. Lech Walesa became the leader of the Striking Committee. An early tactical move on the part of management was to suggest that the committee should be more representative and include people who represented other sections of the shipyards. Management hoped that thus the management's people would enter the negotiations on the workers' side. This manoeuver met with partial success. But the strike gained momentum and the impossibility of stopping all communications (it was summer and people were coming and going to and from the Baltic coast beaches) made increasing numbers of factories in the whole nation join the strike. Gdansk rose to the role of the symbol of the national Polish workers' struggle.

Tactical moves on the part of regional management were supported by low-key but persistent propaganda in the media. A typical instance of this propaganda was provided by "Coastal Evening" ("Wie Czor Wybrzeza," an afternoon paper serving the coastal cities) which published the following cautious admonition:

> We know that there are many painful problems, that troubles are acute, shortages, frictions, and weaknesses plentiful. We could not keep silent—we all care to get rid of them. But the individual, social, and national interest requires us to work during working hours and to dicuss only when time and place are suitable. To mix work and discussion...is an irrational activity, and only rational activities may result in durable, desirable results.

The media are well orchestrated and their saving grace is their low-key strategy. But the media lagged behind the new awareness of the striking workers—the workers read the newspapers and listened to TV but did not pay any attention to them. They realized that something else was at stake and they would not be treated as children again—even if the invisible tutor decided to act in a tactful and low-key manner.

On August 16 negotiations still continued between the striking workers and management, and there was even a chance to arrive at a compromise. One may wonder presently what the Polish situation would be like if the striking committee had actually accepted the compromise that was reached on August 16, namely, that:

—All participants in the strike of 14-16 August obtain full pay for the strike days and declarations of personal safety from police harassment;

—All workers in the shipyards win salary increases of 1500 zlotys per month;

—Activities of the trade unions in the shipyards are to be reexamined;

—Formerly dismissed persons are to be re-employed;

—Memory of the victims of the police massacre of 1970 is to be observed; and,

—Introduction of a four week probation period for the authorities who have to fulfill other postulates in this period is to be enacted. They must furnish better supplies of food, abolish "commercial," i.e. higher, meat prices, and make the family allowances of all groups of employees equal.

At 3 p.m. an official declaration that the strike was over was issued. However, a sudden spontaneous development took place. A group of workers arrived in the conference room and pleaded ignorance of the decision, charging the strikers' committee with treason. They claimed that if Gdansk compromised other strikes in the nation would be easily dealt with, while no guarantee of the fulfillment of other workers' postulates would be in sight. The discussion left the conference room and the workers started discussing matters in the vicinity of Gate No. 2, soon to become the world's most photographed gate, the symbol of the iron will and support of the population expressed with food, money and thousands of flowers. Some people left thinking that the strike was over, but most of them did not. The discussion became heated and there was a risk that after all people would go home and the next day would be a normal work day without any institutional guarantees having been won.

This was the moment of Walesa's most momentous decision: he said that if the workers still wanted to strike, he would stay with them. He would be the last to leave the shipyards. But this decision had to be made with a majority vote. The next few seconds were the crux of the matter, the symbol of a new awareness of political struggle.

—Who wants to strike?

—We do!

—Who does not want to strike?

Silence at Gate No. 2.

—O.K. We go on striking. I will leave the shipyards as the last one.

The gates were closed again. People returned to their posts and improvised shelters. I remember a semi-tent someone built bearing a sign "Hilton Hotel. Dollars only." Spontaneous discussions went on and the Strikers' Committee became a City Striking Committee, which later became an Inter-Factory Striking Committee.

The change of name of this particular body was very interesting—it reflected the growing awareness of the unity of all striking workers. The first name, 14-16 August, reflected the immediate constituency of shipyard workers, the second, a regional association of Gdansk workers, the last, the "inter-factory" formula, included all possible factories with all workers in the country who supported the strike in Gdansk and who would also profit from its victories. A national representation of independent, striking workers was born.

This was already a watershed in the history of the state socialist countries: immediate producers had organized themselves on a national level. No matter what might happen next the slogan on one of the walls near Gate No. 2—"Workers of all factories unite"—reflected this new reality. The ruling class still clung to the old tactical approaches which had worked in the past: for example, a general manager, whom the workers refused to let into his office, appeared in the shipyards, smuggled in by a police motor-boat. But his role was over. And so was the role of the regional representatives of the ruling class.

August 17 was a Sunday, and at nine a.m. a service took place around an improvised altar near Gate No. 2. A local priest fulfilled his weekly duty in front of about 5,000 workers and 2,000 people outside the gate. A wooden cross commemorated the place where people had been killed in December 1970 and it was soon flooded with flowers, brought daily by hundreds of people.

A list of postulates was worked out anew, foreign journalists appeared and political struggle became quite obvious and open, though this did not prevent the academic representatives of the ruling class from declaring cheerfully on TV screens that the workers only wanted more money and that the strike had a purely economic nature. Shipyard workers who left the day before appeared anew as stories circulated of people who went home from the shipyards on Saturday only to be greeted by the disapproval of their families—I managed to confirm two—of sons who were sent back after they related what happened to their families. Right before midnight a few more postulates were added; these were vital. The list of 21 postulates was a mature list of political, social and economic demands, which were a package deal and rationally supported each other, providing for institutional guarantees, political change, and not for a superficial cosmetic facelift of the existing organizational framework of the state socialist society.

There was something more to this development: the Inter-Factory Striking Committee actually assumed authority and ruled the coast. Nobody talked to the ruling class any more—health and all other city services sent their delegates and asked for instructions: how can we support you? The committee made decisions, ordered hospitals and all city services to work, and all special cases were discussed and decided upon. During the strike one of the huge poultry farms supplying the city was short on fodder—the committee thus made the decision to unload one ship in the port specifically for the purpose of getting the fodder, and the order was carried out exactly and speedily.

Money was spontaneously offered for the striking workers. Duty hours were introduced for workers' guards.

Monday, August 18, was a very tense day. Both parties of August 16 tried to win workers who appeared in the morning to their side. The manager of the shipyards used the radio network and repeatedly read out the text of the agreement of August 16, reminding them that they should go to work. A huge body of workers remained indecisively in front of the shipyards. Radio broadcasts began at 5:40.

At 7:00 a.m. Walesa arrived at the head of this huge indecisive crowd in front of the gates and started singing the national anthem. To the managers' admonitions that "management is responsible for law and order and nobody must enter the shipyard before the remnants of those who do not accept the agreement leave..." Walesa declared: "Attention workers behind the gate. Enter freely! We have to fight for what we truly deserve. Come and join us. Nobody will be threatened. The manager says we broke the agreement, but we signed the text which said that 1500 zlotys are for everybody, and now he claims that it will be the average raise. For whom an average? Cheers to those who join us!"

The course of events was thus determined. Workers supported Walesa and their colleagues who decided to continue the strike and to issue new, politically and socially broadened demands. Managers tried their last tactical move and distributed leaflets which encouraged workers to go to work (the leaflets were unsigned) but this proved to be unsuccessful, especially in view of the ever increasing traffic from all parts of the country. Workers' delegates came bringing the news about hundreds of new strikes and total support for the Gdansk demands, Gdansk attitudes, Gdansk's recognized leading role in the political struggle.

The manager refused to give the radio network of the shipyards to the workers. Food supplies were meanwhile organized, while at 9:30 (only hours passed before new, significant developments appeared—but those were decisive hours), when 40 factories were already on the list of those who accepted the demands and the leading role of the Gdansk center under new circumstances, a new message was distributed, a new communique which said:

"As a result of an agreement reached between the striking crews of factories and enterprises a text of demands and postulates which have been jointly agreed upon has been written. Strike has been decided upon until those demands are met. The Inter-Factory Strikers' Committee has been notified that it has the right to represent us in negotiations with the central authorities. The decision to end the strike can only be made by the Inter-Factory Strikers' Committee. After the end of the strike the committee will not dissolve, but shall control the implementation of a future agreement and will organize new independent trade unions as a regional council of new trade unions."

The message was sent to the regional authorities.

At 10:00 a.m. a meeting began in front of the management building; half an hour later 55 factories had already checked in, many more TV and reporters' crews were on the spot, a letter was sent to the regional authorities to close liquor stores, while delegates successively voted on the list of postulates. A huge ovation followed the voting. A general presentation of the situation in the delegates' factories was becoming the rule—every session would listen to the news.

At 11:20 Walesa once again appealed to the manager to give in and to hand the radio network over to the workers, while Gwiazda read out the principles of the strike organization and trade union movement. A kitchen was improvised, a printing establishment (originally with mimeograph only) opened. Some representatives of the opposition, from the Young Poland Movement (coastal youth organization) and KOR (Bogdan Borusewicz) were also there. By 12:10 representatives of 82 factories were already in the shipyards; they all told the same story—workers were on strike and waited for their demands to be fulfilled.

A spontaneous family-bond service was being organized next to the now famous Gate no.2; families came and left messages and food; circulation, timing, everything had to be worked out. A Polish TV crew arrived to interview the manager—the text of the interview was played to the workers who decided against accepting it.

By 2:00 100 factories had delegates in the shipyards. Management became increasingly nervous—one of the managers suggested that he might facilitate contacts with "someone very high up," "who may get things done." This manager was already a laughing stock. A head of the information agency was told to leave the area as the reports from his agency were not reliable for the workers. A decision was made—every day at 10 a.m. and 8 p.m. all representatives of striking factories would meet "in pleno."

At 8:00 p.m. Gierek made his TV speech—he had just returned from a holiday in the Crimea—his story was carefully listened to, but generally rejected as unreliable, unpromising and obviously full of propaganda which had ceased to matter. The response was universal laughter and whistles; everybody understood that Gierek was unable to comprehend the situation and that unless he recognized the situation and started talking in plain language, he could not count on any attention.

At 9 p.m. the committee was coordinating practically all activities and city services. 156 factories were already in the committee, including many non-industrial enterprises like the research institutes of technical departments of the Polish Academy of Sciences. When news reached the shipyards that police were stopping cars which carried the national flag (the government had attempted a few years earlier to monopolize the use of national symbols, a project which never materialized in its original form due to the opposition to constitutional amendments), the response was "not to become provoked, not to oppose the police."

Information in the Polish media was scarce and ambiguous. On the one hand it was clear that the ruling class remained devoted to a low-key response and to a gradual easing of censorship (which meant that the press reported, "yes, we are in trouble, yes, we made mistakes"), while on the other hand there was an unceasing stress on the impossibility of negotiating before workers started working again. It was clear that the ruling class wanted primarily to have all workers back in the factories, and hoped for a gradual dissolving of political demands in bogged-down negotiations with selected and manipulated representatives. There was also a message that the government of the Polish People's Republic and Political Bureau of the Central Committee of the Communist Party had called a special commission headed by deputy prime-minister Tadeusz Pyka, which was to discuss the demands of the coastal workers. However, the communique of the state press agency also stressed the fact that such discussion could only be fruitful if peace and work were achieved.

August 19

A delegation, headed by Bogdan Lis of Elmor Works, went to the city authorities to hand them a list of demands. The authorities did not have time to meet the delegates of the striking workers as they were busy talking to Pyka's people from Warsaw, and thus the list was simply handed over to the secretary who formally acknowledged its receipt.

When the delegates returned, they witnessed an enthusiastic reception of the Elblag regional striking committee, which had joined Gdansk. A small center with its own social order gradually developed—it was noted, for instance, on that day, that food expenses had already exceeded 50,000 zlotys. At noon the faculty and workers of Gdansk Polytechnic University expressed their solidarity with the Gdansk workers. The night session in the regional committee of the communist party records were read out.

It became clear that the government had tried to bypass the committee in negotiations—the Warsaw delegation had rung up various factories and suggested piecemeal negotiations. This tactic was rejected by a majority of the committee in the shipyards. Many protests against the illegal activities of the police and secret police were prepared and disseminated. In the evening the following declaration was issued:

"The range and scope of the Inter-Factory Strikers' Committee (MKS) has already surpassed the limits of the Tri-City area and includes factories in Pruszcz Gdanski, Stargard Gdanski, Elblag and Tczew. All those regions have factories on strike. The only exceptions are enterprises which are socially indispensible. Thus MKS secures proper functioning of health services, water works, gas works, and food producing factories. We can boldly claim that we are the first authentic and free representation of the working masses in our country. This makes us bear a grave responsibility in the face of the whole society. Our major task is to create free independent trade unions, independent of the communist party and employers, since only then will the interests and rights of the employees be efficiently defended. As long as we do not have free trade unions the strike remains our only form of struggle, although this is socially the most costly method of negotiating. But only free trade unions may strive to secure the undisturbed functioning of the national economy and at the same time the actualization of workers' postulates."

Again, this was a great breakthrough in political thinking. The people who wrote the message and circulated it were, until August 1980, passive members of the working class, whose fate was decided by the ruling class as a monopolist in matters of state organization. How long a way had been travelled from the first postulates about dismissed colleagues and pay raises to their awareness of expressing the popular spontaneous political views of masses of the Polish workers. How swiftly and naturally, and how successfully had the workers assumed the actual coordination of daily life in society at large. How automatically and happily had this spontaneous authority of true workers' representatives been recognized by all other workers, by all people in Poland who were not linked to the ruling class by the servile demands of personal interest or uniformed obedience. Yet this is actually what happened. The workers started their struggle and they moved along, winning increasing support and managing an increasing number of activities throughout the country.

The state tried another move: an anonymous messages was circulated to the effect that 17 factories had already talked to Pyka's commission and reached an agreement. The document was well phrased and in other circumstances might possibly have had some appeal—were it not for the fact that the ruling class did not keep in touch with the tremendously rapid growth of workers' consciousness and employed tactics which were already obsolete. The communique said:

"On August 19, 1980 striking committees of 17 factories at the Coast met with the government commission to see to the problems and demands of the workers headed by Tadeusz Pyka. In a joint session postulates were discussed. The chairman of the commission, deputy prime minster Pyka, accepted demands and promised to realize within a specified time over 20 postulates of the striking workers.

A new formula for the privileges of factory trade union units has been accepted. Striking committees are to continue working until a congress of national trade unions votes a new statute in which a decisive voice of the latter in workers' matters will be ensured. The government commisssion guarantees a considerable amelioration of market supplies of meat and other foodstuffs. Two new factories producing housing will bring about a better housing situation at the coast. The working conditions of the health service will improve and there will be more medicines and pharmaceuticals.

In order to secure social care three-year long maternity leaves will be gradually introduced.

From Sept. 1 on all workers will receive payment for free Saturdays, while beginning Jan. 1st, 1981 all Saturdays will be free. Detailed suggestions will be prepared by striking committees.

From Sept. 1st on there will be a guaranteed pay raise proportional to the rise in the cost of living with a particular stress on women and those who earn least.

Other postulates will be discussed during the talks with the factory striking committees..."

The communique closed with the phone number of the government commission which everybody was supposed to use in order to solve the problems. Two things are very striking: a) that the government commission immediately started with an open attempt to destroy the authority of the MKS as an independent agency to deal with the government and with a clear tactic of splitting the factory workers into those who negotiate with the government and those who do not; and b) that while totally ignoring political and social demands the government was ready to outvote the workers as far as economic demands went—more concessions were offered than were demanded, much more rapidly than was demanded, and without any hesitation caused by their overall inflationary effect.

It seemed to be a good move, but it failed completely, primarily because of the above mentioned rapid development of class consciousness on the part of the striking workers who understood the power of their spontaneous takeover of state administrative functions at the coast (many participants of the August events claimed that the Coast was practically a liberated zone in August, giving immense stimulus to all citizen activities and daily relationships between city people). But there were also two futher mistakes inherent in this plan. The first was to try to split the workers' movement which had just begun to appreciate the value of joint struggle—"solidarity" was not yet a popular slogan, but it had already been a lived reality.

The second was to unabashedly promise economic concessions which revealed total neglect of the national economy and of rationality in economic decision-making. It was blatantly obvious that the ruling class wanted to do anything, including ruining the country, in order to regain its monopoly of political power—the economy, rationality and standards of living of the population were just tokens in the power game. This was the lesson that striking workers took very seriously. They were not out to wreck the country's economy to get a few pennies more. They were out to have their say in preventing total chaos in the economy introduced by the very same ruling class which now so lightly disposed of the national budget.

Meanwhile there was a flood of gestures of solidarity with the striking coast. Cars which brought delegates from other parts of Poland to the shipyards were stopped everywhere by total strangers and money, food and words of support were generously offered. Each gesture of this type had an immense influence upon the coastal workers.

At 10:00 p.m. people who had taken part in a plenary session of the old, state-controlled trade unions in their Gdansk regional headquarters related their observations. There was laughter and relaxation—nobody could take these old trade unions seriously anymore. 263 factories were already represented here.

August 20

At 9:15 the national anthem was sung and another session of MKS took place. Each new delegate was already arriving with money, usually between 5-20 thousand zlotys. Almost all of them told the same story of a synchronized nation-wide action and a very militant, determined attitude on the part of their colleagues who sent them. At the same time the media began slow preparation for a hatchet job. An indication of this pressure to defame the Gdansk MKS is found in a commentary published by "Coastal Voice" (Glos Wybrzeza):

"The last two days brought about new symptoms of increasing crisis and made one feel fear about what is happening around us. The free will of citizens is limited or even brutally violated in some cases. People who want to leave striking factories are kept there by force. Workers who want to continue serving the population have their tools destroyed and apartments burglarized. Threats of destruction of indispenable installations are frequent. Cars and lorries are not allowed to transport necessary commoditites. Commercial network employees are threatened. Gasoline is not sold to the drivers of state enterprises. Individuals try to take over the right to decide what is good and what is bad, what is necessary and what is not, what is beneficial and what is not for the daily life of thousands of people. In modern language these activities are described by a strong word, popularly known, which, however, shall not be mentioned here since we feel too much respect for the political culture and dignity of our society. All these activities bring about many questions. The most important question is this: where do the expectations and postulates of the working people end and political games begin—the political games waged by manipulators who hide themselves behind the backs of the shipyard, port, factory and transport workers.

"It is no mystery these manipulators are there and that they are active. Worse—it seems that they know no limit in striving toward their goals, toward further tension and the disorganization of daily life. They feel no remorse in taking advantage of the calm and self control on the part of the authorities, and abuse the fact that all through this period the authorities are ready to solve the problems with political, social, and economic means, that the authorities reveal a self-control and measured attitude which is rarely encountered—even in those cases where a more decisive attitude would be justified."

The text was very revealing: it unveiled a threat of armed intervention and a totally ridiculous view of society, particularly the workers, as docile, hard working supporters of the government who were temporarily blinded and misguided by some "manipulators." It is not quite clear whom the ruling class meant by "manipulators." There were indications that KOR and other (underground or not) oppositional organizations should have played that role and that a scenario of this kind had been prepared. But to treat a nation of 35 million strong as a kindergarten of spoiled kids who are threatened with a stick and promised a candy if some wrongdoers are turned over was the gravest political mistake. It actually contributed to the immense solidarity which was born in August and widened the gap between the ruling class, whose ritual moves were watched with a scornful and amused disinterest, and the working people, the employees of the state enterprises, the laborers in the state-owned means of production.

At the same time it turned out that the 17 factories mentioned by the government communique had been a hoax. A delegate from

"Techmor" arrived to declare that negotiations with Pyka had been conducted by a delegation which had not been instructed nor chosen by the workers; a delegate from "Klimor" explained that the manager and the party secretary of their factory negotiated, supposedly "in their name," forgetting to tell them that they were doing so; Northern Shipyards was still on strike—all those factories mentioned by the government communique were still on strike and nowhere had the ruling class's move borne any fruit.

As far as the obstruction of city services went, it became clear that the police were obstructing everything—they stopped even ambulances rushing dying people to hospitals, for fear that ambulances might be transporting leaflets.

August 21

The media propaganda campaign still went on and telephone numbers of the government commission were broadcast by radio every fifteen minutes, but there was no doubt that the heart of the Polish workers' strike was in Gdansk. Attempts on the part of the media to explain that the workers should really start loving the top party bosses as true representatives of their interests and put an end to the manipulators of KOR and other oppositionists met with laughter—they reminded people of warnings issued to a man in a burning building that he should avoid smokers, for he might accidentally choke to death.

Meanwhile all kinds of professions and branches of industry voiced their support—among them Polish writers, scholars, scientists, and actors—and 347 factories and enterprises were already represented in the Gdansk shipyards. Somebody brought news about an official declaration of the Polish government issued to foreign creditors on the second day of the strike—the statement claimed that the strike was official and that they could thus demand remuneration from their insurance companies.

At 5:20 p.m. a 350th delegation was registered and a team of two priests offered religious consolation. Adam Orchowski, whose diary is the basis of the present reconstruction, noted at 5:40 on the very same day:

"A kneeling crowd bids farewell to the departing priest with a church song. Nobody believes that the strikers can lose. They wait for the government commission. One delegate compares the same information in two papers. Local 'Glos Wybrzeza':

'In the coastal cities—Gdansk, Gdynia Szczecin, and Elblag—
August 20 witnessed further strikes. The attempt on the part of the
management which strove toward an agreement with the strikers
failed to bring any results. Living conditions in the cities have
become difficult, daily problems arise.' And the central organ of the
communist party 'Trybuna Ludu':

'In the coastal cities—Gdansk, Gdynia, Szczecin and Elblag—
August 20 witnessed further strikes, in the maritime enterprises
and some other factories. The attempts on the part of the
management which strove towards an agreement with the strikers
failed to bring any results. The course of the negotiations is made
difficult due to the activity of anti-socialist elements which try to
exert their destructive influence. Living conditions in cities have
become difficult, daily problems arise.' The delegates commented:
They know better in Warsaw, don't they?"

The Strike Bulletin of a week later could be quoted to describe
the strikers' state of mind: "Gentlemen! You are talking to different
people! You are not addressing those who in December 1970
replied to the question, Will you help us? with the answer, We will!
We are different above all because we are united and no longer
powerless. We are different because thirty years have taught us that
your promises are not kept."

One after another delegates from the seventeen factories
which were mentioned in government communiques arrived to
declare that they had not intended and did not intend to negotiate
outside of the Gdansk center. Money flowed in and many enterprises offered printing presses and paper for the striker's disposal.

August 22
     The morning papers brought the news that Pyka had been
removed from the government commission and another deputy
prime minister, Jagielski, had arrived in Gdansk, as had been
decided on the top political level. Neither Pyka's tactics nor
Szydlak's threats voiced in the regional party committee ("We shall
not share our power with anyone") brought any results. Szydlak was
the formal head of the old trade unions, a member of the Political
Bureau and a former chairman of the government commission to
investigate the December 1970 massacre the results of which never
fully materialized.

Shortly before 8:00 a.m. Walesa made a speech in which he informed the world that more than 600,000 zlotys had already been registered and that special aid would be dispatched to the families of those who needed it immediately. It was also known that in Szczecin a government commission under deputy prime minister Barcikowski had already started talking to the local MKS and that the 36 postulates on the list were a recognized topic of the discussion. Printers on the coast announced that they refused to print anti-strike leaflets. People were tired—a principle of rotation was established so that everybody got a chance to spend 4 to 5 hours at home during the day.

At 5:50 p.m. MKS issued a declaration about the role of KOR people in the strike movement, denying the government hints and clearly indicating their auxilliary, advisory role. Delegates from Swidnica brought 175,000 zlotys for the strikers' fund. Finally, at 22:30 the radio network of the shipyard announced "tomorrow—negotiations." The radio was tuned in and all workers could listen to all negotiations—an instance of direct democracy with both negotiating agencies under direct control of the striking workers. Warsaw intellectuals (Mazowiecki, Geremek, Staniszkis et al.) were invited by the strikers to come to supply logistics for technical points which might arise in the course of negotiations.

August 23

Technical preparations for negotiations began. An expert committee of MKS was created. Protests against false and incomplete media information were voiced. The first "Strike Bulletin" appeared and became an immediate bestseller in the whole nation. At 6:30 the first news of the monument to commemorate the murdered shipyard workers of December 1970 was presented. It remained on the table during the negotiations and in December 1980 its opening would become yet another huge patriotic demonstration, broadcast by TV and witnessed by millions of Poles as a testimony to the moral and political victory of Solidarity.

The first round of talks was not very successful. MKS demanded unblocking the city's communications with the rest of the country. The government commission tried cheating on that point—but MKS experts quickly demonstrated the mechanism of police surveillance and blocking. The first communique said that the strike must continue while negotiations went on. 388 factories were members of MKS.

Taperecording of the proceedings of MKS became a standard practice during the whole period of the ensuing negotiations. Hundreds of small taperecorders were used, both within the rooms and outside—and by this means on the very same day one could already listen to the talks in all parts of the country. Thus we can reconstruct some of the developments which took place on August 23, a crucial day in many respects, the day the ruling class decided there was no way out but to talk.

There was, for instance a delegate from Silesia, from Tarnowskie Gory, who made the following speech:

"I do not know how to speak...for... I was not born an orator or anything, I have just been sent here by the workers of the Factory of Mechanized Wall Reinforcements in Tarnowskie Gory with a letter of solidarity with the striking Coast and I would like to read this letter out: 'In connection with the present economic situation in the country the workers of our factory decided to make a statement in the matters which interest us, which interest the whole nation. Our strike has to support the postulates with respect to food supplies and the market situation expressed by the striking workers of the Coast. We support wholeheartedly the postulates to create an Independent Trade Union as a true representative of the working masses. (ovation) Taking into consideration a difficult situation in the country a general assembly of the workers decided to go to work in order to avoid further losses which could make us suffer. At the same time the workers made a list of postulates which have to be met over the next few days. Should the authorities fail to do so, the factory will go on strike on Sept 1, 1980.'"

And then he added privately: "Perhaps...I could talk about the situation in Silesia, for not everybody knows what the situation there really is. Silesia is totally uninformed. They cut us off from the rest of the country. I was sent here by the workers in Silesia in order to find out what is really going on, for some say that only 15 factories are on strike; the radio broadcasts messages that factories cease to strike and go back to work...That is why I am here—and I witness with my own eyes what is happening. And I believe that it is not only the Coast, that Silesia joins the Coast."(ovation)

Zdzislaw Kobylinski read out the text of a protest directed to the Gdansk authorities:

"Demand: we demand very strongly abandoning at present and prohibition in the future of all repression against individuals who aid the Interfactory Striking Committee (MKS). Over the past few days the police and secret police have frequently stopped, interrogated, arrested and beaten up individuals who disseminated MKS leaflets. Here are some instances. The delegates from MKS to invite deputy prime minister Jagielski were stopped by a police unit and their identities checked, preventing them from arriving on time—in spite of explanations. On August 17 Daniel Matyja was arrested for disseminating the writings of MKS. On August 19 Sylwester Niezgoda was arrested for five hours. Miroslaw Chojecki, for 48 hours. On August 20 Andrzej Slominski, Piotr Szczudlowski, Maciej Butkiewicz and the driver Andrzej Madejski—all were arrested in Wrzeszcz and detained for 48 hours for disseminating MKS materials. (A long list of names and incidents follows.) Violence and torture by police and secret police and the tolerant attitude toward these activities on the part of the state authorities are considered by workers and MKS to be an open provocation and crime, totally incompatible with the constitution of Poland and the international pact of citizen and political rights which is valid in Poland. Signed—MKS."

To which it should be added that the international pact on individual rights for citizens and free political agents had never been allowed to function in Poland outside of the underground opposition presses. To sign an international agreement seemed rational to the ruling class—to make the workers aware of their rights was quite a different matter. It is no coincidence that international pacts signed by Poland on the rights of citizens and rights for free trade unions (linked to international labor legislation) became bestsellers in all centers of Solidarity in September 1980 in Poland. There was no way back.

A conversation between the workers' representatives and Jaglielski (subsequently edited in a documentary film "Workers 80" shown all over Poland, although in some cities police managed to forbid advertisement of the movie so that slightly fewer people saw it than otherwise would have) was very instructive. Two different languages confronted each other—the propaganda-laden ritual language of the representatives of the ruling class, and the direct, concrete, unambiguous speech of the workers. Here is an excerpt.

"Lech Walesa: Thank you. Mr. Prime Minister. We listened to it very carefully. But I think that we did not say why is it so that every ten years, let us say—this time it lasted ten years and it may last another ten—we return to the same point, in which we are at present. Thus I think it should be prevented. In order to prevent this repetition, to draw conclusions, one has to know reasons. But you did not tell us the reasons for our nation's vicious circles every ten years—what guarantee do we—the workers—have (and the workers work hard and do not love striking at all) that they will be able to demand what they truly deserve. I think that in this coordination, steering, management, checking and control there is something wrong. I am a worker but this is how I see it. We shall never make up for mistakes if we fail to discover their source. And here—although we said we just want to know where the prime minister stands—you should explain something to us, Mr. Prime Minister: what does the government think, what do they think we should do in order to abandon this vicious circle and in order never to enter the vicious circle again. Thank you.

Mieczyslaw Jagielski: I can answer that. You had said, I have made a note, I did not note everything, that the reason for this development here and for our discussion of them—means, among others, that is, that it is linked to something wrong in managing and coordinating. I agree. Something is wrong. Something is wrong. I suggest that we accept the following. The following. Let us make an agreement. Trust me. The coming plenum of the Central Committee will answer this question.

Lech Walesa: We shall prompt them how to answer it. There is only one solution. We suggest what we see, we observe, we notice. Free trade unions! Strong and dynamic, as the workers would like to see them. This is no political matter, this is actual counter-balance and check and control. We shall control ourselves, we shall see mistakes and prompt solutions, but not with the means which are presently employed, i.e. not by silencing the people who want to voice their opinion—not by arrests, imprisonments, and huge enlargement of the power and violence machinery, i.e. huge development of police forces. Thus this matter should be controlled. For if everything goes ok, if the government is ok, if the power structure is ok—then the government doesn't need many police and secret police to be protected. Thank you. (ovation)

Jagielski: I suggested and I still suggest that we do not..the topic that you mentioned...I told you I agree, didn't I? What you said about the system of coordinating, managing, control—that there is something wrong in it. Thus a complete, full and profound evaluation of all reasons (those that are not within our power and those that we control) should be made. In other words—quite simply—all these reasons are to be explained. This is number one. And I want to say—well, that this problem shall be explained by the plenary session of Central Committee of our party, that a full evaluation of these reasons shall be presented and directions and programs of reforms, of action, shall be provided.

Lech Walesa: In order not to prolong, not to play those little... I suggest that we stop here for today and establish the next date for our future discussions which can take place upon the condition that you fulfill our above mentioned two demands. That is, we may talk if you finish blocking phone connections of Gdansk with the rest of Poland and stop arresting and imprisoning. Only then can we talk seriously. We shall prompt you, we want to help and we will. We shall make things that will make the world wonder how is this possible. For we want and we shall demonstrate that this can be done. But only when we understand... that things are done as we see them, as they appear to us, i.e. through independent free trade unions, which can make us prompt you in a rational, logical, reasonable way. Then we shall bring the nation out of this mess. Thank you. I suggest we end the discussion here and agree to the next meeting. Just one thing more. I would like our communique to be announced and discussed jointly, for we do not want to see things in this communique which might astonish and surprise us. Thus we shall edit it together. Maybe not here with all of us, but together, after both sides have accepted it. It should be nice, fair and just, for we want to play fair. And I suggest the day and hour of the next discussion. We shall wait here, in the shipyards for we have to finish this business in a true, human way. And not postponing it, going back to work, for then we might never meet again and never again have the chance to meet and discuss everything.

The above quotation shows clearly the difference between the speakers and the quiet determination of the workers to have their way. It is also clear that Jagielski, albeit one of the very few members of the top political body of the ruling class who did not cry fire and think in terms of hundreds of thousands to be shot, failed to understand what was going on. He still announced news about coming decisions of party executive organs as if they mattered, as if anybody cared for the new style or tone of the ruling class's manifestos. He failed totally and his numerous tricks met with laughter and were easily disarmed by the MKS delegates. It is, at the same time, also clear that in spite of the immense political power wielded by the MKS and the thorough support of the whole working class, the MKS people managed to refrain from political manifestos and played all their vital demands in a low key—a curbing of hyperstrong Polish police and secret police forces was suggested as a clinical measure, a simple return to the observation of law and order which was threatened by law enforcement, while the crucial demands for independent trade unions were put forward with a suggestion that an alternative might be found to the tired, disorganized and thoughtless ruling class (for a thoughtless ruling class it was in 1980, with no actual program acceptable to anybody apart from a narrow inner party clique). The carrot and the stick were both present but a framework of non-political strike negotiations was thoroughly observed: a historical instance of revolution which curbs itself in order not to lose; a late lesson of how to draw conclusions from 1956, 1968, 1970, 1976—late, but well learned.

August 24, Sunday.

Holy Mass was observed by almost twenty thousand people on both sides of Gate No. 2, which already had become the object of national pilgrimages. Every day made the government's tactics appear more ridiculous. For instance, on this very day local leaflets (this time signed by the National United Front, an umbrella organization created after the war and maintained to prepare and conduct all elections to preserve monoparty rule) were distributed to persuade workers that though negotiations continued they should return to work, since everything was just a matter of technical refinements from this moment on. This was a laughable invention, but it was definitely pursued on that day, probably because the top elite were divided on the issue of how to deal with the strikers. The coordination with Szczecin followed. Szczecin MKS united 134 factories and had a list of demands very similar to the Gdansk list.

In the morning a stranger handed over a grey envelope to the workers' guards at Gate No. 2. Inside was a statement allegedly written by the regional party committee of Gdansk to the Warsaw-based Central Committee. The text of this statement which has never been officially disseminated, could mean that either the regional party people had been instructed to move in a manner which did not deprive them of the remnants of their authority (the tactical move selected was to oppose the Warsaw top people just in time to welcome decisions to be made the same evening, but enough to create a shade of independence) or that the ruling class had already decided that trade unions would be won, and was looking to slowly reconstruct a power base within the party with the pretence that they had always wanted democracy within the party and had always alarmed the top comrades. Whatever the truth may be, the statements directed to Warsaw's party functionaries by Henryk Bartnicki and dated August 24, 1980, are as follows:

"The socio-political situation has not been basically trans-formed, a tense disorganized situation has not been basically transformed. The question arises: who will put an end to this improper situation? Why are no consequences drawn with respect to this improper situation? People already criticize the speech of Szydlak in the Gdansk trade unions, especially his views on the subject and object of power. The whole voivodship is presently under the direct control of MKS as far as gasoline distribution goes. There are increasing troubles with repairs of agricultural machinery, society is increasingly convinced that some definite negotiations with MKS have to be made. Further strike committees in other factories spring to life. The number of institutions which express their solidarity with MKS grows. The members of MKS claim that they espouse no political slogans. The number of factories in which money is collected for the strikers grows, too. Striking workers think that changes in the top ranks of the party and government are to be made. At the same time that all economic losses will be made up for in two-three months due to a more effective and efficient labor effort. Society becomes convinced that talking about losses is a weak political argument. Yesterday and today all major factories in the coastal area had Holy Masses. The action of sending the old ID cards of old trade unions back has become a broad reality. The ministerial teams of the government cannot succeed in winning a single factory over to persuade it to start working. These teams have, as a matter of fact, contributed to the stimulation of other heretofore non-striking factories, which presently start compiling lists of demands. Regional committees of the party tried to enter the striking factories with a very partial success. We failed to enter the majority of factories because of—as has been said by local strike committees—lack of acceptance on the part of MKS. Explanatory activity on the part of the party and administration functionaries becomes increasingly difficult in striking factories. Our functionaries who try it are simply removed by the striking workers. It is increasingly difficult to act politically on behalf of breaking the strike for solidarity of the workers with the postulates of MKS grows increasingly. In Pruszcz Gdanski part of the party membership went over to the MKS and expressed solidarity with their postulates. Party members are universally convinced that it is high time to put an end to this complex and difficult social situation. Yesterday night a meeting of the government commission and MKS took place in Gdansk Lenin Shipyards. Under the shipyard gates two thousand people listened to the negotiations and expressed their attitudes by cries, whistles, etc. The delegates of the various strike committees declared to their working constituencies after the first round that the government commission is unprepared to negotiate but talks will go on. Tapes from the negotiations have been replayed in many factories. The view is being disseminated that beginning these negotiations is a success for the striking workers."

A strange document. If it was a coincidence that the workers got hold of it, then it reveals an inability to think of the political process in any other way than in terms of personal cliques and police-like reports on the consequences of the growing power of the strikers. Party functionaries are unable to communicate with workers, for the workers just tell them to go to hell whenever they try to speak down to them and "explain" the situation. The mixture of true facts reported in the document and overall pattern of party intrigue thinking is astounding. In all probability the document was an attempt on the part of the local party functionaries to present themselves as the forerunners of a major change, a personal transformation in the Political Bureau, but the mistake of this thinking was that personnel changes in top party echelons had ceased to matter; nobody was interested in appearances anymore.

August 25

The government tried cheating again: the authorities informed MKS that telephone connections between Gdansk and
Szczecin were restored, and the connection to Warsaw was
underway. The rest of the country's connections would be restored
along with progress in the negotiations. MKS rejected this move
and voted against having another negotiating session until all
phone connections with the country were reinstated.

After midnight, Opera and Philharmonic artists gave free
concerts for the striking workers, and Walesa's name appeared in
the local newspapers for the first time. The Warsaw connection was
unblocked, and all other blockades were to end the next day, and the
media were to inform on progress in negotiations. The new session
was to begin at 11:00 the next day.

August 26

9:30. One of the MKS members explained that the government had to be told everything, to have everything explained, for
they did not understand yet that MKS had real power and was able
to call for a national strike if their demands were not met.

11:00. Both groups met. Jagielski suggested that the old trade
unions should remain but be reformed—popular, secret and
democratic elections would be held, and that should help. MKS was
against this move and declared openly that they wanted quite new
trade unions and were entitled to have them. No progress, but no
breakdowns, either.

Norwegian and French trade unionists came with words of
solidarity and financial support.

The TV news featured a sterile party columnist, Wojna, who
threatened the workers with the next partition of Poland if they
still opposed the ruling party's will. "Wojna" means "war" in
Polish, so the next morning a new slogan appeared: "Wojna—
never more." In thematic commissions it soon turned out that the
government's experts were simply not up to the MKS experts
level—the latter were the cream of what Polish people of
knowledge could offer, the selected elite of the intelligentsia, while
the former were paid courtiers and failed to compete. The MKS
team was headed by A. Gwiazda and included T. Mazowiecki, J.
Staniszkis and B. Geremek, while the government team included J.

Pajestka (the author of many disastrous moves in the Polish economy, former advisor to many Polish cabinets), A. Rajkiewicz and A. Jackiewicz.

August 27

The functionaries of the old trade unions became scared. They published leaflets in which they claimed that those former members of their organization who rejected their membership and left their ranks would automatically lose their savings and a number of social privileges linked to membership. This was illegal, untrue, and caused by a million-strong desertion from the ranks of the old trade unions.

Gossip had it that Giereck had been dismissed. Jagielski spoke on local TV and radio and announced that there was a grave disparity on the topic of independent trade unions and that the government thought it wise to reform the old ones, not to allow for the new ones—however painful the cure of the older trade unions might be. No progress.

August 28

Peasants supported the strike, bringing food and money. In, Zbrosza Duza, a famous village where the independent peasant trade union movement started along with some attempts to organize the peasants politically, the priest was dispatched to bring money and words of solidarity to the workers. There, even before August 1980 the government had harrassed the village in a typical heavy-handed manner—searching households, arresting the priest, harrassing children on their way to school through nearby woods and farmers on their way to neighbours or markets—with police units encircling the village during weeks of intensive prosecution as if it was World War II. The Polish fleet radio network notified all Polish ships of the situation and accepted daily solidarity messages from overseas.

The session dealt with censorship—the workers were decisive and unyielding. Gwiazda nailed Jagielski on the topic of arrests made by the secret police during the past few days. Those people would have to be released or no further negotiations would be conducted. "Mr. Prime Minister," asks Gwiazda, "this is crucial, shall our system be described as democratic or as a police one? What guarantees do we have that the 1968 or 1970 arrests will never happen again? There is fear of voicing opinions. We want to put an end to this fear."

W. Gruszecki added, "No wonder so many people mention injustice, and illegal actions of the police and government. The Government Commission has no right to plead ignorance on the subject. We speak the truth and we want these things to never happen again."

The Prime Minister made an attempt to remove foreign journalists. MKS opposed the move explaining that it was mainly due to their efforts that the world learned about the actual course of the negotiations.

MKS registered 600 factories.

August 29

Electronic engineers completed a device which enabled shipyard workers to eavesdrop on police communications.

Bogdan Lis and Andrzej Gwiazda declared that the government commission delayed discussion by arguing that their people were unprepared.

Delegates from Wroclaw and Bytom arrived, workers of the copper mining industry sent their messages of solidarity, and miners of one of the largest coal mines, in Jastrzebie, started a solidarity strike.

The film director Andrzej Wajda appeared in the shipyards and told of his first impressions:

"The first impression which reaches Warsaw and all other cities is one of immense calm, absolute self-assurance; an impression of a feast, something solemn, dignified, and extraordinary. I feel I am witnessing some part of our history, which rarely happens to me. Most often history walks by, and here history can be felt. History's presence is directly experienced."

Poznan's "Cegielski," the largest industrial plant in the city, waged a twenty-four hour long warning strike—should the shipyard workers' postulates not be met, a full-fledged strike would be proclaimed. The "Solidarity" symbol became an overnight national treasure and was displayed everywhere.

Five million zlotys had already been collected to construct the monument commemorating the victims of December 1970. "Trybuna Ludu" voiced an official attitude about the strikers:

"During party meetings and discussions—for instance in Elblag—there is an increasing desire to unmask the other party, to say openly who are the people who guide the strikers, and who is hidden behind them."

Solidarity's information bulletin answers this question:

"The people who guide the strikers are workers themselves, including members of the Polish United Workers Party. Behind them there are the masses of the workers, including many Party members. The strike committees are an achievement of the working class which demands the right to have its own tribune."

August 30

News about the arrests of opposition activists in Warsaw reached the shipyards. It was a disturbing message in view of progress achieved in the expert teams and during negotiations.

Lodz delegates announced the support and strike of the Lodz textile industry and the whole region.

At 10:15 the last round of talks began. This was the grand finale. But there were still unclear points. There was no certainty that top party bureaucrats in Warsaw would still accept the results.

Walesa: Welcome for the fourth time. The text of point one we have agreed upon is being typed out.

Jagielski: We can give you our copy.

Walesa: We prefer our own. Meanwhile we can start talking about point two.

Jagieski: The time has come to reach conclusions. Negotiations were difficult but they refered to basic matters. What matters is not only that we solve the social conflict but also that we solve problems of our country's future. The first point is the cornerstone of the agreement but economic problems should not be viewed as marginal. I gladly notice that MKS has unambiguously stated that the new trade unions will accept social ownership of the means of production and accept the leading role of the communist party and the system of international alliances. This means that they will accept the constitution of Poland.

Gwiazda demanded the release of all political prisoners who had been lately arrested, as did Pienkowska. Jagielski objected to granting immunity for individuals who "supported" the strike. Walesa insisted that they should also be granted immunity from prosecution—"they have done well."

Gwiazda: These are people who aided us out of their own good will.

Jagielski: But I have thanked them. Only I want to give you a guarantee of supreme political power...

Jagielski then signed the agreements and suggested that everybody should go back to work. Walesa said that everybody would go back to work on Monday—so far there were too many unsolved problems.

Jagielski: But the agreement will be printed today for all the world to see.

Walesa: Will be? We want to have it. Another problem. We are reaching an agreement so would you please stop arresting people from KOR. They have helped us though they were not with us. Should they do anything wrong, we shall stop them ourselves.

Gwiazda: We have news of new arrests in Warsaw.

Jagielski: I am leaving now, please work the communique out, and we shall sign it in the evening.

The prime minister did not return in the evening. Tension began to grow after the initial release caused by signing the vital points of agreement. There was news that practically the whole country, including all vital industrial centers, was threatened with a solidarity strike if the ruling class did not work out the agreement.

August 31

Sunday—the third Sunday in the striking shipyards, and a crowd was at Holy Mass. Radio news was enigmatic—the central committee had "approvingly acknowledged" the new agreements reached in Gdansk and Szczecin.

At 11:30 the last round of talks began—or the one after the last, the one that should have happened an evening before. The radio network broadcast the discussion all over the shipyards, and news agencies from all over the world as well as private tape recorders followed every word.

Walesa: We begin this meeting with hope. Please explain the cases of people being arrested. And I have doubts about points 1 and 2. The end of the strike will be announced 3 to 4 hours after all questions are answered.

Jagielski: What news? I am also glad and I believe that today we shall close our talks with success. According to my promise I was in Gdansk yesterday at 7:30 p.m. and I was ready to finish the matter—the 21 points are accepted, and to end this I want to make a statement, and then to sign with you the project of a communique and a statement.

Walesa: OK

Jagielski: Who will read the points out?

Walesa: We can do it.

Bogdan Lis reads out point 3 about freedom of speech and printed word (points 1 and 2 had been signed the day before.)

Jagielski: I accept this point.

Then Lis read the point on political prisoners.

Jagielski: In the spirit of understanding I accept and sign it.

Gwiazda: I have received an appendix with a list of individuals who have been lately arrested. Please explain.

Jagielski: This I would like to discuss at the end. Point 5 has been accepted.

Walesa: We want to know about those who had been arrested. People want it.

Jagieslki: I have just got the list...

Walesa: We gave the list yesterday to the local authoritites.

Jagielski: They notified me yesterday that the list had been handed over to the Prosecutor General. I represent the government and these are matters dealt with by the Prosecutor General. I can accept and sign the agreement. I will come back to Warsaw and explain.

Anna Walentynowicz: Mr. Prime Minister guaranteed security to the strikers and those who supported the strike. Miroslaw Chojecki taught us how to print. We could not do it, we are workers. And now he has been arrested.

Jagielski: With full responsibility I promise that I shall convey this matter as it has been presented. Other rights I do not have.

Gwiazda: If you, Mr. Prime Minister, are so full of good will, then why are these arrests going on? We have another list of names. Those people supported the workers with good will. They had been released and just now they have been rearrested.

Jagielski: I shall do what I can to explain this in Warsaw.

Walesa: But we have to talk. Since we have the right to strike and our place on Marchlewskiego 13 we shall begin a new strike if you fail to release them.

Finally, the climax came—Walesa's closing speech, broadcast, along with the last statements by both Jagielski and Walesa, by the Polish TV and by all major TV networks in the world, with the notable exception of those in the state socialist countries:

"Dear people! We go back to work on September 1st! We all know what this day means to us, what we think of on this day. Of motherland, of national cause, of common interests of a family called Poland. We have thought about it a lot during our strike. We think about it even more ending this strike. Have we achieved everything we wanted, we desired, we dreamt of? I always speak openly and honestly what I think. And I will answer honestly this time too—no, not everthing, but we all know that we have won a lot. You trusted me all this time, so please believe in what I say now. We achieved everything we could have achieved in the present situation. The rest we shall also win, for we have the most important thing—our independent, self-governed trade unions. This is our guarantee for the future. We have fought not only for ourselves, for our interests, but for the whole country. We all know how great the solidarity of working people has been. Thank you all for supporting us. We have been together, we fought for you, too. We have won the right to strike, we have won full citizen rights, and what is most vital—the right to independent trade unions. All working people have a guaranteed right to associate in such trade unions if they wish to do so. And now, with the same solidarity and courage we had in our strike, we shall go to work. From tomorrow on a new life for new trade unions begins. Let us care for their self-government and independence, for the sake of all of us, of our country, of Poland. I proclaim the strike is over."

And during the broadcast signing ceremony Walesa added a few words which also reflected the spirit of victory and were received with immense acclaim by millions of Polish workers:

"I would like to thank Mr. Jagielski and all those forces which did not allow for a violent solution of the matter. We have struck an agreement as a Pole with a Pole, only in talks, negotiations, with small compromises, and this should always be so. We do understand our common cause and we have to repair everything that has been wrecked previously. We have to feel it and work for it. I shall do everything in order to bring it about, as you trusted me. And I know you shall help and we shall succeed."

A few minutes later Walesa returned to the conference room to excuse his forgetfulness and to thank the experts: Takeusz Mazowiecki, Bronislaw Geremek, Tadeusz Kowalik, Jadwiga Staniszkis, Waldemar Kuczynski, Andrzej Wielowieyski, Bogdan Cywinski, Prof. Stembrowicz, Jan Strelecki, Prof. Stelmachowski.*

*The above reconstruction is based on an excellent account provided by Adam Orchowski in "Przebieg strajku okupacyjnego w stoczni Gdanskiej im. Lenina w dniach 14-31 sierpnia 1980 roku" published in a special issue of Gdansk almanack "Punkt" in Nov.—Dec. 1980, and on other documents assembled in this excellent publication. (Eyewitness accounts of Solidarity members were also used.)

Chapter Five

The Aftermath of Gdansk
Politics, Economy, and Culture

a) Politics

The history of political struggle in post-August 1980 Poland is a history of regular crises which occur roughly every two months as a result of the enormous pressure and tension produced between the ruling class's systematic attempts to reinstate total state power and the working class's stubborn refusal to yield to every technique employed in order to force society into the state socialist mold.

It is a very clear history with very visible class attitudes. On the one hand we have the three attempts to submit the newly organized working class to the state's control; on the other, we have not only resistance but also a systematic broadening of spontaneous activities and associations.

The major attempts on the part of the ruling class to reinstate its control were: a) to insert (against Polish law) into the text registering Solidarity submitted by the workers a clause on the leading role of the communist party; b) to impose a government elaborated system introducing free Saturdays as a one-sided decision and thus as a precedent for deciding how to take care of workers needs in the future; and c) to introduce selective terror by letting police beat Solidarity members and activists, thus making it clear that the police would go unpunished and Solidarity should beware, especially if it did not stop calling for trade unions for peasants.

It may be observed that all three major conflicts almost resulted in general strikes—the third one being the most serious— and failed to develop into a general strike only because of the threat of Soviet military manoeuvres, the Church's pacifying influence and the worker's awareness of the economic situation of the country.

All three conflicts resulted from illegal decisions made by the ruling class and by attempts to check whether such blatant violations of democracy and obvious attacks on the working class could have a chance of success. The first attempt to compel Solidarity to register with an "innocent clause" added to its statute was so clearly an instance of provocation that the public universally supported the struggle against it. As the Polish solicitors' and bar members' conference was also taking place at the time, the role of a corrupted judicial system came under criticism as well. The ruling class had to yield; there was absolutely no justification for the claim that a new trade union must unequivocally recognize the right of the ruling class to supremacy over everything in the political landscape of the country. However, this illegitimacy did not prevent the ruling class from announcing that whoever failed to recognize this claim meant to destroy socialism in Poland and even ventured to state openly that those peasants who support independent trade unions for individual farmers had to be former landowners.

The situation was tense: there were rumors that the secret police had prepared special lists of people to be arrested and that there were orders to consider the possibility of mass arrests with the employment of city sport stadiums as short-term prisons. But the propaganda onslaught was finally broken down due to a very decisive stand taken by all Solidarity members and by thousands of people who flocked into Solidarity precisely because they did not wish to acknowledge the right of the ruling class to a monopoly of political power.

The ruling class thus learned that it was impossible to press with impunity for recognition of their title to sole authority so the next decision, which precipitated the crisis in late January, was made as a matter-of-fact technical one. It had been annnounced that the government would observe the August agreements and that it wanted to increase the amount of free time enjoyed by workers. However, the country's difficult economic situation was said to make it impossible to stick to the letter of the agreement, and thus the government suggested that only two Saturdays in January would be free.

This was a more reserved and skillful trial-and-error probing. The government announced the plan knowing perfectly well that the trade unions could not accept the arbitrary and unnegotiated decision. But it wanted: a) to discover the extent of the actual influence of Solidarity on the masses of workers, by testing who would and who would not show up at work on the crucial Saturdays, and b) to blame eventual opposition to the scheme on Solidarity's unwillingness to feel a spirit of responsibility for the nation's well-being and to its sticking to bare economic demands of a very selfish type, limited in applicability to some sectors of the working class only.

The scheme did not work, but it meant that the ruling class was already using more subtle weapons than those employed by the court which registered Solidarity only after arbitrarily changing the submitted document. The outcome was a disaster for the ruling class—the first of the two Saturdays in question brought about 40-50% of the labor force to the factories, although most of them expressed support for the Solidarity policy and claimed that they worked only because of the particularly hard situation in the production of their commodity, but the second already found 70-80% following Solidarity's lead, in spite of none too gentle manipulations by the managers.

During that time a famous TV debate between government people, Solidarity experts and the reformed branch of the old trade unions (a small insignificant group which the government wanted to slowly build up as a counterbalance to Solidarity) took place. It turned out that the representatives of the old trade unions (the so-called "reformed branch-unions") out of habit sat down on the government representatives side of the moderator's table, just as had happened during the negotiations at the Wroclaw railroad workers' strike and hunger strike, indicating by this slip the true nature of the old unions. But more important was the clear TV impression that the government had no valid arguments to back the decisions it made, and that its experts were far inferior to the ones furnished by Solidarity, not to mention the very vital fact that the TV demonstrated the ugliness of party bureaucrats and the openness and natural ease of the Solidarity people. The very next day one heard a popular comment that it was hard to expect any other outcome of a TV discussion—after all, if world champions meet with a third rate local team, the result can generally be predicted...

The latest confrontation to date (I am typing this section in late May 1981) was a result of two latent processes which had only partially been solved so far.

The first was the problem of the institutional framework of the absolute monopoly of political power: although this monopoly had been questioned and had been practically denied by the daily spontaneous activities of millions of workers, the ruling class hoped to sit this through and to wait until the day when all the mechanisms of subjection and terror could be switched on again. The technique of starving people to the point where they will accept a ruling class with some bread and butter was strongly believed in and scrupulously followed. Therefore the ruling class was desperately trying to both prevent the police and secret police from any activity which might bring about another confrontation, and to preserve these forces for a better opportunity.

This strategy proved successful until mid-March, for although in many cities society won back huge investments the police had allowed themselves (people usually demanded that the luxurious buildings and facilities thus funded be turned into city hospitals and community centers), there was really no clash except for the Lodz crisis in a hospital of the Ministry of the Interior. This case is interesting; it broke out as a result of the head of the hospital stealing few kilograms of ham which were sent to the hospital to give every patient a piece as a gift from the Pope. A few younger doctors noticed the theft and made a case of it, founding a Solidarity chapter and demanding distribution of the ham. The head laughed them off and fired them. They appealed. The case became a cause celebre, for the hospital belonged to the Ministry of the Interior. The doctors won—but a million people had to go on strike in Lodz to secure the right of Ministry of the Interior employees to organize in Solidarity and the dismissal of the head of the hospital.

However, the situation again became inflamed when the government decided that society should be reminded that a) there would never be peasant trade unions—this was expressed very definitely—"we shall never allow that." This was a mistake, as society asked immediately, who is "we" and why not? and b) there will never be a change in police structure which might diminish the police's capacity to effectively subdue any portion of society at any time—including Solidarity leaders.

Thus a clumsy second-rate thriller movie plot was staged by the local authorities, the judicial state functionaries, and the secret police. When local Solidarity leaders assembled to talk to local authorities about registration of a peasant trade union—this negotiation was linked to an occupational strike of the farmers from the Bydgoszcz area of the city—the authorities first pretended that they would talk, and then left suddenly as if following orders.

As Solidarity members left the building a group of policemen in civilian clothes, accompanied by a passive but watchful group of uniformed policemen, attacked the Solidarity leaders with the usual weapons, clubs and knuckle-dusters. The aim was to attack the Solidarity leaders in the period of the Warsaw Pact armies' exercises in Poland, and thus to provoke riots against the government to provide a pretext for armed intervention, and to blame Solidarity itself for the outcome. Indeed, Solidarity had already been warned that the ruling class was preparing a special plan to announce a state of emergency with martial law and foreign troops. Special handbooks of "What to do if martial law is declared" were distributed in millions of copies—perhaps a major reason why the Warsaw pact armies did not intervene nor was martial law declared. However, the calculation to create terror was totally mistaken. The mass distribution of the abovementioned handbooks assured an effective mobilization, while the mass distribution of pictures of police atrocities served to muster popular support for Solidarity and to increase the pressure to deprive the police of their privileged position, but without inciting riots.

b) The Economy

It is popularly admitted that the economy of socialism is among the least known economic mechanisms and that no successful description has been provided, although some methods of practically limiting the disadvantages of a centralized, planned economy have been tested with varying degrees of success. The most promising description of the impossibility of market balance of supply and demand under socialism has been put forward by a Hungarian economist, Jonas Kornai. In his paper "Resource-constrained versus demand-constrained systems", he claims that a socialist economy cannot be regulated by the condition that supply and demand must be balanced (which is what the Polish ruling class always sought by introducing increases in food prices). Kornai follows a very traditional distinction of economic systems into demand-limited and production-limited, with the socialist economy clearly falling into the latter category. It is clear that the growth of whole branches of the economy depends only on the human and material resources commanded by society. Kornai's novelty is a new analysis of the limitations imposed on economic agents.

Economic agents whose budget constraints are "hard" have to make their expenditures in the context of their incomes—for instance a householder has a "hard" budget constraint and cannot spend more than he/she earns. The threat of financial bankruptcy determines the possibilities the agent can undertake. However, an economic agent who has "soft" budget constraints does not have to take care of the balancing of expenditures and incomes and does not have to be afraid of the threat of financial bankruptcy. Money is an auxiliary measure which does not play a significant role as an indicator. Demand is only very weakly limited, since it is not dependent on financial limits and on incomes.

Kornai says that in the capitalist economy practically all economic agents and units have hard financial limitations, while in a socialist one only household economies are regulated by hard limitations, and almost all other economic agents have soft limits imposed on their activities. Thus the state enterprise, which knows only soft budget limitations, sucks up all available markets— intaking all available labor, all raw materials, all production goods, all consumption goods, all services. It is quite clear, says Kornai, that household units and state enterprises are competing on the same markets for the above articles—and it is not hard to see who is bound to lose.

Kornai's point is well taken. It was quite clear in Poland in the seventies, for instance, that the coming crisis of the world economy meant practically that the institutionally secured economic units— state enterprises—would not diminish their "sucking up" of the market. It is not enough to raise the prices to reinstate a market balance—one needs an institutional change to lower the pressure of "softly" limited state enterprises upon the market.

The crisis is grave and definite—but the crisis is simply a manifestation of a much more basic crisis of the guaranteed ir-responsibility of economic agents in a state socialist system. Nothing suggested by the state commission of economic reform even barely touches the real reasons for the crisis. Cosmetic shifts and patches are all the ruling class may comprehend or suggest. The ruling class most probably does not understand the economic situation at all. There is an understanding that some structure of state expenditures has to be maintained if the ruling class is to preserve its power (the ruling party regularly steals state funds to finance itself), but there is not much recognition of the continually weak economic results in the state-ized economy or of an analysis of what went wrong.

The introduction of food rationing, originally demanded by Solidarity as a result of the egalitarian postulates of workers outraged by high free market food prices and the ensuing availability of some foods to the upper crust only, soon became a touchy point on which Solidarity tried to back down, but the government conveniently stuck to the letter of early proposals.

The food rationing, basically of meat, sugar, butter and milk, means that there is much left over beyond what is bought in the market, so that the government does not have to work really hard to raise food production and can easily acquire the surplus it needs for export. It also means that the inefficiently run state owned farms do not have to fail immediately as the state can finance them out of its surplus sale in the West.

The programs of reform are varied; the most interesting ones come from Wroclaw, Poznan, and Warsaw's younger faculty members of the "Main School of Rural Economy and Statistics," i.e. the local economic college. While there are some important differences, the crux of most proposals can be best understood if we consider the following situation. In order to suggest that Solidarity will not be able to function effectively in the state socialist system, the ruling class has undertaken a program of rapid disorganization of an already impoverished market, the idea behind the program of this kind being that the masses will tire of democracy and the hopes brought about Solidarity. The calculation is probably wrong, especially in view of a broad front of economists' explanations and educational activities which have resulted in a quite sophisticated public understanding of economics and in view of popular demands for real economic reform. Moreover, the economic team of Solidarity, the Polish Economists' Society group (headed by Leszek Balcerowicz), became very popular, and has had a proposed project for over half a year, the crux of which is a criticism of the state socialist economy from the point of view of its "soft" limits, i.e. the irresponsible waste with respect to everything and irresponsible impoverishment of the economic opportunities of individual consumers.

The order-based and distributional nature of the mechanism of economic guidance is followed by a suitable organizational structure. The latter has a number of features which either autonomously or together with this mechanism influence the functioning of the economy: 1. The concentration of many detailed decisions on the central level and a labor-intensive method of "writing off" these decisions into directives for lower executive levels, which calls for a strongly developed central administration. This, in turn, requires even greater development of administration on lower levels, since it is needed for further "writing off" of the directives and "limits" sent from above and for preparation of reports to the center. This manner of directing the economy thus involves a bureaucratic multiplier: every additional official at a central level requires employing a few more officials on each lower level, down to the plant level.

As a result the economy has to bear the burden of maintenance of a huge administrative apparatus, which at the same time hampers the economy's functioning, limiting its possibilities with a jungle of rules, orders and limits.

2. Among the central administrative agencies the branch agencies fulfill a special role: for instance ministries such as the Ministries of Machine Building Industry, Light Industry, Metal Industry, Construction, etc., and central agencies administering cooperatives. They are most closely linked to an order-rule system of guiding the economy from a central point. Each of these agencies has a group of organizations to direct and at the same time to represent in a struggle for means allocated by the top. Thus the huge lobbies so characteristic of our system arise—enormous organizations guided by branch ministers. They break the economy down into around 15 isolated "mini-states" ("Polska resortowa") immensely hampering cooperation between producers and compe-

ting over minute details in economic policy, the general social interest notwithstanding. They fight for themselves. The very fact that huge lobbies—such as heavy industry—take part in this struggle means that other domains are predetermined to lose—such as health services, education, culture, environmental protection, apartment construction, etc. Hence the systematic underinvestment in these areas.

3. The lobbies ("resorty") are huge organizations insensitive to all pressures from consumers, hence they contribute to the extreme monopolization of the economy. Monopolization has further vital sources in the making of multi-factory organisms (unions or "combinates") within the abovementioned lobbies. Each of these organizations usually includes within its bureaucratic domain all factories which produce the same article. Each actively strives to include all factories which produce this article, and at the same time does not allow for the existence of those which would remain outside of the lobby framework. The latter practice stems from the relative facility of order-rule guidance of the economy if all agents are united—the number of addresses of directives radically diminishes.

At the same time the consumers of particular products are forced to agree on a single supplier, with its whims and fads. This contributes to constant disturbances in cooperation since the factories grouped within a single lobby cannot for technical reasons cooperate with each other but have to cooperate with an array of other factories from outside of the lobby which requires overcoming high organizational obstacles.

4. The managers of economic units, including the managers of factories, are subordinates of the managers of upper echelons, in that they can be recalled from their posts by their superiors with the help of political functionaries. This makes managers very susceptible to the often informal directives from many various sources, which destroys the autonomy of their organizations and makes the guidance of the economy more complex.

Order-rule guidance mechanisms for the economy and appropriate organizational structures reinforce each other which makes one impossible to remove without the other. On the one hand the mechanism needs this structure for services. The need is increasingly great because the mechanism itself results in a lack of balance in the economy which requires the mobilization of growing numbers of administrators. The administration fights against the lack of balance and replaces some rules with others, attempting to prove it is indispensable. On the other hand key points of this structure, especially on a central level, being unable to switch to another guidance mechanism, support the present one in order to defend their own interests. In this coupling and feedback of the mechanism of the centralized guidance of economy and of the organizational structure lies one of the major reasons for resistance to all reforms. None of the previous reforms managed to alter either of these two. And without such change the immense daily waste, constant crises and periodical outbursts in our economy cannot be removed. One cannot improve lastingly the situation of consumers interested in better living standards, the situation of workers who want well organized and meaningful work, of citizens who want to have their share in making decisions which determine their future.

On April 17 the national weekly of Solidarity published a number of statements entitled "Tendencies of trade union activities in the present situation" and the section on "economic matters" included a very sharp criticism of the basic economic structure with its organized and planned waste. The system was blamed for the current crisis, diminishing rate of growth of gross national product and decline of living standards in the past two years. Among lasting disadvantages of current economic policy the following was mentioned:

"Inefficiencies of the system and inefficiencies of economic policy have been compensated for by growing foreign credits. Capitalist bankers have had to finance the economic inefficiencies of our state planned economy. However, these loans have to be repaid, with interest, which is possible only if the economy is effective. But given economic failures, compensation cannot be made for a long time and becomes another factor in the crisis. The ultimate effect is a gigantic Western debt of over 24 billion dollars, not to mention short term loans. The country has to pay more for interest and loan backpayment than export brings in return for commodities. This means that all imports have to be paid for by additional credit. This additional credit is increasingly difficult to obtain; interest is higher on it and the terms of payment harsh. We are considered bankrupt and treated accordingly."

Solidarity presses for a rapid economic reform, democratically introduced but profoundly affecting our system. We want to abolish the coupling of the huge administration and the petrified, semi-monopolist "isolated islands" of the state economy, and reinstate some approximation of market balance. And a stress on the individual farmer as the basic supplier of foodstuffs is definitely the only rational agricultural policy at present.

c) Culture

On December 16, 1980, Polish TV broadcast the solemn dedication of a monument to victims of the police massacre of December 1970. A few hundred thousand people gathered on the spot, many millions watched the opening on their TV screens.

Plates commemorating the dead shipyard workers bore inscriptions saying that "they gave their life so that you can live in dignity," and an appriopriate fragment of Milosz's poetry was also quoted: "You, who had wronged a simple man..." The nation had its symbols ready—the ruling class had to broadcast this ceremony commemorating its crimes and praising heroes of the working masses. All attempts to thwart the opening of the monument and the public broadcast were met with suggestions that all media "go over to the nation" right away. The ruling class yielded, hoping that this would remain an isolated case, and that everybody would be too happy to see Walesa and the ceremony on TV to remember anything else and to fight for a further de-censoring of the media. This hope did not last, but it must be admitted that it turned out that the relatively long grasp of the ruling class on the media (except for the clandestine and trade unionist ones—though the nation-wide weekly of Solidarity is censored) has not been an entirely negative phenomenon. For there has been an element of continuity in all external elements of public life and public opinion making, and this has prevented the Soviets from declaring that the mythical "anti-socialist forces" have materialized from TV tubes, radio networks or printing presses.

The cultural aspects of the social changes following the August 1980 political breakthrough are probably most interesting of all because here the immense class meaning of the workers' struggle has become crystal clear and borne the earliest fruit. First the young intelligentsia and the students have overwhelmingly supported Solidarity. The national student strike from February 1981 was not, contrary to what has been thought, a safe repetition of what had already been accomplished by the workers, but a very significant broadening of the achievements won by the workers in the sphere of citizen rights and in the sphere of national education.

The two major victories won by the students were a demo-cratization of university structure (including the free election of presidents of universities by the faculty which will mean a very considerable reduction of party front men) and a profound change in the curricula and general educational profile. They have practically won back everything that the ruling class had managed to annul in recent years and they have also legalized and registered an independent student union (NZS) which has assumed the guidance of student strikes and shown itself a spontaneous response to the state attempt to remodel the state controlled Polish Student Union (ZSP) as the major student organization.

The newly elected president of Warsaw university, professor Henryk Samsonowicz, a prominent historian, wrote in an interview for a Warsaw weekly "Politika":

"...what happened in March 1968 in the university started events which were more meaningful than the mere fact that there was a student meeting, that it was broken up by the police, that students had been beaten up. What I mean is a certain model of supervising science and culture originated in March.

I would be more cautious as far as non-scholarly priorities of faculty staffing are concerned. After all, no first secretary ever made a solitary decision whom to leave and whom to fire. It was more complex. Personal and group characteristics were important. And what is even more vital we must associate with some forms of propaganda which are shameful to our recent history—lack of tolerance, chauvinism, not to mention anti-semitism... And I am afraid the matters of 1968 are linked to the crisis we are going through nowadays. Marginal positions were given to some people who naturally became bitter and radical. The need to make up for the wrongs is especially clear in this case."

Polish literature was already in the struggle as of 1968. Many contemporary writers were already committing their works to underground publications and this is especially true with respect to the poets and critics of the 1968 generation, for whom it was the only solution anyway. For example, novels by Konwicki and Kazimierz Brandys, Julian Stryjkowdki and Dazimierz Orlos appeared in considerable numbers of copies. Most of them also supported the striking workers even before August 1980 and KOR itself, which was staffed predominantly by well known writers of whom Jerzy Andrzejewski was the most famous.

Of the younger generation Stanislaw Baranczak, Adam Zagajewski, Julian Kornhauser and other members of the 1968 generation merit attention. Their works have appeared both in ordinary and underground publishing houses (except for Baranczak who paid for his prominent role in KOR) and helped organize the new Polish imagination. Baranczak wrote a series of essays on mass culture in People's Poland. The most decisive of these tells of an attempt to produce a culture depriving individuals of all vestiges of independence and autonomy and is entitled "Red Banner over a Disco" and it closes with a political anecdote: Two peasants are sitting on the bank of a river when the Soviet army pours into Poland in mid-1944. One of them asks another, "Well, do you think those bolsheviks will make us starve?" The other replies, "Starve they will not make us, but bore they will us to death."

How different is this statement by Baranczak (who belonged to a selected team invited by Milosz to Stockholm to take part in the Nobel Prize ceremony in December 1980) from a book by Milosz written in 1952 entitled "Takeover," in which the march of the Soviets into Poland is described in the following manner:

"The riders stop their horses. In front of them a huge country won over, given to their power. They look at rivers blinking in the sun, at the ruins of deserted cities, quiet in blue mist. Small figures move in the valleys, ignorant of their destinies. Round mountain tops with castles, powerful ones, touching skies with the fists of their towers. They will rule out of these castles. By circling with the blades of their swords they point to places where according to their plans new towns will spring into life, new splendid constructions, dams, circus arenas. It is enough for them to nod and crowds of people will march forward, will carry wooden blocks and stones. Over their daily toil, over their meaningless physiological life there will be a penetrating idea, victorious in disputes..."

The difference is crucial. The new generation considered the impact of state socialism in terms of a new perspective—the vague Hegelian appeal of Soviet tanks rolling through Poland in 1944 was meaningless and dead.

An interesting development, on which one should say a few words in order to appreciate the cultural consequences of what happened in Poland after August 1980, is the new wave of spontaneous creative writing—especially visible in poetry, songs, pamphlets and columns published and disseminated during the strikes. One of the universities had, for instance, a huge poster made by the old student union, which tried to sound courageous and anti-authoritarian and wrote "We demand guarantees of democracy —signed SZSP." The members of the independent student organization wrote underneath: "That's great. We *are* this guarantee."

The Gdansk poetry of the workers has already become a subject of separate studies. Poems like the ones I quote below are simple and direct forms of committed art if there ever were any; they are the actual proletarian poetry of 1980.

Polish recipe

Take what you have not
add salt and some pepper
then mix with that which
has not been on the market

Mix it well and thoroughly
stop when getting bored
then sprinkle with that which
you can not afford

Then roast it or fry it
or put it on a grill
pouring out something
you do not even dream of

Everybody eats this daily
everybody gets enough
this is precisely the meaning
of the Polish economic miracle.

Apart from the satirical tone there was a strong propaganda content:

Only free ones!!!
New trade unions—they precisely
are the nation's future
the old were sick and pushed us down
to hunger and poverty

But the new ones are not enough
for in a few years
they will also give birth to
newer bloodsuckers
Free, free, only free
trade unions for us
the nation needs them
to lift its head up

The nation wants to go to work
boldly and without fear
Only free can the country last
and Poles survive.

   Both poems are anonymous and I quote them from "Punkt."
The most frequent tone was a critical assessment of the propaganda
and the actual situation of the worker and the voicing of support for
the struggle for independent trade unions. The last of the poems I
quote reveals, in its Polish original, vivacity and lightness; with a
wonderfully simple mixture of irony and a strong, straightforward
stand:

From a lie to a lie
from a madness to a madness
from the mountains to Gdansk
we are fed up with this mess

October and December
August after August
how many repressions
how much suffering?

The posts change again
the names switch all over
but we are fed up with promises
if the bowl is still empty

No Gdansk and no Radom
no Lublin, Warszawa
the whole of this Poland is fed up with lawlessness
fed up with repressions
false promises bygone
wants bread for their labor and true authority

The demands we are voicing
with no others, no new ones
but of authority independent
—our trade unions.

One social psychologist, who had spent a few years studying the effects of TV news on audiences (these interesting studies show the public's total disbelief in TV "facts") said that Solidarity's meaning for culture consists of the fact that it created a platform for a very broad scope of initiatives and that individuals saw this chance and started to fight for those values which are still top priorities: dignity, freedom, truth. No culture can live without the struggle for these values.

Chapter Six

The Process Continues

The following is an attempt to summarize developments in People's Poland up to the end of July, 1981 and it is based more on facts than interpretations, since the latter are available to readers from all sides and the former are less easy to find and also more central to reachng an informed personal understanding. Before indulging in further pursuits, let me state very briefly the order of presentation:

a) From the ordinary to the extraordinary party congress: a synopsis of dates and events from January '80 to July '81.
b) The cultural renaissance or the making of a post-Stalinist socialist working class consciousness: films, monuments, and history handbooks.
c) The way it really was: an insider's story of selected strikes after the Gdansk agreements were signed.
d) Peripheralization and its discontents.

A) From the Ordinary to the Extraordinary Party Congress

The following dates and descriptions show the direction of political changes in Poland and the response of the party to the political pressures of a society in rebellion.

February '80
The eighth congress of the Polish Workers' Party witnessed Gierek's speech on "Further development of Poland, further welfare of the Polish nation; and basic tenets of economic growth in the years 1981-85," in which it was stated that the party had managed to elaborate a socio-economic strategy for "man's sake," responsive to the needs and hopes of the Poles, and that this strategy would be implemented. Principles of social justice were stressed and each family's good was seen as the major social value.

The parliament or Seym heard prime minister Piotr Jaruszewicz ask to be relieved of his duties, and a new prime minister, Edward Babiuch, was nominated.

March '80
The election campaign developed candidates for the Seym and for the national councils, and local authorities in Poland made many speeches. Edward Gierek claimed in Sosnowiec that "we are all responsible for Poland...in spite of the troubles of which we speak honestly and openly, we have the necessary stamina to reach our targets." Elections took place on March 23rd.

April '80
The new prime minister, Edward Babiuch, opened parliament by announcing the new goverment's program. He appealed to the unity of all Poles around mutual interests. Gierek traveled the country.

May '80
Edward Babiuch made his first foreign trip, to the Soviet Union to be received by Brezhnev.

June '80
In the Seym sessions on the 23rd and 24th the analysis of economic troubles revealed that the reason for the economic ills was a negative trade balance and excessive financial and productive debts to foreign creditors.

July '80
The first strikes, which the mass media called "work stoppages"

broke out in the Mielec airplane factory, the Tozev automobile plant and the Ursus tractor production plant as protests against new salary principles and higher meat prices. 71,000 workers went on strike in 177 production units.

August '80
On August 14 a strike broke out in the Lenin shipyards in Gdansk headed by a former shipyard worker and a former active member of the strike committee of December 1970—Lech Walesa. Edward Gierek returned from his holiday leave in the Crimea. On the 30th in Szczecin and on the 31st in Gdansk an agreement was signed between striking workers and the authorities. A plenary sitting of the party's central committee accepted these agreements. (This month's events are described in more detail in Chapter Four)

September '80
On September 1 almost all previously striking factories started functioning. Only the coal workers in Silesia were still on strike; the mass media did not inform the populace of their strikes although their agreements had not yet been reached. They started working once their agreement was signed on September 3 in Jastrzebie. On September 5 the Seym acknowledged, for the first time in its history, with mass media coverage, the massive influence of the workers' strikes in all areas of social life. On the evening of the 5th and into the morning of the 6th, a special 6th plenary sitting of the party's Central Committee convened in Warsaw and dismissed Gierek (absent because of a heart attack) from his post, unanimously nominating Stanislaw Kania to take Gierek's place. New strikes continued in various parts of the country as local authorities began to openly express their disdain for the Gdansk agreements.

On the 13th, the State Council announced the principles of registration of the new trade unions. The first application was received on the 16th. The official (pre-Solidarity) trade unions, previously centralized within the Central Council of Trade Unions, decided to break relations with the latter. Ordinary and extraordinary congresses of trade unions were called for.

In Torun the first "horizontal party structure" came into being. Writers and activists around Krakow "Kuznica" appealed to the Central Committee to get rid of the remnants of arbitrariness and bureaucracy, to broaden inner party democracy, to stop individual authoritarian measures, to oppose cliques and to secure open, free, and complete information for all. They urged that party and state functions should also be separate henceforth.

Most party members called for an extraordinary congress of the party and a tentative date in December was discussed. Negotiations with top party leaders produced another date in May. Finally, July was suggested.

On the 24th the representatives of the independent self-governing trade union, Solidarity, from Gdansk, headed by Lech Walesa, applied for registration of their organization in Warsaw's district court. At the same time, the first rural Solidarity chapters sprang up under the names Rural Solidarity, Peasant Solidarity, and Individual Farmer's Solidarity.

October '80
The leaders of Solidarity announced an hour long warning strike on October 3. In the context of sudden social tension and many local strikes, the second half of the sixth plenary session of the General Committee met on the 4th—the session lasted till the early morning hours of the 6th. The Central Committee evaluated the causes of the crisis and made the party's targets for the future more clear. It dismissed from the Central Committee persons who were responsible for "weakening the link of the party with the masses" and "causing the severe social crisis."

The Seym met on the 8th; a bill subjecting the Supreme Chamber of Control to parliament passed—in the seventies the chamber had been illegally subjected to the prime minister whose authority was thus uncontrolled by anyone. Mieczyslaw Moczar returned as the chamber's head official. Personnel changes in the State Council and the Council of Ministers were announced; after the top leaders, a second rank of victims was carefully selected—large enough to attract attention but not large enough to mean any profound change in the structure of the ruling class.

Warsaw's district court registered Solidarity on the 24th, but sneaked a few points onto the statute—on its own! This unheard of procedure of the court being at the same time a "corrector" of legal documents (the new additions concerned the "leading role of the party") increased tensions as the trade union appealed to the Supreme Court for a new registration without corrections. The next day all public transport vehicles bore the sign "registration yes; corrections, no."

November '80
On the 10th the Supreme Court finally recognized that the statutes allowed for registration of Solidarity without corrections and a compromise formula was invented—the trade union promised to obey the constitution which has had this phrase written into it since the mid-seventies. A relief.

Kania received Walesa to talk on the socio-economic situation of the country and on Solidarity's actions for the sake of the country. This was an early attempt to make Solidarity a better whip to discipline the labor force.

The Seym nominated Jerzy Ozdowski, a professor of economics, a catholic politician, and head of Poznan's Catholic Intelligentsia Club, to the post of deputy prime minister. Other ministers were forced out of office as agricultural production became the topic of many heated discussions.

December '80
The ruling class developed a new strategem in order to save former trade union functionaries who had meanwhile attempted to improve their image by refusing to be "united" by a central body and by nominating themselves branch trade unions. The new "Cooperation Commission of Branch Trade Unions," headed by Albin Szyszka, appealed to Walesa to meet and talk things over. The appeal ended with the words "A Pole should be able to talk things over with a Pole." The registration of branch trade unions, needless to say and in contrast to Solidarity's experience, met with no obstacles—and thus the Central Council of Trade Unions ceased to exist by the end of 1980.

January '81
In some regions of the country spontaneous massive elections of party officials and representatives at different levels began to take place, removing previous functionaries. The action became nationwide with mixed responses from local party committees as no decisive policy was expressed by either the central or voivodsip committees. The ruling class panicked and withdrew from party appearances, offering no comment.

New instances of "horizontal structures" within the party appeared—that is, party members of various plants and regions simply met and cooperated without party functionaries and outside formal structures. This happened in Gdansk, Poznan, Krakow, Katowice, and Szczecin, following the example of Torun.

In a TV speech, Deputy Prime Minister Mieczyslaw Jagielski suggested two free Saturdays per month and an eight hour day, or all free Saturdays and an eight and a half hour working day. The suggestion was a brutal violation of the Gdansk Agreements on two counts:

a) all Saturdays were to be free, and no compensation was to be sought.

b) the decision to suggest this alternative was made suddenly, without any attempt to consult with working people.

The result was that many production plants simply stopped working on Saturdays; that is, on the first Saturday which the government declared a normal working day about 60% of all workers failed to obey the government's orders. The percentage given officially, 30-40% is lower as a result of a managerial trick: writing this particular Saturday off as if workers had made a collective choice to make it up in February. On the next Saturday almost all workers were off, that is, about 90%. There was no doubt, therefore, that the ruling class test of the possibility of slowly withdrawing the concessions granted to the working class in August '80 misfired.

Stefan Olszowski, a hard-liner from the Political Bureau, in a TV speech said that: "The party says yes to the development of socialist democracy, yes to new activity of trade unions, yes to the reforms and perfection of planning and management, yes to all actions which aim at the amelioration of society's living standards; but it says decisively no to all attempts to introduce chaos and anarchy to public life. It says no to those who want to attack the party, socialist state, international alliances and obligations—the bases of Poland's existence as a state. We say no to all counter-revolutionary attempts."

Stanislaw Kania opened a national session of the first secretaries of the party from all major production plants in Poland. Kazimierz Barcikowski, who headed the government delegation to Szczecin, says that: "There is no way to emerge from the present situation, both for the party and the state, without a reinforcement of the basic working class units of the party, and a securing of a proper place in the socio-political life of the state and the nation for workers and industrial employees."

A new Solidarity protest took place in Nowy Sacz (since "Nowy" means new, the slogan runs "Old methods in New Sacz") where the town hall was occupied. The reasons were presented in a list of grievances, and especially emphasized was the notorious corruption of the officials who still held all vital party and state posts in Nowy Sacz. The police intervened and cleared the town hall. The protestors continued their protest from the buildings of Solidarity, but their negotiations were artificially prolonged by the very officials in question who wanted to present their critics from Solidarity as irresponsible trouble-makers and thus to save their own skins. This attempt was allowed by the central authorities who were anxious to find some remedy for the growing wave of social grievances and accusations of misdemeanors and corruption against party and state officials.

The Pope received a Solidarity delegation headed by Lech Walesa (who also honored the graves of the Polish soldiers under Monte Casino, a symbol of the military triumph of the non-Communist Polish units during World War II). Walesa announced that there shoud be no contradiction between the self-rule and social initiative of working people and the structure of a system which claims to see labor as the basis of social and state life.

Ustrzyki Dolne, a remote, south-eastern town of Poland, witnessed a farmer led strike: the farmers wanted to have their rural Solidarity registered.

Many factories waged short warning strikes as a response to the government's manner of dealing with free Saturdays.

The National Coordination Commission of Solidarity appealed to all factories to stop strikes, but upon the condition that the government begin negotiations with the commission about free Saturdays. The negotiations were to be held in Rzeszow (the largest town in the vicinity of Ustrzyki Dolne) and the demand for farmers' trade unions was part and parcel of Solidarity's demand for a coherent free Saturday policy. On the third, a warning strike propelled the government toward negotiations—the strike's organization and scope left no doubt about the workers' support for Solidarity.

In a vain attempt to win over the public, TV commentators tried to organize an open discussion on free Saturdays with government representatives, Solidarity people, and "branch trade union" representatives. The TV debate, albeit an unheard of phenomenon in the "socialist countries," clearly demonstrated that the government had no arguments and no specialists to speak of, and that the branch unionists were theatrically attempting to oppose the goverment while having actually no counter program. The TV managers made the latter sit on the government's side, which provided an adequate visual symbol of their role....

The negotiations between Solidarity and the government brought results: the working week had to consist of 42 hours, and three Saturdays of each month had to be free, while the last one would remain a normal working day. A nation-wide Solidarity weekly was agreed upon, and a joint commission to continue working on the farmers' union was established.

February '81

An occupational strike organized by the Rzezow chapter of Solidarity in the former buildings of the local trade union authorities started under the slogan of "a just division of the wealth and property of the former trade unions." Inasmuch as the ruling class wanted to offset the results of the free Saturday agreement by a conscious effort to starve the populace and "prove" that Saturdays should not be free, here the division of wealth left by non-existent trade union structural levels favored the government-formed branch trade unions at the expense of Solidarity. Nothing was said about the unjust division of the property of former trade unions which should go to the members who paid for it.

Another major demand was to register rural Solidarity. The government speaker answered publicly that trade unions can only represent employees and individual farmers, as agricultural producers can only organize themselves in "agricultural circles," a facade for a state monopoly of agricultural control and investment.

120 Bielsko voivodship factories went on strike because nobody wanted to relieve a clearly corrupt and incompetent local state head officer of his duties, and the prime minister even insisted that he should not resign. The negotiations stuttered; local papers in Poland asked "how much does a voivoda cost" because of the cost of the strike. Finally, church mediation resulted in removal of the officials and an end to the strike.

The students went on strike in Lodz and other centers—after a round of negotiations with Minister Gorski a new, Independent Student Association was registered, and the students' postulates acquired popularity.

Government commissions had to negotiate in various places in the country, especially with farmers who decided to go on a hunger strike in Swidnica.

A typical phenomenon of the period was that many brand new buildings changed owners and purpose: they were not police, party or luxurious government centers any more, but became generally accessible public places, hospitals, sanatoria, kindergartens, schools, etc.

Villas and even whole settlements of luxurious houses inhabited by previous functionaries were the subject of public discussion. The tendency to take individual action was very strong. The ruling class responded with cynicism and indifference: Grabski, a hard-liner from the June counter-Kania attack who was nominated for a search commission to prove the corruption of Gierek and co., was himself, for example, an owner of a luxurious villa near Poznan, next to the former almighty Poznan secretary Zasada, whose demise was quick, and whose crimes have been legendary.

The 8th plenary sitting of the party's central committee announced that Pinkowski, prime minister from September, would resign to be replaced by Wojciech Jaruzelski, heretofore Minister of National Defense. Apart from this personnel decision the plenum reported nothing but cliches about the need for national unity and avoided a clear committment for a new date for the party congress.

The Supreme Court failed to register the individual farmers' Solidarity and gave the case over to Warsaw city authorities.

The Seym assembled to confirm the nomination of Prime Minister Jaruzelski by the party, and the new prime minister offered nothing but a plea for 90 days without a strike plus a very contradictory, uncertain and vague government plan for ending the crisis; most economists dismissed it as verbiage.

The strikes in Rzeszow and Ustrzyki Dolne were over but their resolving agreements covered only certain legal checks and balances against an unjust agricultural investment policy and the state's infringement upon land ownership, not a recognition of rural Solidarity itself.

Kania visited Moscow's Soviet party congress but nothing interesting was revealed about the discussions: banalities abounded about "true faith in our solutions expressed by our eternal friends."

March '81

Poznan was the seat of the First National Congress of the independent trade union of individual farmers' Solidarity which united all three major forms of rural Solidarity. The congress took place in the middle of Poznan, in the Opera, but the authorities decided that it was illegal and allowed no mention about it in the press. No journalist could comment, and the citizens of Poznan passed unknowingly by the decorated Opera about which even the local TV program kept silent.

In order to try and reach a compromise without actually recognizing rural Solidarity, the government began a whole array of TV programs about progressive changes within the existing structures and had the Seym discuss a new bill on rural self-government which still stressed state controlled "agricultural circles" and allowed for no independent farmer organizations. The Seym also called a special commission to organize and observe the authorities' honesty in fulfilling the obligations which resulted from the Gdansk, Szczecin and Jastrzebie agreements. There were heated debates on a new bill on censorship, whose early drafts as prepared by the government were laughable in their attempts to maintain the status quo and to introduce penalties for anything that went to print uncensored.

Meanwhile, although the ruling class systematically tried to present the KOR activists, especially Kuron and Michnik, as dangerous elements of which Solidarity should beware, it focused its central attack on KPN (The Confederation of Independent Poland) led by Moczulski. The district attorney of Warsaw made a formal case in Warsaw court against this organization.

Lodz announced a strike standby due to the police hospital policies, while Radom announced a standby too in order to hold the authorities responsible for their 1976 policies of repressing the workers' unrest.

The church bishop's conference expressed support for individual farmers being granted the right to associate, just like the workers.

A minor democratic political party showed the way to political modernization. During its congress almost all previous office holders were rejected by the democratically chosen delegates. The ruling class decided to postpone the Polish United Workers Party congress and to aggravate the economic situation of consumers as a means of gaining leverage against this anti-functionary tendency.

In a censored speech, Walesa appealed to society to stop unnecessary strikes, and announced the opening of negotiations with deputy prime minister Rakowski.

The example set by the democratic party and the wave of strikes against local authorities who did not respect the agreements made the ruling class act. The strongest confrontation since the period of struggle over "free Saturdays" came with the "Bydgoszcz massacre." where the top Political Bureau leaders in conjunction with the secret police (SB) decided to demonstrate that the core of their power structure must remain untouched. They did so by applying violence openly and with the cooperation of local authorities and central officials of the ministry of justice. Indeed, the scene of the brutal physical assault by secret police agents against Solidarity leaders was filmed by the uniformed police. One of the uniformed policemen watched it with inner struggle, and finally wept publicly because of his impotence to prevent it. Information in the mass media was grotesquely distorted—but Solidarity responded with a massive and detailed description of the events and a wave of protest swept the country astonishing the authorities who groped for a way back from their initial actions. The threat of a general strike grew as the police refused to turn in the agents responsible and officials refused to confess which top leaders ordered the action. Negotiations followed.

The events had an unplanned effect on party members themselves who now demanded an extraordinary party congress in May. The top party leaders did not yield, but decided that if they did not call the congress at all, the party would simply dissolve as it would have nothing to offer. The 9th plenary session of the Central Committee thus issued the following announcement, having already decided that the congress would take place in July and a nation wide campaign for party posts and delegates would be held. "It is the basic duty of the party and of all social forces which guard socialism to secure leadership for our nation as it emerges from a profound crisis, and to create the preconditions for peace, order, and national and citizen's security." The party declared it wants an agreement, a truce with society—a recantation of Bydgozcz policy—and at the same time the opposition of top leaders against "horizontal structures" grew fierce.

The Warsaw talks between Rakowski and Walesa resulted in a compromise on the thirtieth: the general strike was averted though the Gdansk commission of Solidarity had yet to accept Walesa's compromise, which it did, however, after a stormy discussion and vote: 25 to put the strike off, 4 for the strike, 6 abstentions.

Meanwhile the crisis within the party grew. Almost all members expressed the opinion that the party was unable to even define sources of tension, unwilling to forbid terrorist activities by the secret police, and promised no plan for the future. The ruling class wanted to prepare basic documents for the congress—"assumptions and directives"—but the latter were laughed off by the party base.

April '81

The government resumed conversations with the bishops—a joint commission of both sides was reinstated, dialogue was stressed. The government thanked the Pope, primate, and bishops for their help in the peaceful solution of the Bydgoszcz crisis, but did not give the culprits away.

Apart from sugar rationing, meat rationing was also introduced. It turned out very soon that although rationing secured a minimum of meat per capita, the government had issued two million cards too many, trying to preserve privileges even in times of scarcity. This rendered Rakowski's TV claim that he was also living only off his rationing card ridiculous.

The weekly, *Solidarity*, appeared and its popularity was established immediately. It was, however, censored. Krakow witnessed the first national congress of the Independent Student Association.

The Seym voted in favor of Jaruzelski's plan for two months without strikes but was shocked by the attempt to use this moratorium period to repress Bydgosczc's Solidarity leaders, and also called for a registration of rural Solidarity. So finally, the Bydgoszcz negotiations produced a compromise—the punishment of police agents was postponed, but rural Solidarity was accepted; the legal steps were to be over before May 10th. The pattern of these negotiations was a model of all ruling class responses: never let the society touch the actual political power base (the secret police and the Soviet Union's support of party leaders), but yield after much blood and pressure to everything else.

The Seym also discussed two censorship bills: one prepared by the government, another by a spontaneous association of those who had been harmed by censorship in the past.

The censorship debate and peasant advances together increased Moscow's uneasiness and the Soviets sent Suslov to Warsaw to discuss party problems. The results were not known to the public.

The trade union parliamentary bill was presented in the press and underwent a general public discussion which exposed it as a ruling class attempt to thwart the trade unions.

The tenth plenary session of the Central Committee finally decided to call an extraordinary party congress on July 14-18. There were personnel changes in the Central Committee. Gierek's closest allies were ousted but there was still a prevailing force of hardliners. For example, the special commission to investigate corruption and power abuse was headed by Grabski, a hardliner whose only supposed saving grace was that he had once criticized Gierek; but no one mentioned that he did so as a part of a plot implicating some regional first secretaries, not out of general social concern.

May '81

For the first time, May Day passed in People's Poland with practically no celebrations. There was a very modest and unobtrusive walk of party functionaries to the monument in Warsaw and practically nothing elsewhere which meant a significant change from previous enforced manifestations of the unity of the working masses and its beloved functionaries.

In a joint effort of major centers of economic research (especially Warsaw's Main School of Planning and Statistics, the Poznan Economic Academy, and the Wroclaw center) Solidarity developed a number of possible projects for economic reform. But the government was not ready to accept anything more than a vague appeal for order and for necessary reforms of an unknown kind.

The third of May, which was traditionally, until 1945, a Polish national day to celebrate the anniversary of the famous Polish Constitution paralleling the American and French ones, became a day of national unity, with a gala concert in Warsaw attended by state authorities and church officials. The church celebrations evoked Polish history and became a symbol of hopes for a better future.

The Seym passed a number of bills, including the one on individual farmers, thus paving the way for registration of their Solidarity trade union. The Polish Peasant Party, so far a front for communist manipulation, changed its top functionaries.

The Warsaw police manipulated a scene in Otwock (a small town about 20 miles from the capital) and arranged for a battle between two drunks and a police patrol in which the latter lost. The aim was to persuade society that the police have too little to say in social life and cannot even protect law and order—it was a response to successive revelations about the private investments and economic life of the Ministry of the Interior. A similar event was arranged in Katowice, but people at the main railway station there spontaneously disarmed the paid trouble-makers whom the police failed to stop, thus rendering the whole scheme invalid.

Prisoners went on strikes and protests against their exploitation in labor centers and the horrible conditions in prisons—instances of extreme and systematic cruelty were cited. This drew attention to the fact that there are over 100,000 prisoners in Poland, that the Polish punitive system is one of the harshest in Europe, and that prison terms are long even for relatively petty crimes while large cases of blatant corruption and theft go unpunished. The ideas of amnesty and abolition were voiced by Polish lawyers and solicitors and the Poznan congress of the latter became a huge accusation of the juridicial and penal system in Poland.

Meanwhile the ruling class decided to lower living standards: butter, flour, and cereals were rationed. In some centers cigarettes were added to the list.

On the twelfth the Warsaw District Court registered the Independent, Self-Governing Trade Union of Individual Farmers' Solidarity. The importance of this event in a country where state socialist accumulation has been achieved primarily at the expense of the peasant masses can hardly be overestimated—see, for example, the description of peasant strikes below.

Over the next two days the Pope was seriously wounded by a Turkish rightist extremist whose illegal clandestine organization had links to both Soviet and American secret services, and the primate of Poland, Cardinal Wyszynski, fell ill.

Students, workers, and all segments of the population protested against the imprisonment of KOR members (Moczulski, Szeremietiew, et al.) and against the principle that political views can lead one to prison. The government announced that they were being held not for political reasons, but juridicially speaking the police presented no coherent case against them apart from political deviance—they were against Soviet domination in all spheres of life. Solidarity announced that it did not share the views of the imprisoned, but was strongly against political imprisonment. "They go now, we shall go next," is the prevailing mood. Students in Warsaw sold T-shirts with abbreviations for "anti-socialist elements" and kid's T-shirts with "slouching imperialist" tags to ridicule the attempts of state propagandists to call every spontaneous social activity an anti-socialist imperialist diversion.

In Sosnowiec, Silesia, people went on hunger strikes to protest political imprisonment and Solidarity organized peaceful protest marches.

The ruling class began to stir: as its test balloon, it set up the so called Katowice Party Forum, a secret assembly of hardliners who called themselves true communists, published incoherent blubbering about anti-socialism and the weak resistance of central party functionaries, and praised the Russians as a model, all the while failing to reveal their own names. But the test failed. It soon turned out that almost everybody—from bottom assembly line workers to top party leaders—condemned the Forum as an open invitation to mass terror and/or the Soviet army. Of course, on the other hand, the Forum was immediately hailed in the Soviet, Czech, and East German press, even before it was known in Poland. However, despite the failure, the ruling class stuck to pattern and tried to found the same sort of "forums" in Poznan, Torun, and other centers. People whose names were given as members of the forums usually protested loudly in the press against having their names used this way and no one ever knew who was for the forums apart from some former party big shots, but the policy was nonetheless pursued.

On May 28 Cardinal Stefan Wyszynski, the primate of Poland, died in Warsaw. His death became both a celebration of the role the church plays in Polish life and an opportunity to remember his life history of persistent struggle against the Sovietization of Polish life.

June '81

The regional party conferences in most cases lasted much longer than intended, and only a few of the centrally imposed voivodship party secretaries remained in their posts. However, Kania's direct interventions saved the skins of a number of top hardliners who otherwise would never have been selected as party delegates to the congress and this demonstrated clearly that the so-called split in the Political Bureau and Central Committee was not real, but staged. Were it otherwise, Kania would have no reason to defend people who ostensibly sought his demise as a man who was too soft on "anti-socialist elements."

Czeslaw Milosz, the Nobel prize laureate of 1980, visited Poland for the first time since he emigrated in 1952. His visit and a ceremony granting him a doctorate honoris causa in the Catholic University of Lublin, became manifestations of an independent Polish culture. Underground publications of his works were finally slowly matched by state published versions.

Walesa visited Geneva and was hailed at the ILO session there.

The ruling class decided the "forum" technique was insufficient and founded *Grunwald*—an anti-semitic supposedly mass organization of former Stalinist secret police who happened to be mainly Polish Jewish communist post-1945 police and party staff members—of which little was known except that it was supported by Political Bureau member, Stefan Olszowski, who had his own ambitions. The organization is virtually secret although some party hardliners with nationalist beliefs became mildly associated with it. They publish their own weekly, "Reality," anonymously, but in 150,000 copies—unheard of in a country where the press cuts circulation because of paper shortages, and where the 11 million strong Solidarity fought for a weekly for almost a year. It is a melange of cheap mudslinging against liberals, Jews, progressives, and reformists—everybody who is not absolutely authoritarian and loyal to a party power cloaked in nationalist slogans.

The ruling class and secret police decided that neither the "Grunwald"/"Reality" technique nor threats of the anti-socialist nature of Solidarity activities were enough. Therefore the secret police undertook the action of smearing the monuments of Soviet soldiers of WWII in order both to accuse Solidarity of anti-Sovietism and to invoke the Soviet threat, more clearly and palpably. This action, which was universally understood as a threat from the secret police and a possible invitation to the Soviets, failed as a provocation but succeeded as a pacifier: society became more afraid of Soviet intervention than before.

The pressure of society made the court decide to release KPN members from custody—the attorney general was even notified by the court to prepare a more convincing case. The release was propelled both by public pressure and by a decision of the ruling class that the release of openly anti-Soviet activists would put some credibility into the police provocations against the monuments and graves of Soviet soldiers fallen in WWII.

The ruling class got new wind. The Soviets pitched in with a letter of warning and a personal attack against Kania and Jaruzelski which very conveniently boosted the popularity of both and gave Jaruzelski an opportunity to give up possible suggestions of parliamentary reform he had ostensibly prepared, among others that top party people would form a higher chamber of the parliament, where only long range strategies would be discussed, while democratically elected delegates would manage the state daily in a lower chamber—an interesting project. Meanwhile, the Soviets warned about threats to socialism. At the Eleventh Plenum of the Central Committee Grabski openly attacked Kania and the latter called for a vote. However, he also managed to convince the regional party secretaries that he and Jaruzelski were best for the party, Poland, and the situation, and so finally no personnel changes were made within the Central Committee. The discussion revealed that top party functionaries did not care about public developments, the economic situation, or anything at all except for their own political careers. Most of their speeches were either attacks against newspapers, Solidarity leaders, or imaginary anti-socialist forces. The Plenum also showed a split between "hard-liners" like Grabski, Zabinski, Olszowski and "liberals" like Rakowski, all of which worked to Kania's benefit and provided a convincing explanation for party members of the almost total inactivity and lack of imagination and programs on the part of the party leadership. Rakowski made an interesting speech about the necessity to avoid a repetition of 1956 and 1970 because, as he phrased it "the party would not last through it, nor would any Polish communist."

Bydgoszcz finally announced that the general strike was recalled—it would have been another protest against the lack of an explanation of the March events as so far the government had still refused to identify the police agents responsible for the physical assault and had removed only the attorney general, minister of justice, and some local authorities responsible for the developments.

Kania enjoyed the benefits of the Soviet's letter: he got himself elected as a Krakow party organization delegate to the extraordinary congress.

Walesa met with Solidarity organizations and explained the necessity for a more coordinated action against the Bydgoszcz secret police gangsters and for other aims. However, as usual, the press broadcast his calls for peace and little else.

Poznan lived through its great day on June 28, commemorating the 27th anniversary of the tragic Poznan June of 1956. There were significant changes—"Dzherzynski" street disappeared and was replaced by "28 June" street, while the name of the youngest victim of the police brutality of 1956, Romek Strzalkowski, also was given to a street. A huge monument, very much in the style of the one in Gdansk, opened in the heart of Poznan, next to Mickiewiczmonument, close to the regional party headquarters, and in the most visible spot in the whole city. Over 200,000 people attended the ceremony of the opening of the monument and there were numerous sessions and discussions as many documents and sources were prepared. Quite by coincidence, for example, it turned out that some Poznan sociologists had preserved genuine questionaires they had given to the Gegielski workers in 1956, immediately after the events; others brought private photo albums; and the documentation grew daily. Walesa visited the ceremony and spoke of the significance of 1956 and the monument.

A day later he was present in Radom, where a foundation was being laid for a future monument to the victims of the police brutality of 1976.

However, one element of the project to organize national unity failed. The British government did not allow for a transference of the body of General Sikorski from England to Poland, so that the latter could not be ceremoniously interred in Wawei royal castle in Krakow on July 4.

July '81

The party congress opened on July 14 and lasted till July 20. No economic reform was in sight, and the whole proceeding involved more statutory and backroom power struggles than actual care for the country. The results were mixed. On the one hand, there was undoubtedly more democracy in the proceedings than ever before, though its basis was uncertain. For example, Kania's election was more a matter of careful Polish (and Soviet) policy orchestration than of outright domination of the voting machinery. On the other hand, the best speech produced at the congress, the one made by Mieczyslaw Rakowski, the deputy prime minister and editor in chief of *Polityka*, whom the hard-core ruling class members distrusted and never allowed to enter top party circles, nonetheless indicated that the ruling class wanted not only to preserve existing privileges but also to recover what was recently lost. The following are extensive excerpts which speak for themselves:

"Almost daily I ask myself why the policy established by the 6th Plenum of the Central Committee, the one that we think the only correct one, the one we all assembled here at this extra ordinary congress to support, why has this policy failed so far to solve our crisis? If our policy is correct than why does the crisis go on? This is the major question which the congress should answer, and other questions depend on this one—answers to questions of what should be changed so that our policy becomes more effective.

There is a demand that our party turn the course of events back. *We all desire it* (italics mine—S.S.) but what does it practically mean? It means that we can not reverse the agreements and the conditions which they created, but we can prevent further crisis.

The greatest threat, I think, consists of the fact that if the crisis lasts, it may become permanent, both society and government getting used to it. It would then become a lasting life style. We would continue to speak of overcoming the crisis, but we would remain within its grasp. Danger over the country and worrying over national survival would then assume another, not necessarily explosive character, but remain very thorough. Under the agreement's protective umbrella, among the various national celebrations and popular symbolic gestures, we shall slowly get used to a lack of basic products, we shall start thinking that labor is not the most important matter, that other states should care for our well-being, and that our national specialties are celebrations and discussions.

I do not know what would have happened in Poland if a number of years ago suddenly there were no detergents, meat, milk, butter, vodka, cigarettes and coal, if money lost value daily, people stopped leaving for holidays, newspapers would be out of reach, subscription impossible, etc. I do not know what would have happened, but remember that in the past even smaller reasons, attempts to raise the prices of meat, for instance, were enough to stir the nation. Today it turns out that under new circumstances, due to new policy, the nation demonstrates much more patience and rationality than we would have expected. But one should not overdo it. This patience is not unlimited. This is the credit, for which we have to pay increasingly high political interest rates.

I claim that the political line of the agreements was and is indispensible, for its alternative was a major conflict, authorities struggling with the majority, a bloodbath and national drama, after which all our problems would still face us and in a more intensive and dangerous way. This conflict would not fix anything—we would all be fixed for good, we, the nation, the state, and Polish communists.

Among the reasons for which our policy failed to close the crisis phase off I would like to point out first a general unpreparedness of the party for the completely new situations which resulted from the working class protests. We have been surprised by the scope and political effects of the making of Solidarity. The party was not ready, neither ideologically, nor politically, for this development. It is thus quite understandable that millions of party members who had no influence upon the leaders' policies anyway, that these millions were stirred up by the attacks of the angry people who headed many local chapters of Solidarity and turned against their own leaders. This anger brought a huge wave of concern about the responsibility of former leaders and a demand to state this responsibility in an unambiguous manner....

The first reason for the inefficiency of party policy with respect to stopping the crisis I see as conservative forces within the party, not very numerous but strategically placed in the party and state apparatus. They did not allow the party to get ahead of events, to express social strivings, to be the avant garde of the transformations. They acted to call all agreements and reforms "concessions" and turned them into acts accomplished only against the resistance of authority structures: all this in a situation in which forces definitely unsympathetic to our social system worked for the dismantling of socialism.

The second reason was the not very numerous but very vocal forces in the party which denied the latter's marxist-leninist nature and invoked democracy to try to dismantle the party as an organized power and political identity.

The third reason was radicals within Solidarity and opposition members working under Solidarity's shield, who wanted to have confrontations and to threaten the system.

The other reason lies in the Central Committee and the Political Bureau which often failed to make clear statements and form coherent views. The latter was especially half-hearted and indecisive.

All these factors not only paralyzed reforms, but contributed to a lasting state of tension so that all party efforts went to defusing daily conflicts; policy making was replaced by seeking tactical survival from one crisis to another....

I want to call again, here and now, for formation of a special commission to objectively evaluate the history of People's Poland—both the crises and the achievements.

Yes. Achievements. For we have nothing to be ashamed of. We can be ashamed of some mistakes of our leaders, but not of People's Poland.

Nobody should harbor any illusions in so far as our decisive power in a new National Unity Front goes....But our decisive leading role is no dictatorship but honest partnership.....

Polish reform, let us not be afraid of this word, let us stop thinking of it as of a dirty one, is an acute problem for the whole socialist camp. If we move wisely, we shall turn Poland which could be seen as a sick man of Europe into, instead, one of the sources of hope we have in socialism."

These excerpts from *Trybuna Ludu* of July 16, 1981 make clear that the ruling class still refused to accept the independent political expression of society's strivings, and that it could hardly comprehend its loss of control over the working class. It is also clear that no solution, no policy has been suggested by any member of the current power elite, and that the comedy of a struggle between hard-liners and liberals is all that society is supposed to swallow as a positive proof that the ruling class seeks change and reform. The only interesting suggestion found in this, the only interesting voice among ruling class representatives during the congress (all the others came from below) especially in questioning Kania's role in the bloodbath of December 1970, was to separate the state and party and it was rendered meaningless by the domination over political machinery which enabled the party to put anyone it desired into any post from prime minister to local village community official.

B) The Cultural Renaissance or the Making of a Poststalinist Socialist Working Class Consciousness—the Films, the Monuments, the History Handbooks.

One of the symbols of new Polish consciousness, Wajda's artistic reflection on the years 1970-1980, "The Man of Iron," which shocked the Cannes international audience in June 1981, was also presented for the first time to Poznan audiences during the celebrations of the June 1956 anniversary. There was still no official distribution copy by then, so that only Wajda's personal copy was used, and it was presented for 48 hours in two cinemas simultaneously, with couriers exchanging reels day and night between the two, the theatres being packed for the whole 48 hours. This was a film made, so to speak, because of a social demand voiced by the shipyard workers when Wajda visited the striking shipyard in August 1980. It was already the place where most intellectuals went on pilgrimages by then. The public demand went so far that Wajda even assembled actual film reels of police brutality from December 1970—candid cameras of amateurs had caught scenes which censorship subsequently found too ugly and revealing to be presented to society at large. A compromise was that Wajda had to trim them for Polish distributors. The main protagonist of "The Man of Iron" is a son of "The Man of Marble" stakhanovite worker, Maciek Tomczyk, who begins his active social and political life the second he hears that his father has been killed by police in the 1970 workers' riots in Gdansk. Here is what Wajda says about his protagonist:

"My problem was to create Maciek Tomczyk—he could not become the leader of the Gdansk riots, for we knew that Walesa was one and he appears in documentary segments of the film. But if Maciek is no leader, why would the secret police send their man to "fix" him? What we want to say is very important. We want to say that one cannot "prepare" the workers. The workers either act or they do not. And if they do, they do so in their own cause. Had they not moved in their own cause, no leader would be able to move them, no representative of any political ideology. Thus I had understood that Maciek has to be a worker like his father, but on another level. For Maciek begins to be a political man the minute he learns his father was murdered."

Wajda's film is symbolic of a renaissance of interest in Poland's recent history, for the mass movement to analyze, understand and to speak openly about. The Poznan celebrations of the opening of the monument to commemorate victims of the 1956 police terror included, for example, theatre shows prepared by former participants in the riots. They used their private archives to reconstruct the parody of justice which followed the street scenes—the state archives had been emptied of court records by special units of the secret police headed by the former mayor of Poznan, Cozac. They left a note "materials with no historical value"...

There is more. In education, for instance, negotiations of Solidarity teams with the ministry of education revealed the latter's total incompetence and vanity—"we have always wanted everything Solidarity wants, so what is the problem?"—asked the same officials who never cared for any change and still do not, while teachers and intellectuals started preparing new curricula and handbooks on Polish history, etc. The low investment level in education over the past decade in Poland means that Poland is close to what UNESCO terms "educational death," which is what occurs in societies in which no more than 4 percent of the GNP goes for education. Here Solidarity had simply to provide the program and execute it, for the ministry was totally unable or unwilling to suggest anything.

Thus, in short order, history handbooks will appear and children will be able to learn about the history of their country without injections of state propaganda and scorn for the truth. Moreover, the daily history which happens before everybody's eyes nowadays, is also a strong support for educational reform. It is, of course, also heard from hard liners and top police officials that all these monuments should be destroyed and replaced by monuments to commemorate fulfillment of duties by secret and uniformed police agents, but it is hard to imagine how this "enlightened proposal" could possibly be accomplished. It is also hard to imagine what history handbooks one would have to employ to convince even a single thinking human that power should be paid homage in this particular manner.

The term has not surfaced yet, but it is more or less evident that Polish society is a poststalinist one in the particular sense that no future political elite, no matter what ruling class calls it into being, can rule with the ambition of exercizing the kind of total control that the present ruling class has desired till 1980. It is far from clear whether the ruling class understands this—Rakowski's speech would rather point to the contrary, and his is the most rational and broadminded one—but it is quite clear that none-theless the ruling class will be kept in check by a system of checks and balances that have slowly and painfully emerged. Not least of the latter is the new awareness of the working class, a truly poststalinist social consciousness.

The latter is a result of a "happy coincidence" of workers' political maturity and sophistication, and of a proliferation of semi-legal and clandestine or "underground" publications and conscious-ness raising actions (for example, the "flying university") on the part of the intelligentsia and the young. The police harassed the participants, but the breaking point was crossed and repressions proved either ineffective (when too weak) or counterproductive (when too strong). Miroslaw Chojecki, the master of the most prestigious "Nowa" underground publishing house, has been, in mid-1981, suggested as a likely candidate to receive the "Dough" prize granted by the *Polityka* weekly headed by deputy prime minister Rakowski, for the most stimulating idea or activity.

There was no single centralized plan to proliferate these publications, organize these lectures, etc. But they grew, and they harmoniously melted into a vast social upheaval of post-August 1980 Poland, a poststalinist country in culture if not in all other areas.

C) The Way It Really Was
An Insider's Story of Several Strikes After August 1980

Bielsko-Biala—On February 6, 1981, at 4:38 a.m. negotiations between the government commission and the Solidarity regional strike committee were completed and an agreement was signed. The negotiations referred to over fifty cases of charges by Solidarity against the local party and state administration. The strike had been long, over two weeks, and could have been avoided if the local administration had not clung to their posts in spite of documented corruption, and if it had not received support from Warsaw.

On November 20, 1980, 501 delegates from various factories of the Podbeskedzie region formulated a 120 page document which proved charges of abuse of power on the part of practically all police commanders, voivodas, city presidents, mayors and some managers in Bielsko-Biaka, Ustron, Zywiec, Golesow, Zawoja, Wilkowice, Stryszawa, Brenna and Porabka. The charges were that the persons mentioned in the document had acquired financial and real estate gains at the expense of the social and private property of the citizenry, and at the material and moral expense of the workers in whose name the authorities acted.

Typical instances are: "purchase and letting to nine families of voivodship officials and functionaries of nine buildings in Bielsko-Biala which cost the city 14,275,000 zl subtracted from community housing funds by the city voivoda," or "city president Antoni Kobiela had applied a compulsory relocation of the owners of buildings at Wodna St. 3 and 5, letting these subsequently to the voivodship commander of police Byszard Witek and deputy voivoda Antoni Urbaniec which is clearly illegal since compulsory relocation can only be applied for public purposes."

All the cases were well documented. However, the local authorities first tried to charge only a top official, then accepted the visit of a Warsaw delegation but the latter turned out to be incompetent to do anything against the local authorities, and finally, in a rare attempt to abuse Walesa's name, faked a phone call from Gdansk in which Walesa ostensibly asked for a peaceful solution by a simple mailing of charges to Warsaw—but a delegation drove to Gdansk and found out the trick.

A mixed commission to investigate the charges was then formed and Solidarity members were in it. All the charges were confirmed, in spite of sabotage on the part of the local authorities with respect to financial data.

The local party committees tried to divide the workers and disseminated leaflets calling the Solidarity investigation political blackmail. No consequences were drawn from confirmation of the charges. Thus Solidarity, pressed hard by its members, decided to announce a state of preparedness to strike. Since subsequent leaflets from the local party and state officials not only revealed their unwillingness to respond to the charges but also the fact that they knew the contents of a report supposedly delivered only to the Supreme Control Chamber and Prosecutor General's Office, the strike broke out on January 27th. Communique number five said: "Friends! How much do we have to pay for the authorities' attitude towards the conflict? TV and radio will probably reply in the near future. The precision of their calculations will probably assert how much Solidarity contributes to the destabilization of public order. The truth is different. The lack of good will and the indecisiveness of the government contributes to an unnecessary prolongation of the strike...."

There was a stalemate. The government did not want to recognize the responsibility of the local power structure for abuses, the workers did not want to have thieves as their ostensible representatives. Meanwhile, working people from all over Poland expressed their solidarity with the Bielski-Biala workers.

The TV tried another sabotage and announced that the Solidarity chapter in the striking region was not obeying the national coordinating commission of Solidarity. Meanwhile the local government authorities held a session of the voivodship council from which they emerged unscathed, with—as their communique claimed—"full support of their voters"—this was asserted for a region which was on strike against them!

A government commission arrived but the prime minister had given them tough instructions: he would not accept the resignation of local authorities, who meanwhile understood that they would not last, and he asked the workers to return to work, promising that perhaps within a month he would try to analyze their charges.

Finally, after an intervention of bishops and grudging support from Walesa, who had arrived in Bielsko Biala with mixed feelings, he supported the regional strikers, but had doubts about this manner of punishing every culprit among the rulers—the following agreement was reached:

—all guilty representatives of the authorities would be immediately deprived of their posts.
—administrative and punitive measures would be taken against those found guilty of charges.
—A thorough oversight of local administration would be conducted.

The government commission confirmed the principle that strikers should not be repressed nor their salaries diminished. A mixed commission to observe the execution of the terms of agreement was established.

At five Lech Walesa spoke:

"There are neither winners nor losers, and what we made proves once again that we are capable of solving hard problems. It was hard, as you all know... We shall now rewrite the agreement, sign it, and then let us have a thanksgiving holy mass...."

The delegates stood and sang the national anthem.

After holy services a member of the regional commission of

Solidarity, Mieczyslaw Barteczko, made a statement:

"In spite of those fifteen odd days of slow decay—both physical and moral—on our part and on the part of our brothers and sisters in the factories, we survived, for we had much support..."

Walesa made a final statement.

"Thank you that you have made it, it was a fine struggle, a hard one, but somehow we made it...."

Ustrzyki Dolne—Instead of the list of events I shall quote a fragment of the negotiations between the striking committee of the farmers' Solidarity headed by Wojnarowicz, and the government delegation with the Krosno voivoda Kruk.

"It's a beautiful scene, fit for a movie. On one side of the table are gentlemen in formal dress, polite, pretending to be free and easy, to feel normal. They have a sad role. On another side of the table are farmers in unironed trousers, not always shaved, sometimes wanting to match the other's politeness.

...The strike committee suggests that the postulates should be discussed one after another, and that successive problems can only be tackled if prior postulates have been negotiated. Wojnarowicz informs the government delegation that new postulates have been prepared.

Government Commission: Do we have to negotiate the postulates we do not know yet?

Wojnarowicz: All the postulates are known, since we, the workers and peasants, have made them simple and clear. The only difference is that our lawyers have modified their expression.

The lawyers had arrived lately from Krakow Solidarity and worked out more precise formulas for the postulates.

The chairman of the government delegation: Can't we just talk to the presidium of the strike committee?

Wojarowicz: The strike committe has decided that the negotiations will take place only in the presence of all those assembled. I guarantee peaceful conditions in which to negotiate.

So much for the entrees. Antoni Wojnarowicz read out the first postulate about stopping the repressions. The chairman of the government commission asks for justification of this postulate.

—We meet here—says Wojnarowicz—since the spirit of the Gdansk agreements is still unknown to the local authorities of Bieszczady. Since September 1 various conflicts have broken out.

The founders of rural Solidarity have been hampered in organizing independent trade unions. The local authorities think that the rural Solidarity of peasants and federation of workers, farmers, and other professional groups of Bieszczady do not exist. Had the federation been recognized, and had the voivoda accepted our delegation, which we suggested a number of times, no strike would be needed.

Wojnarowicz cites instances of repression, attempts to break up meetings of the peasant Solidarity by a village mayor in Czarna, confiscation of trade union printed matter held by Leszek Karubin, and then his own trial in court for making criticisms during a meeting of agricultural circles. Wojnarowicz speaks calmly, in full sentences, as if he was not tense at all. But he must be. These talks are not only a test of psychological resistance, but also a test of successful argumentation. Will he manage?

Voivoda: There are a few postulates about myself. There are also charges against party secretaries, functionaries of the police and of the activists of state agricultural circles. In cases of the agricultural services and officials the immediate superior—a village mayor, for instance, should respond. In so far as police functionaries go, commanders of police are competent. If secretaries of the party are concerned, this should be discussed with the voivodship party committee. I do not feel competent to judge persons elected within the party.

Strike Committee: We do not want to discuss these facts with anybody else. You are responsible for the voivodship, the police commander is your subordinate. All the cases in question are under your responsibility. We are an apolitical organization, you are the authority both for party members and non-party members. Experience teaches us that if we just hand these papers over to you, you will return them. So we disagree. You wanted to cheat us, either consciously or by coincidence. We do not care about charges against the party, we charge the people. In the legal meaning of the term, you, as a voivoda, are the authority here. The commander of police and other services are subjected to your decisions.

Voivoda: I insist.

Wojnarowicz: OK, let us discuss those two secretaries separately.

Voivoda: That is the secretaries in Ustrzyski and Czarna...

Wojnarowicz: Those two.

Government Commission: OK.

Voivoda: Answering the charge that I did not show good will and did not seek contact with you, Mr. Chairman, and with the federation of farmers, workers, and other professional groups of Bieszcady...I received the first letter from you on September 7, and it was a very direct one. I answered on September 19: ...the legal organizational bureau kindly informs that voivoda or one of his deputies receives citizens in individual cases every Monday from 3 to 5 p.m. Registration in room nr.... I quote this letter as evidence that I wanted to meet and make contacts. Then I received another letter, also a direct one, without my name, with only my function on it. This is not grave, but still I want to say it. This letter asks me to establish a dialogue with Solidarity and to come for a meeting in a village office...My head of legal office wrote in reply: I inform kindly that the delegation of farmers from Ustrzyki Dolne can be received in voivodship office on September 17, between 12 and 5 p.m. I waited, and neither in the first or second case was there a visit from the federation.

Strike Committee: It is a surprise for us that you have informed us that complaints can be voiced in some room. Mr. Voivoda, for the first time in postwar Poland a social contract has been made, and you still refer us to a routine bureaucratic complaint scheme. We differ. We mean a trade union, its organization, principles of cooperation between you and us, and you just want us to come and voice complaints. We have nothing to complain.

Voivoda: Let us remain with our different views...

Strike Committee: We suggest signing the first point: to stop all repression of trade union activities...

Voivoda: Excuse me, but the expression 'to stop all repression' suggests that the latter were there, and we still do not know whether these charges are true.

Strike Committee: We understand that you feel uneasy to sign something like this.

Voivoda: This is not the question of uneasiness or easiness...

Strike Committee: So maybe we shall use another formula?

Voivoda: We can agree that there were some cases but not that they can be generalized so far...

Strike Committee: Maybe the game would be a trifle in Warsaw, but here in Ustrzyki Dolne...

Voivoda: I am not for this comparison. Warsaw is Warsaw and what is characteristic for Ustrzyki has been explained. Let us not divide Poland!

Strike Committee: Poland has already been divided. If this society learns that social contracts are just and good, maybe we shall need no further guarantees.

Voivoda: You have doubts whether social contracts are observed?

Strike Committee: If you want me to tell you something I can do it during the break.

Voivoda: What do you want? To observe the Gdansk agreements?

Strike Committee: Yes!

The next day nothing happened. The government delegation disappeared and the strikers were offered an explanation that everything was in order, for they invited the government people—expressis verbis—for talks, not for signing an agreement...."

This instance of negotiations demonstrates clearly with what attitudes the local power structure accepted the Gdansk agreements, and how difficult a year Poland has been through. Historical instances of Marie Antoinette saying "Let them eat cake" are superbly equalled by the Krosno voivoda's response to Solidarity's appeal for cooperation—"complaints can be voiced by individual citizens from 3 to 5 p.m."

D) Peripheralization and its Discontents.

That Poland is a periphery with respect to the political core of the Soviet Union, and that it is also doubly a periphery in the economic sphere—being subjected to peripheralization by both Western capital—French banks have been especially aggressive in over-lending Poland in the mid-seventies—and by the Soviet economy, especially in strategic and military matters, is presently in no doubt.

The problem, therefore, is whether Poland can emerge from this peripheral status to show that state socialism is not irremediable and that it can and should be turned around and made to serve human individuals united in solidarity over joint efforts to live better, more justly, and more socially. Solidarity is, indeed, a beautiful concept.

My tentative answer is that with the present political ruling class it is impossible to change the peripheral status. The raison d'etre of this very class is its total subjection to the Soviet ruling class. But it is possible to introduce a complex and hardly predictable network of checks and balances which might, in the long run, contribute to a slow dissipation of the ruling class's prerogatives.

This is a revolutionary idea, and indeed making a revolution without displaying any violent outward symbols of the revolution has become a Polish specialty. It is revolutionary, for within the poststalinist social awareness of the workers 'in the long run' does not mean too many years. Furthermore, economic shortages also contribute to the disappearance of the buffer social strata between the ruling class and the class of state employees, a buffer stratum who could possibly have obscured the social landscape if consumption was more normal. It is also revolutionary, for no other ruling class in the Eastern state socialist camp can feel secure any more.

I am writing these words at the end of July 1981. No major economic problem has been tackled by the Polish ruling class. This may, after all, have one saving grace—that is, it may turn out that this class has managed to get rid of those members who wanted to profit from direct Soviet intervention. For its fumbling around with ideology and statutory matters may have provided enough feeling of security in other state socialist countries to offset any hostile measures.

But unfortunately the latter is not very probable. Poland—in spite of slowdowns in production—has kept up all quotas of exports to "socialist countries" including the Soviet Union (contrary rumors notwithstanding), but has not gotten the same treatment in return. Instead political punishment has assumed the form of an economic cut in Polish imports from socialist countries and this is occurring on top of natural cutbacks in imports from capitalist producers due to an unstable credit situation. So it may turn out that economic peripheralization is more important than other factors. But even then, does not the organization of our labor force offer a better alternative for the political organization of society than a party which loves the secret police and has no coherent economic policy, to speak of, and no power base inside the Polish border?

The last sentence suggests that perhaps peripheralization can last no matter what revolutionary socialism comes to mean in Poland. But it also suggests that Poland is caught in a dilemma: if the ruling class remains in power in spite of new checks and balances, there will be no major changes for world socialism stemming from the Polish experience. But if it does not remain in power and if Solidrity designs the future scene, there may be uneasiness in both cores about the revolutionary Polish periphery. Still, the latter case is more promising. But it remains to be seen whether a society which has freed itself of the state's political monopoly can also find the way out of a world system which binds it in a multifold way.

Relatives of strikers wait at Gate No. 2   (Jan Kups)

...affitti on the wall of the Gdansk shipyard.   (Jan Kups)

Polish construction workers   (Boguseaw Biegansk

Time runs out for Gierek and Jaroszewicz   (Bogdan Lopienski)

Strikers' meeting inside the Gdansk shipyard   (Jan Kups)

ss at Gdansk   (Jan Kups)

Lech Walesa rallies his co-workers. (Jan K

Party leaders at a local festival (Krzysztof Baranski)

ayday parade (Krzysztof Baranski)

Church and State (Krzysztof Baranski)

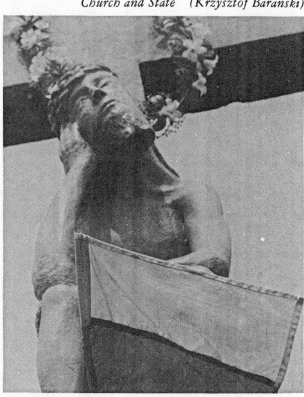

Industrial pollution overshadows rural life   (Bogdan Lopienski)

Picnic by the railroad   (Bogdan Lopienski)

Chapter Seven

One Year After
August/September 1981

The following commentary was written in early October 1981 when the first national congress of Solidarity passed its bills and elected its leaders, and when the major trends and tendencies in the political, economic and social transformation of Poland showed more clear-cut outlines.

There is, first of all, an almost complete inconsistency between the international framework of dependencies and influences and the dynamics of Poland's inner development. There is also an understandable delay in deciding upon and executing designs and reforms, due both to the inconveniences of democratic procedures and to the not-so-subtle obstacles mounted by the ruling class and its foreign allies.

The two most important international developments connected to Poland's situation and likely to be quite important in the long run were (1) the successive letters from the Soviet government to the Polish state leaders on the eve of the second round of Solidarity's national congress, and (2) the prohibition expressed by Soviet Russia indirectly (by means of a leak to a West German banker who represented it in Washington) concerning the possible participation of Poland in a relief program linked to World Bank activities. The former was a serious threat aimed at terrorizing a sovereign state; the latter was a repetition of the post-Rapallo policy of German bankers in the twenties which discouraged Americans from investing in Poland as a potentially unstable "bastard of Versailles."

Neither of these events had a direct immediate bearing on inner Polish developments, although the former precipitated a KOR decision to voluntarily dissolve and the latter will contribute to the seriousness of the economic crisis over the next decade. Every Polish citizen employed at present owes over a thousand dollars to Western capitalism, and each Polish citizen, of any age, is threatened by Soviet intervention.

However, the climaxes of Polish political life in August and September 1981 had little to do with these external events. The two most burning issues have been self-government by employees as a new principle of economic reform, and the ability of Solidarity to both preserve its position in protection of employee's rights and to control the social movement which, apart from political excesses to the left and right, tended to organize itself around the issue of self-government.

The problem of Poland's present situation should thus be tackled by means of a threefold discussion (1) of the program of social ownership of the enterprises (with two rival self-government bills, sponsored respectively by the government and by Solidarity, vying for both parliamentary and extra-parliamentary support), (2) of the course and results of Solidarity's national congress, and (3) of the forecasts for political and economic trends in the near future, especially in view of almost unavoidable shortages of food, energy and most other commodities in the coming few years. (This shortage will result both from the accumulated effects of the suicidal economic strategies of the ruling class, and from the ruling class's unwillingness to understand that by opposing reforms, out of fear that the latter will increase Solidarity's significance, one risks much more: that hungry and despairing people will topple the ruling class entirely, having not much to lose or at least thinking that there is not much to lose.)

The problem of economic reform triggered a wave of unrest in mid-August 1981, when a TV presentation of the long overdue government program revealed the latter's total inadequacy to the country's situation. An alternative reform program had been suggested, but it was prevented from reaching a wide audience by means of mass media avoidance. The government refused to consider it a bill to be discussed by the senate and this provoked an angry confrontation. Finally, Vice Prime Minister Mieczyslaw

Rakowski decided to break the negotiations by blaming Solidarity for an unyielding stand. After pressure from Solidarity membership a minor Watergate occurred, namely, the typescripts of the negotiations were broadcast twice on the radio, automatically making Rakowski unpopular when his manipulations to break negotiations became clear, and adding to the tension. Thus emotions came to focus on two bills. The two bills, the government's and Solidarity's, merit attention in so far as they reveal interesting differences even though it is true that 90% of the rhetoric is similar. Here are the most important contrasts:

Government Bill—Art. 1: The state enterprise is the basic organizational unit of the national economy, created in order to produce economically effective results and to satisfy social needs by means of production of goods or services. As an autonomous economic unit it has legal personality and includes the work force and a surplus part of the national material wealth.

Solidarity Bill—Art 1: The social enterprise is the basic organizational unit of the national economy which produces goods and services in order to satisfy social needs, autonomously and accounting for the principles of economic calculability, possesses legal personality and includes an organized work force which disposes of the respective part of the national wealth entrusted to it, and manages the social enterprise with the aid of the organs of the employees' self-government.

G—Art 7: The state organ which created the enterprise controls it with the help of decrees.

S—Art 52: The state influences enterprises by means of legal and economic parameters—taxes, credits, customs—established in a general manner.

G—Art 26: The manager is called by and removed by the founding organ with the approval of the council of the crew of an enterprise... the council of the crew can present a candidate or candidates. The candidates can emerge from a competition. The calling and the removal of a manager requires approval of the founding organ.

S—Art 36: The manager is the executioner of the decisions made by the organ of the employees' self-government. —Art 42: The manager is called by the council of the crew by means of an open competition. He can also be removed by means of a referendum.

G—Art 25: The manager directs the enterprise and represents it to other parties. The manager makes autonomous decisions in the enterprise's matters and is responsible for them.

S—Art 38: The manager's competence includes making all decisions in matters of an enterprise which do not fall under the competence of the organs of employee self-government.

G—Art 33: The enterprise works with allotted and acquired national wealth, secures its protection and works according to the requirements of economic efficiency.

S—Art 5: The organ which founds the enterprise secures for it part of the national wealth. The enterprise managed by its self-government organs disposes of this wealth.

G—Art 4: The organs of an enterprise make autonomous decisions and organize activities in all matters of an enterprise acording to law and in order to accomplish enterprise tasks.

S—Art 10: The enterprise is managed by its crew by means of employee self-government. The self-government manages the enterprise's wealth and decides upon major lines of the enterprise's development and activity and about the division of profits.

G—Art 40: The enterprise works according to its plan compatible with the national socio-economic plan. The manager works out a plan consulting the crew's council and acquiring the latter's approval.

S—Art 2: The social enterprise works economically in order to win economic aims and accomplish social tasks rationally employing its means.

G—Art 60: The bill does not apply to railroads, posts, banks, insurance companies, energy production units and enterprises subjected to the Ministries of Justice and National Defense.

S—Art 60: The bill does not apply to railroads, airlines and the posts, banks, insurance companies, and enterprises subjected to the Ministry of Justice.

It is easily noticed that the major differences result from the state's attempt to secure control of the enterprises through control of management and legal attribution of rights to "the founding organs," i.e. to the organs of state administration. However, the discussion which broke out clearly demonstrated that although the ruling class may win recognition of its claims for absolute control in isolated cases of enterprises vital for national defense, it will certainly be unable to win recognition for the vast majority of its demands. From a legal point of view the situation was thus a complicated one: the parliament had only a government bill officially submitted, but there was no point in passing the bill if most of society was critical of it. Solidarity naturally called for a fair discussion of both bills. Legally the government bill could be passed, but a substantial compromise had to be reached if it was to become an observed law. The first round of the national congress of Solidarity ended with a statement by the delegates of the working class demanding a popular referendum on the bill on enterprises and employee self-government and threatening new parliamentary elections if the parliament continued to be a puppet show managed by the ruling class.

As usual, a compromise was reached at the last minute. On September 25, 1981, a new, corrected bill was passed which accounted for some of the objections raised by the trade unionists. And even then, the ruling class tried to intervene at the last moment and to change the bill between the commission meeting which had worked out the compromise, and the plenary session. But this was too much for the parliament and even party members were outraged and refused to acknowledge the secret, last minute corrections the ruling class sought to attach. Yet, after much heated debate Solidarity did accept the new bill, which was definitely a significant compromise. Here are some of the notable articles of the adopted bill:

Art 4: Organs of enterprise make autonomous decisions and organize the enterprise's activities according to the law in order to accomplish the enterprise's tasks. State organs can make decisions with respect to enterprises only within the framework of this bill.

Art 10: The statuses of the following state enterprises requires acceptance by the founding organs: public utilities, foreign commerce, radio and TV stations, telelectronic industry, automobile transportation and communication, state bus lines and railroad industries. Decisions about acceptance of status should be made as quickly as possible, not later then three months after submissions.

Art 34: 1) The manager of a state enterprise is called and removed by the founding organ or Employee's Council. These organs have a mutual right to veto the decisions made by each other and to submit material supporting vetos within three weeks. 2) The council of the ministers will negotiate with the trade unions making a list of enterprises particularly important for the economy, where a

manager is called and removed as described in paragraph 1.
3) Managers of enterprises in public utilities are called and removed by the founding organs according to paragraph 1. 4) In case a veto is ignored, the vetoing organ has a right to go to the court whose verdict is final. 5) In newly founded enterprises the manager is called by the founding organs. The same happens if the employees' council of an enterprise did not make use of its rights in the period which would secure continuity of the enterprise's activities. 6) The manager of state enterprises is called for five years or for an indefinite period of time.

Art 35: 1) The manager of an enterprise is called from among the candidates participating in a competition. 2) In order to stage a competition, the competition commission is organized with three representatives of the employees' council and one representative of each of the following: founding organ, the bank which finances the enterprise, trade unions, political organizations, youth organizations, and principal technical organizations present in the enterprise. 3) The commission makes a list of candidates, evaluates their skills in managing the enterprise because of their education, morals, and ability to deal with people.

Art 37: The employees' council can apply to the founding organ for removal of a manager called by this organ if the manager acts against the law or prevents the enterprise from reaching satisfactory results with his decisions....

Art 54: The founding organ is entitled to force an enterprise to introduce a new task into a plan or to execute a task outside of the plan if this is indispensable due to the national defense, natural disaster or in order to fulfill international obligations....

Art 70: The bill becomes a law on October 1, 1981.

The passing of this bill was not the only element of a dramatic struggle between the ruling class and the social movement of the working class in September 1981. However, this was among the major elements of this struggle, and the results of this new compromised solution remain to be seen. It should be stressed that the compromise was reached against fierce criticism by extremists on both sides. Hard-liners in the political bureau, especially Albin Siwak, a puppet of the secret police and pro-Moscow fraction within the party apparatus, openly advised banning Solidarity and forcing it underground, while the broad masses of members of the union called for less restraint and the open removal of a ruling class now clearly depending only on the Soviets for its survival. The ruling class understood their situation and gratefully accepted the non too subtle hints expressed by the Soviets—a huge military buildup in the Baltic Republics and unannounced military games next to the Polish border, and the above mentioned letter from the Soviets which condemns an anti-Soviet campaign in Poland. In fact, of course there is no anti-Soviet campaign in Poland. Although the secret police try to arrange cases of provocative anti-Soviet activity, Solidarity is always quick to point out the circumstances under which the provocation was enacted, if at all. A number of times, for example, Tass mentioned the defaming of monuments to Soviet soldiers in Polish towns where no such monuments even exist. The only anti-Sovietism there is exists universally in Eastern Europe and expresses recognition of the class nature of the military and ideological alliance of local ruling classes with the ruling class of the Soviet Union. And this anti-Sovietism does not express itself in acts against monuments, but in a conscious effort to ease the pressure from the Soviet Union aimed at terrorizing the local working classes to the benefit of local rulers. This was, in fact, the background of the open letter from the delegates to Solidarity's national congress to the working people of Eastern Europe. The letter was greeted with hypocritical awe in the West: journalists were quick to point out that this was a "provocation" of Soviet military might and that Poles were "intervening" in inner affairs of their allies. The same journalists kept their mouths shut when for a year Soviets blamed Solidarity for everything thinkable, openly calling its leaders fascists, landowners, crypto-capitalists, and criminals, and when the Soviet Union openly intervened with blatant threats on the eve of both the Party and Solidarity conferences. The letter was not a political mistake—the mistake was that this letter and this kind of attitude still existed so late in the history of Eastern Europe.

The battle for a bill on the self-government of state enterprises was accompanied by another struggle which culminated with a unanimous prohibition against Polish TV taking part in the proceedings of the national congress of Solidarity. This prohibition itself is an interesting phenomenon—although the nation was deprived of the TV coverage, there were no complaints. Most people realized that it is better not to see TV news on the congress than to have the news manipulated. And manipulated it was and is. Never has the political strategy of the ruling class emerged more sharply and definitely than in the case of the mass media.

It started with a hatchet job by a number of second-rate reporters who tried to present Solidarity in general and its leaders in particular as people of more or less criminal or upper-class background. The lies and manipulations of filmed material were so obvious that in some cases the reporters were openly chased from further interview spots. The head of state radio and TV, Wladyslaw Loranc, appeared on Polish TV as late as September 13, 1981, and explained why the first round of the national congress was not broadcast and why the government was still unyielding thereby ensuring the continued absence of Polish TV for the second round of negotiations as well. Here are excerpts from his speech:

"In the whole country over 40% of all journalists and over 60% of all TV technical crews belong to Solidarity and in this sense the union's access to TV is a fact. For the trade union is already present in TV and radio centers. Local TV stations inform their audiences quickly and efficiently on local Solidarity activities. But managers of state TV think even that these local stations pay too little attention to the initiatives of local "branch" trade unions and "autonomous" ones....And this allows me to say that although radio and TV do not flirt with Solidarity, neither do they fight against it....When we speak with the leaders of the union they say clearly: we are not interested in programs on Solidarity or with Solidarity participating. We are interested in Solidarity's programs, i.e., programs we shall prepare ourselves.

Two solutions have been suggested to us. The making of a central alternative office and local chapters with people subjected only to the trade union, not TV managers; or acquisition of time slots by the trade union—the latter to be filled with programs prepared by the union in their own TV and radio stations. Each of these suggestions would mean a profound change since they would divide our institution between two centers of authority. Our state, as most states in the world, has a monopoly for creating and broadcasting radio and TV programs.... In the twentieth century radio and TV are for public life what energy is for the economy.... No social movement, no matter how large, is a copy of a state.... Poles did not stop needing a state only because a million strong social movement came into being.... Therefore we defend and shall defend the indivisibility of Polish radio and TV. We know that if we allow for a division of each factory and each institution between the state and Solidarity there will be no one to protect the agricultural reform, nationalization of industry, and international treaties which guarantee Poland's borders and socialist system. Europe will face this question: what political future is forged for this continent by a country which made its state organization insignificant replacing it with parliamentary-like local trade union chapters? This is not a phantasy. This is what happens. The slogan on access of Solidarity to mass media is supposed to precipitate this process. And this should be opposed.

Thank you very much for hearing my arguments, too."

This speech is very interesting. First, it closes with a thank you for listening to the government's arguments, too, unconsciously admitting that the state monopoly of the media is maintained against overwhelming majority opinion of the audience. It offers some quietly phrased lies about Solidarity's fair share in programming, forgetting that if there is a conflict between Solidarity and state managers, the former gets three minutes, the latter three hours to present their arguments. The whole program is then counted as "representing Solidarity to the mass audiences." The quotation also offers some interesting views on the nature and role of mass media in modern society.

According to the government interpretation, a state media monopoly is normal and acceptable, while any attempt to undermine it would make Europe unstable in the future. In other words—if the ruling classes maintain control of the media everybody is safe and will live in a world with a brilliant future; if the monopoly is questioned, national disasters in countries where this questioning occurs could follow. This argument has some validity: it is indeed quite possible that an alliance of the ruling classes both in capitalist and socialist states may contribute in the long run to the "international punishment" of Poland for attempts at alternative social organization. However, this is not an argument that has stopped social movements and revolutions anywhere.

The fact remains that Polish TV crews were conspicuously absent from the national congress both in early and late September. The cars and buses in the area were parked behind hand-painted words: "TV lies" and but a few minutes of film of the daily proceedings of the congress were obtained through foreign TV stations.

Before discussing the course of Solidarity's national congress, let us mention three major events from outside the congress, timed to affect its deliberation. First, the attempt to demonstrate that the penal system and judicial affairs were still firmly controlled by the ruling class. This attempt brought about the provocative announcement of the Attorney General of the Polish People's Republic on the eve of the second round of the congress that the investigation of the Bydgoszcz massacre had failed to bring any results because the secret police had done their beating in a dark staircase, so that policemen could not see them, and neither could the victims. Major Bednarek, who supervised the action of evacuating the building of the local government in Bydgoszcz and who secured the passive aid of uniformed police to the plainclothed hacks was reprimanded for failing to switch the light on in the above mentioned staircase. The decision of the Attorney General was questioned by the Legal Commission of the Council of the State which meant that it would have to be reconsidered, but this move of the Council of State seemed more like a concilliatory step than any actual attempt to bring the secret police under the law. This was undoubtedly a provocation, and only with the utmost care and restraint could the leaders of Solidarity prevent their members from proposing an open referendum on the radical reform of the judicial system. Another event was a carefully staged provocation at Bydgoszcz prison: a riot of the prisoners broke out when one of the guards shot a prisoner who allegedly attempted to escape. The police who arrived on the scene, headed again by major Bednarek of the Bydgoszcz massacre, did nothing to prevent over 100 prisoners from fleeing. Instead, they restricted themselves to beating up the crowd which slowly congregated arounded the prison and to a violent crackdown on those prisoners who blockaded themselves in cells, although the latter happened *after* it was agreed that Solidarity representatives would be allowed in to negotiate with the prisoners. The affair failed to bring about more serious riots in the city, thus making it impossible to declare any special emergency status—the obvious aim. But it did disclose the inhuman tortures regularly applied by the Bydgoszcz police and prison guards.

Second, prices for flour, bread and all baked products went up considerably, emptying people's pockets but failing to bring about any economic balance in the marketplace. The regimentation of rationing was extended to many new products—especially to sweets, cigarettes, and vodka. The standard of living of over 2.5 million retired persons fell below the official minimum subsistance level in mid-September, mostly due to the price increases. Further increases were planned, and a second round of them was timed purposefully to go into effect on Monday, September 28, during the second round of the union's congress—another provocation. This second wave of price increases brought about a 90% increase of tobacco prices and higher vegetable, fruit and fish prices. The government offered negotiations with respect to the compensatory increase of payments for those with lowest salaries and pensions, but refused to discuss the methods by which the price changes were accomplished.

Third, the new Roman Catholic primate of Poland, Jozef Glemp, turned out to be more firmly in support of Solidarity than his predecessor who was older and much more cautious in his public speeches. This progressive Church trend was further reinforced by the papal encyclical "On Human Labor." Together, this might mean that a rough balance of power between the ruling class, Solidarity and the Catholic Church could come into being, especially in light of the ruling class' shakiness. This would help explain the unusual threats of military maneuvers and open letters about anti-Sovietism coming from the Soviets at just this time.

The first round of the national congress of Solidarity took place between September 5 and 10, 1981: all information quoted below comes from the official bulletin of the congress called "Glos Wolny" [Free Voice]. The delegates issued a declaration:

"The superior aim of Solidarity is to create decent living conditions in economically and politically sovereign Poland. We mean a life free of poverty, exploitation, fear and deception, in a democratic and legally bound society.

Today the nation expects:

1. Amelioration of supplies by establishment of control over production, distribution and prices, in cooperation with Solidarity of Individual Farmers.

2. Economic reform by establishment of authentic employees' self-

government, abolishment of party nomenclature and the stimulation of effective economic measures.

3. Truth by social control of mass media and taking the lies out of Polish schools and culture.

4. Democracy by free elections to the Parliament and national councils.

5. Justice by securing equality of all before the law, freeing those imprisoned for their beliefs, defense of those who have been oppressed because of their editorial, trade unionist and political activities.

6. Saving of the threatened health of the nation by environmental protection, greater expenditures for health services and securing a full participation of handicapped persons in social life.

7. Coal for population and industry through a guarantee of proper living and working conditions for the miners.

We shall reach these aims through the unified effort of the Union and the solidarity of its members. The activities of various forces which provoke external threats shall not deprive us of the will to fight for the ideals of August 1980, for the actual realization of the agreements from Gdansk, Szczecin and Jastrzebie."

Apart from plenary sessions, the delegates worked in the following teams:

1. democracy and forms of trade unionist activities
2. union organization
3. information, schooling, opinions and expert reports
4. negotiations, protest actions, propaganda
5. economic stabilization, reform, employees' self-government
6. markets, prices, costs of living
7. labor and employment, salaries, labor protection, labor law
8. citizens' rights and legality
9. man (sic) and environment—social policy
10. education and national culture
11. union vis-a-vis state authorities and PUWP
12. union and other social movements
13. mass media

The first statements approved of by the delegates and issued along with the open letter to the laborers of Eastern Europe included a statement on elections to national councils —the basic units of state administration on all levels—on education, the

Bydgoszcz affair, and on the self-government of higher schools and universities. The first of the above mentioned statements questioned the political monopoly of FJN (National Unity Front), a front for the ruling class monopoly in making lists of candidates and voicing political programs. The statement was especially important as the scheduled elections were to take place on February 5, 1982.

There were also statements on "foreign trips and returns from abroad" which called for the restoration of the free movement of Polish citizens in the world, currently restricted by the use of passports as a special bonus for political conformism, which in effect has forced many Poles into exile. There were also statements on the trade unionist rights of employees of radio and TV—which had been systematically violated by the authorities—and on the same rights of civilian employees of the police and the army.

The message to the working people of Eastern Europe also merits closer attention, because it is a mild document which gained greater fame than warranted, and because it demonstrates a spirit not of provocation but of restraint and caution:

"The delegates assembled in Gdansk at the first national congress of the delegates of an independent self-governed trade union Solidarity send greetings and words of support to the workers of Albania, Bulgaria, Czechoslovakia, the German Democratic Republic, Rumania, Hungary and all nations of the Soviet Union.

As the first independent trade union in our postwar history we feel deeply the profound closeness of our fate. We assure you that contrary to the lies disseminated in your countries we are an authentic, 10 million strong organization of employees, created as a result of the workers' strikes. Our aim is to fight for the amelioration of living conditions of all people of labor. We support those of you who have decided to enter the difficult path of a struggle for an independent trade union movement. We believe that before long your and our representatives shall be able to meet to exchange trade unionist experiences."

The statements were issued by delegates from 42 regions, a total of almost 900 persons.

To counter the lies disseminated freely by TASS and other Soviet-inspired mass media in Eastern Europe—namely that the delegates were mostly political adventurers who had nothing in common with the working class—some journalists managed to conduct an incomplete survey of the delegates and it showed that workers provided about 60% of the delegates, peasants about 20% and that only 20% belonged to the so-called intelligentsia, with the exception of the Warsaw region, where the proportions were 27:15:58, differing sharply from the proportions in all other regions. For example in the Silesian-Babrowski industrial region the proportions were 60:20:20; in lower Silesia 64:16:20; and in small regions generally they averaged 53:16:31.

The theme of political repression was dominant throughout the congress. On top of the above mentioned affairs there remained unsolved the problem of the three leaders of the "Confederation of Independent Poland" (Moczulski, Szeremietiew, Stanski) who had been released after protests early in 1981, but then arrested again after a hasty and illegal ruling of the Supreme Court. The Court failed to study the case at all, ruled in an hour and failed to listen to the lawyers representing the plaintiffs. Further, it did not allow a trial, since police investigations could not produce materials supporting the state's accusation of an attempt at the armed overthrow of the regime in People's Poland. Immense difficulties on the eve of the second round of the congress were best summed up in a delayed issue of the Solidarity weekly, which had its circulation increased to 1 million copies for September due to the congress, where Krzysztof Wyszkowski wrote in a marginal note entitled "Extremists and stupid children": "One of the members of the Political Bureau loudly discussed delegalization of Solidarity and concluded publicly that it is enough to issue the appropriate orders to the police and the army....

One of the experts of the National Coordination Commission of Solidarity wrote that PUWP has practically been deprived of power already and one should look for some replacement....

On the eve of the congress it turns out that the goons from Bydgoszcz are not to be found because they had done their beatings in the darkness...

A delegate to the congress, arrested and released after the printing of anti-Soviet leaflets, confides that they could be useful if the Soviet Union actually intervened....

One could ignore all this if it was not for the fact that all these people represent influential political groups and interests which cannot be ignored and can turn out to be very dangerous for society as a whole.

The situation of a country split between these contradictory attempts is very difficult. The question arises—is it also hopeless?

Certainly not. The fate of a huge and experienced nation cannot depend on the games of extremists or stupid children.

The responsibility of the authorities is unquestionable. On them to a large extent it depends whether they can emerge with authority and social trust or be lost. But the responsibility of Solidarity seems to be even greater. The union which represents, more than any other group, the expectations and will of the nation, has to notice on the horizon of its activities—apart from its role as a defender and guarantor of the rights of its members—the interests of the state as a whole, with all the consequences. And if the good of the state required the union to refrain from or even give up some or even most of its demands, Solidarity has to be capable of the required force and endurance."

Among the most vital achievements of the congress was a decision to agree with the parliamentary way of deciding a debate on employees' self-government and elections to the union's top leadership. This secured Lech Walesa's position and, generally speaking, the position of "the moderates" represented mostly by Walesa himself and delegates from the regions of Szczecin, Poznan, Wroclaw—that is, Lower Silesia as opposed to the Gdansk and Warsaw regions where extremist tendencies were more prevalent, and Bydgoszcz, where immediate political struggle had prompted a desire for more radical solutions. The second round, which started on September 26 and continued until October 8, surpassed all deadlines, mostly because of struggles over inner-union democracy and over the above mentioned provocations which naturally reinforced the position of the extremists. The final document resembled the declaration with which the congress opened, though it had become more concrete due to the discussions and proceedings. It declared that Solidarity has the double nature of both a trade union and a social movement, thus recognizing the specifity of the political situation in Poland and calling for:
1) political pluralism of opinions and transformation of the economy and the state according to the spirit of democracy. (At the same time, however, the trade union voted against the formation of

a political organization within the ranks of its members—the arguments for which had been disseminated by a recently returned from exile 1970 strike leader from Szczecin, Baluka.)

2) socialization of the economy with the ultimate aim of a self-governed Poland, the division of political and economic authorities, abolishing "nomenclatura," limitation of military spending and militarization of the economy, and overcoming the present crisis through speedy investment of superfluous money in the production sector;

3) social control of the mass media and abolishment of the state monopoly of the latter, especially with respect to TV and radio;

4) a new limitation of and clear definition of the competence of the police force, which should be prevented from intervening in political activities of citizens;

5) the foundation of a social court which would hear the cases of those who have led the nation to the brink of economic disaster.

Meanwhile, the economic situation of the country remains precarious, especially with respect to foodstuffs and—with the coming winter—energy supplies. The government failed to meet most of the conditions it promised to meet in agreements with rural Solidarity and this prompted, on September 17, 1981, the following announcement of the press agent for rural Solidarity:

> The press of September 17 announced a statement from the Minister of Finances to the National Founding Committee of Solidarity of Individual Farmers. The statement refers to the action undertaken by our union which protests, by refusing to pay the third installment of the annual tax, the government's failure to comply with the agreement of August 17 on turning the Agricultural Development Fund over to individual farmers, and the public announcement of its expenditures over the past three years and annuling of baseless price increases for services rendered by "agricultural circles" to individual farmers.
>
> The statement of the Minister of Finances includes lies with respect to the state of affairs and illegal threats. It is our duty to point out these lies in public. Continuation of protest is justified in view of none of three obligations accepted by the government on August 17 being met until

the present date. The statement of the Minister of Finances that "part of the obligations have been met" is not true in view of the facts we know and in view of the Minister's further argumentation. The charge that our action will cause a financial gap in the state income necessary to finance the villages and farmers is baseless. These gaps can only occur as a result of the premeditated activity of the authorities since our action consists of withdrawing from current payments until the government fulfills its obligations.

It is laughable to claim that our action will deprive the individual farmers of means within the Agricultural Development Fund, since our action itself aims at the turning of this fund over to the farmers, not the bureaucracy.

It is not true that the rise in insurance rates by the insurance company was agreed upon with our union. This statement is not connected to the topic and brings false data, with the explicit aim of discrediting our union in the eyes of the farmers whose just rights we exist to defend. The rates have been introduced unilaterally by the Minister of Finances and the insurance agents have just informed the union about them. If acknowledgement of this information is to be viewed as an acceptance of the rise, then any negotiations or letter exchange are impossible....

The protest action is in accordance with the statutes of the union. It is a quiet action and does not take the farmers away from production. Threats and their implementation can provoke a different course of events. Responsibility for this will remain with the authorities....

This statement is an important one, for it shows the tactical manipulations of the ruling class which at the time concentrated on four types of activity:

1) driving a wedge between rural Solidarity and urban Solidarity by depriving individual farmers of equipment and financial support, thus hampering their food production. Usually this was accomplished by destroying the tractors which state farms had to give away or sell to the individual farmers, or by refusing to let individual farmers profit from credits remaining in the Agricultural Development Fund, or by artificially reducing food supplies for the market,

often digging trenches to dump foodstuffs. A number of these trenches have been discovered by members of Solidarity.

2) driving a wedge between workers and the intelligentsia, which resulted in, among other things, a change of the principles according to which experts were to be employed by the trade union and, generally, in weakening their position in the movement.

3) retaining a firm grip on the mass media, which would rather lie than serve the public. The only difference in the period is that "black propaganda" replaced the "rosy" kind: the locus of control, however, remained firmly lodged in top party circles, with Olszowski, the hard-liner from the Political Bureau, personally censoring programs.

4) coordinating the propaganda activities of all other socialist countries which, with lies and vengeance, were attacking Solidarity as an enemy of socialism, as Poland's disaster, and as an anti-worker, un-democratic evil social force. The cooperation of Polish and Eastern Bloc media was great enough so that when Solidarity staged a protest in August and announced "days without press" to protest vicious state propaganda, "ersatz-papers" were printed in East Germany and Czechoslovakia to create an impression that not all printers were supporting Solidarity's action.

In the present situation there is definitedly a serious lack of foodstuffs. There is no hunger, but there is no feeling of security as far as continuity of provisions goes. Therefore, the state indulges in all sorts of operations which aim at maintaining a firm grip on the distribution of food—especially the so-called "battle against specu-lation" which is a ridiculous attempt to disguise a lack of state will and ruling class interest in stimulating production—and main-taining firm political control. It is also clear that the situation of shortage of foodstuffs is artificially prolonged and that no effective measures are being taken. The government's huge team of experts failed to produce even a preliminary outline of economic reform after a year of work! The ruling class considers it safer to deal with reinforced control of necessary distribution of insufficient quan-tities of food than to stimulate economic growth and food production which would strengthen the rural and urban Solidarity.

The trade union, from whose top authorities extremists like Gwiazda, Solidarity co-founder from Gdansk, Rulewski, one of the victims of the Bydgoszcz massacre, or Bujak have been removed by majority vote of the congress (October 7 & 8, 1981), settled on a moderate political course, but managed to preserve its double character as a trade union and as a social movement, understanding correctly that its limitation to either of the two would be a disaster. If Solidarity limited itself to trade unionist tasks the political context would be left for the ruling class to contain, pacify and recover. But if it announced itself as a social movement, the acceptable platform of trade unionism would be gone, and there would be a direct confrontation between Solidarity and the combined forces of the ruling class and the armed aid of other ruling classes of the Soviet bloc.

Polish society is, indeed, treading a very thin line but there is practically no other choice left. Marx defined a revolutionary situation as one in which the ruling class is unable and the masses unwilling to live in their former manner—and from the point of view of this aphorism Poland is, indeed, undergoing a revolution. However, this is a very particular revolution: it is occurring in a quite different society from the ones that existed before the advent of state socialism, and it has not defined its allies and aims in language free from traditional masks and misunderstandings.

One of the most important misunderstandings concerns the role of the capitalist world and of the Catholic church. It is true that delegates to the Solidarity congress decided on having a Holy Mass before every morning session, but it was a continuation of the spirit of August 80, when this was the only organized liturgy available to the workers which was not monopolized by the state. The Church has a very important "moderating" role, but it has no influence upon the leaders of Solidarity. Catholic intellectuals did play an important role in the founding of Solidarity's press, being experienced in combatting monopolists of state and party type.

On the whole the capitalist world views Polish developments favorably, from a political point of view, since they mean trouble for the Soviets. But this does not mean that Polish workers look to western capital to save them from the jaws of the Polish ruling class.

As a matter of fact, quite the contrary is true. Solidarity understands that there is a double bondage of capital and imperial dependence which makes the Polish situation so serious. However much they despise the Soviet imperial reign, they reveal no desire to return to a capitalist type of economy.

This awareness of the double threat to Poland's sovereignity contributes to the difficulty in formulating a more concrete and detailed program. The program that was announced by Solidarity's first congress will probably be carried out with the following contradictory tendencies trying to win the upper hand within the union:

1) a tendency which seeks to work out a reasonable economic system with as many incentives as possible to make Poland's economy effective but which does not always see eye to eye with another tendency that views alternatives to state socialist inequalities in terms of a radical, populist egalitarianism;

2) a tendency which would like to leave the ruling class in positions of political representation in the state and respect the army as embodiment of international obligations resulting from the Warsaw pact, which is opposed by another tendency that has as a priority a political solution preventing the ruling class from winning back the political monopoly all other ruling classes in the area still enjoy.

The first contradiction is the legacy of state socialism from the very outset. The exploitation of the working class (which, as a matter of fact, includes also exploitation of the sectors of population traditionally called peasants and intelligentsia, although there are specialized forms of this exploitation in both latter cases) assumes a form which does not have to depend on threats like those that exist in the capitalist system. There is, for instance, universal job security and health protection. However, the widespread tendency to egalitarian measures, combined with shortages in the market, may very well turn all economic initiatives into something less than incentive-like for the individuals involved. What route should Solidarity take, assuming it does not want to simply care for the state's diligent execution of its employees' rightful dues? This is going to be one of the most interesting moments in the implementation of any fragments of the present reform and it is also going to provide the decisive testing ground for Solidarity's ability to draw conclusions from its double role, to step over the limitations imposed by the traditional understanding of the role of a trade union.

Mobilization of social energy can only happen due to the joint impact of two factors: immense moral support for a new plan of social and economic reconstruction which Solidarity clearly musters, and a reasonable set of rules of the economic game which will restore faith in the worth of productive labor. The ruling class proved totally incapable of wresting moral support from Solidarity and from this point of view the whole government effort to keep a close check on the mass media misfired and will continue to misfire in the future. However, due to holding key positions of political power the ruling class can wreck at least some of the reforms introduced and supported by Solidarity by trying to persuade the population that labor does not pay and that following new reforms can only make the situation worse. This would then be considered a preparation for a wholesale return of the "ancien regime." Unfortunately, this possibility cannot be ruled out. For instance, the Solidarity team of experts (Bugaj, Janas, Kazanczuk, Renski, Kuczynski) has suggested that Poland join the International Monetary Fund, a suggestion immediately torpedoed by the Soviets before it even had a chance of being discussed by Polish economists and politicians. Another team of experts (Adamczyk, Karwowski, Palka and Kurowski) suggested a two-variant project to balance the market: the first foresees sharp price increases, with the exception of meat, economic conversion to market demands and high income taxation, while the second opts for currency exchange to get rid of the inflationary gap and also for IMF membership.

Apart from the search for IMF aid in paying off the debts, there is a tendency to level off incomes, either through taxation, as in the latter project, or through high pricing of the so-called "luxury goods" which would then include probably most of what falls outside of the "social minimum". This will not necessarily be very helpful in mobilizing social support for proposed reforms. However, Solidarity is the only organization capable of introducing this program of saving, severity and sacrifice, while the ruling class wants both to threaten Solidarity into submission and to prey on its willingness for reforms by introducing price changes on its own.

The situation, with the ruling class left intact in key positions, with a decision to fight for broad representation in national councils elected according to new principles and to postpone the struggle for parliament, is also a potential source of powerful conflict. Within Solidarity heated discussion took place between "fundamentalists" and "pragmatists". The former claim that the very existence of the ruling class, which monopolizes economic, political and ideological power, is incompatible with any attempt to build a juster, more promising social order, while the latter recall the route from Gdansk strikes in August 1980 to Solidarity's national congress. In the most general terms—the former want to reject the system and base their opinions on the growing radicalization of the masses, while the latter want to ameliorate the system and transform it without a violent shakeup. During the discussions the pragmatists gained support through the voices of Bogdan Lis, Karol Modzelewski, Seweryn Jaworski, Leszek and Jaroslaw Kaczynski, Andrzej Gwiazda, lawyer Sila-Nowicki, Maciej Sewerynski et al. This demonstrates, among other things, that government propaganda which blames Gwiazda and Lis for excessive extremism is totally baseless and boils down to no more than a hostility for tough negotiators the government wanted to oust from the other side of the table.

The fundamentalists were defended by Andrzej Rozplochowski, Ireneusz Kosmahl, Andrzej Wieczorek, Kazimierz Firlejczyk, Waldemar Gil, et al. The pragmatic line, which, generally speaking, won due to the moderate outcome of both the elections of the leadership and the voting for the documents of the congress, had modest formulations:

"...Ours is the struggle for bread which has to be waged by a trade union, and not a political one. We have to initiate and support new organizational forms, which will enable the working masses to take over matters of production and distribution of goods. We mean self-governments. Only they can liberate social initiatives, the energy of the masses, only they can save the country and all of us, secure bread for the nation....

Guarding, according to the Gdansk agreement, a right for a free expression of opinion, we shall protect independent political activity, stimulate rebirth of independent political thinking, and support their clubs and publishers. At the same time, accepting the principle of unity of the union we cannot agree to create political parties within Solidarity since this could threaten the above mentioned unity."

The situation is stable and quiet in mid-October. Not that there are no tensions left or that food supplies grow, but the Solidarity congress, in spite of many tiresome and excessively detailed polemics, especially on matters of intra-union democracy and procedures of leader election, was definitely a success for the pragmatically oriented and very much reform-minded part of the activists of the union. It is also true that the political restraint showed by the congress was not uniformly popular, especially among the broadest masses of the population, which would very much like to see the whole ruling class either punished for 35 years of continuous war against their own society or totally pushed off the political stage. However, as has also been pointed out by other participants in the congress, it would, indeed, be very bad for the future of the union if its activists danced exclusively to the tune of broad expectations and never had the courage to decide against the grain of commonly felt desires when they were convinced that it is to the ultimately better cause of general good. As Walesa summed it up in an interview:

"Government is the partner for our Union. 36 million Poles will not write to the Prime Minister. We have to hand one common letter to the government. Let us remember that at least 80 percent of individuals will not become parliamentary delegates nor elected members of national councils and they will not be particularly interested in who is there—Walesa, Kuron or Geremek. They want to have bread and they do not want to risk too much. Trying to realize our postulates on the bottom level we have to say that we are striving towards a grand solution, and that at the level of an enterprise the solution consists of a struggle for self-government. This is how we should work it out."

Walesa's statement is probably one of the most succinct formulations of the union's double role and the complexity of the economic and political tasks it should perform in order to actually make the dreams of its supporters come true. The unprecedented struggle of the Polish workers goes on.

PART TWO

THEORIES OF
CLASS STRUGGLE

Chapter Eight

Theoretical Diagnoses

The first attempts to provide a theoretical analysis, or the first stimulus to come up with such analysis, came from the workers themselves. The main line of attack [in 1956] indicated the class they considered antagonistic and the privileges they thought undeserved and harmful in the long run to the development of society as a whole.

The workers attacked the party functionaries, the secret police, and the economic managers, who were given a ride out of their factories in wheelbarrows. One of the first acts of the riotous Poznan workers was to smash the interference devices preventing Polish radio audiences from listening to non-Polish broadcasts. The only unattacked fortress was marxism itself—not because it did not need criticism, but because this criticism had already been taken care of for a year or two by many young philosophers, columnists, and sociologists, mainly in "Po prostu." But it was not only because of this spontaneous "social division of labor" that marxism was not attacked as a whole. It was also a result of the fact that class awareness of both sides in the conflict of 1956—as has been indicated above—did not allow for the rejection of a dogma and an elaboration of a completely new approach to marxism both as a theory and as an ideology.

167

So parallel to a very sharp criticism of what was being done by the ruling class there was a very ambiguous attitude towards marxism. The final outcome of this theoretical struggle to get rid of the dogma but to preserve the orientation was a kind of theoretical compromise. Reality was blamed for coming up with a non-revolutionary political party monopolizing revolutionary ideology and turning it into a smokescreen for its reign, while marxism was criticized for failing to acknowledge the subtlety of human life and its supraeconomic anxieties and features.

Two symbolic spokesmen of this double development in the theory of marxism of 1956, a period when a compromise was struck strongly in favor of the new wave, a new generation, and a new lobby of the ruling class, were Leszek Kolakowski and Adam Schaff. Both had been stout marxists with a strongly marxist image in the eyes of the academic world, where they had been the "angry young men" after the war and especially after 1949.

Kolokowski developed a very interesting criticism of the ruling class stressing the critique of ideology. His passage from early serialized essays (printed in "Po Prostu" mentioned above, and in another popular weekly "Nowa Kultura") of which "The Ideological Meaning of the Concept of Left" is the most famous one, to a generalized analysis of the philosophical doctrines functioning as ideologies of earthly institutions (most notably in "Religious Awareness and Ecclesiastical Bonds"), and finally to a wholesale analysis of eschatological and metaphysical assumptions indispensable in the legitimation of cognitive ("The Presence of the Myth") and political ("Main Currents of Marxism") pursuits, is very telling. Kolokowski has never rejected marxism—he has always sought to determine the responsibility of this political ideology and this theoretical approach in shaping a particular social system, the state socialist system.

However, his analysis has always remained academic in both the positive and negative meaning of the term. In the positive sense, his writings are highly sophisticated and coherent, and much can be learned from them. In the negative sense, he viewed his theoretical approach as a finite pursuit not necessarily linked with actual developments in social and political life.

His basic theme is an idea that metaphysical hopes, especially the ones which are elaborated into designs for making people lastingly happy during their earthly existence, usually result in justifications of institutional solutions adverse to valuable and desirable aspects of individual and collective life.

It is a very profoundly and unambiguously non-revolutionary attitude. For Kolakowski revolution is a myth. As a dream it is prerequsite for a sound social development but dangerous and even evil in real social relations. Revolutions always fall short of their aims. It is almost as if Kolakowski views 1956 as a traumatic experience that convinced him for the rest of his life that nothing could be done and that after a wave of revolutionary enthusiasm everything eventually has to fall victim to increased terror and repression by either the old or the new ruling class. Yet he has written in his famous "Theses on Hope and Hopelessness" that a widespread belief in the non-reformability of the state socialist system is dangerous for societies caught by it, since it is a self-confirming, self-fulfilling prophecy. He argues it is much better and more beneficial for those societies to believe in reformability and to strive for every inch of reform which can make life better and more bearable.

But at the same time there is a profound pessimism which E.P. Thompson tries to locate in his "Open Letter to Kolakowski" (reprinted in the "Poverty of Theory and Other Essays"). Thompson rightly senses that Kolakowski should not be considered a leftist any more, but he fails to recognize that it is not because of any theoretical view or any charge that Kolakowski brings against the communist parties or Marx, but because of his profound distrust of any major social change achieved through effort mobilized by eschatological slogans, best summarized in his late essay "Revolution As A Beautiful and Fashionable Illness."

"Hope for New Times, Absolute Beginning, Total Youth is, it appears, a constant and never dying form of human spiritual life. It should not be thought that this hope can ever be removed from our culture, or that this would, indeed, be desirable. It is a desire to wipe the past off. Revolutionary fantasies of the modern epoch are a historical embodiment of this hope. They had originally appeared as religious eschatologies, where belief in New Time, i.e. Salvation, assumed that sins will be redeemed, mistakes and faults wiped clean.

The Hope for New Time is resistant to rational arguments, since in its proper form it is not a "theory" or an intellectual attitude, but a spiritual passion. Religious eschatologies do not require rational grounding, they are not based on prediction and theory, but on trust in a promise that people were given once upon a time, in the beginnings of time. The promise sustains their hope that the past can somehow be wiped off in a moral sense, that a chain of suffering and evil can be radically broken.

Secular eschatologies of revolution are variants of the same faith, disfigured for two reasons. They present their hopes—for one thing—as beliefs based on rational premises, which cannot be done without mala fide. Secondly, since salvation has both to be collective and to happen due to some special social technique, wiping the past off cannot be moral, but political, which means that Apocalypse consists of the destruction of culture and in its perfect form aims at enforced forgetting of all inherited cultural treasures. Not in all revolutions we know of was the destruction of the past carried through equally coherently and not in all revolutions were the ideological premises of this destruction spelled out equally clearly. From the present day perspective the Russian revolution has to be considered a relatively mild and incoherent variant of cultural apocalypse. Most of the pre-revolutionary intelligentsia has been killed or exiled; falsifying history has become a daily routine; religious tradition has been mercilessly persecuted; literature, philosophy and art have dwindled and died off as a result of repressions, massacres and restrictions. In spite of all this the exterminations and repressions were not consistent enough to break cultural continuity completely, and the radical will to destroy everything in the inherited culture has never become an offical policy of the rulers. It turned out that a slight easing of the repressive policy gave Russia a chance to produce new cultural energies, to manifest its link to the past and resistance to the beauties of the New Time.

The Chinese Apocalypse has been more radical, especially in the period of the so-called Cultural Revolution. It was not only that the actual destruction of the past, of inherited art, philosophy, religion, science, school, university, etc. was much more consistent; there was also a more orchestrated effort to destroy the family as the social bond which is most resistant to state-ization. Maoist revolutionary ideology has also spelled out the tasks of the New Epoch much more clearly—a total denial of cultural continuity, the shaping of a New Man (sic) in a cultural desert. We cannot presently evaluate the degree of success in this activity, and we are unable to tell to what degree the Chinese have succeeded in preserving—in spite of horrible destruction—the capacity for spiritual rebirth. However, it seems that there, too, an attempt to create a New Man has failed.

Revolution in Cambodia (the liberation before the last) seems to have come closest to the ideal. Preparation of the New Epoch, i.e. destruction of the old society, has known no limits. Towns, schools, family, religion, all forms of social life, all cultural treasures have been destroyed—the new rulers have justly thought that a New Man, if new he is to be, should never be addicted to the past cultural forms. Practically it meant that all literate individuals had to be killed and the others locked in concentration camps. The effort was to a large extent successful; massacres of thousands and systematic destruction turned the country into a desert, and the foundations of the New Time had been laid.

But one thing could have never been done in Cambodia, since there was no appropriate techology in sight: one could not make people forget the language. But a consistent destruction of the past would require forgetting the inherited language, which carries in itself the cultural tradition, imposes a certain structure of thinking and thus limits the possiblity of creating a New Man. Language contains words and grammatical forms, which should not be known by a New Man. Perfect Revolution would thus require a perfect cultural desert and should command technologies for throwing people back to the pre-linguistic stage.

Human youth: troglodite, anthropopithecus. Total liberation: a cage.

Apart from this difficulty, the revolution in Cambodia achieved, it seems, the best results of all. As a result the definitions of Total Revolution, New Time and New Man can be much more precisely defined than ever before: genocide, slavery, bestiality. Apocalypse has almost happened, the revolutionary idea has almost turned into reality. The Idea of a return to an Absolute Beginning, to the beauty of youth has been embodied best of all."

Kolakowski was not alone: he was a leader of public opinion and he clearly generalized and expressed the attitudes and ideas of a huge part of the Polish intelligentsia of his time. Another representative of the latter, a poet Alexander Wat, wrote in 1956 in a poem he dedicated to "his fellows of political thaw":

And blood his own he pumps
into a dark chimera of his illusion
and he sings "alleluya" to her
and scarlet with gold to adorn her he gives
And Jagganatha jumps the wagon
strong with your weakening.
Thus ironic history
will play a cruel trick upon you."

The poet explained in a footnote that Jagganath (Juggernaut) was an embodiment of Shiva. On the day of the god's festival the faithful threw themselves under the god's carriage and died.

Disillusionment, disenchantment, without a major effort to undertake another attempt, perhaps in a different institutional form, to change the social order, was the main theme. I find it symbolic that Kolokowski developed his studies of religion, Husserl, analytical philosophy and the forms of metaphysical assumptions our culture makes us accept tacitly in all walks of life, without ever coming back to an active political life. The next wave of theoreticians of state socialism was to be different in this regard.

Schaff is a different kind of a theoretician. Not quite of the same stature as Kolakowski, he has nevertheless written two interesting books. One of them, very much praised at the time, appeared in the early sixties, and resulted from the 1956-1960 philosophical arguments and polemics. Its title "Marxism and the Human Individual" summarizes it neatly. The major thesis was that marxism as a theory furnishes an approximate image of the workings of macrostructures while totally neglecting the individual and especially the psychological sphere of human existence. This in turn results in grave inconsistencies and cruel distortions of the social order with respect to its effect upon individuals and with respect to understanding the subjective impression of the workings of the system that any individual gets.

Schaff's thesis was not a banal one; it came along with the wave of existentialist philosphy and opened the way for a very interesting discussion of this philosophy. It also paid close attention to social-ization which Schaff showed always to occur in individual variants and for the understanding of which it is, indeed, very important to notice individual strivings and suffering. Does suffering stop under socialism? was one of Schaff's major questions. He answered with a thundering "No!".

But Schaff also became ever more academic, even while indicating that existence under state socialism yields little happiness for the individual and that something must be done about the way the psychological needs of individuals are left unaccounted for by this society organized along faulty, or more cautiously, negligent lines. He gradually withdrew into a more remote region of semiotics, semantics, and academic philosophy in general, gradually losing popularity and producing nothing new with respect to the theoretical image of state socialist society.

It may appear to the reader that I dispose too harshly of two thinkers who have been justly praised for their penetrating and brilliant studies. I do not intend to do so. I simply question their work from the perspective of a theoretical penetration of the workings of state socialist society and with regard to future benefits for the left, the reformers, the resistance, the opposition—the people who changed state socialism in 1980. For comparative purposes it is worth recalling that this by no means downgrades their achievements; they were the first postwar Polish generation of theoreticians who strove to solve the problem of the entangled Marxist semi-legitimacy of the ruling class. Their contemporary, Molovan Djilas, said in 1979 that he was himself very much in the dark during that period. He had already understood that Stalinism was not a direct outgrowth of Marx's ideas, though it was a legitimate heir of Lenin, whose "leninism" and "party organization" clearly could only result in a genocidal, totalitarian society. But, admitted Djilas, he was wrong in calling state socialism a state capitalist system—no elements of capitalism could emerge in a state-ized structure, where the political sphere of influence and familiarity with those who have this influence determine most activities and options, while the economic laws of capitalist economy clearly do not apply. He later spoke of "industrial feudalism" which indirectly confirms my thesis that there is a rough analogy between the introductiuon of a manorial serf economy by East European gentry in the 17th century as opposed to the birth of capitalism in Western Europe of the time.

Another problem which obscured the development of a clearer awareness of the class nature of Polish society in the mid 50's was the nationalistic context in which Polish and Hungarian strivings for social and political liberation of the workers had necessarily to emerge. Success or failure to win national independence—or more justly, relatively lesser dependence—were important, tangible social targets. But in order to win these one had to accept the local ruling class at least as a go-between from the society to the Soviets. The very same element which had actually helped in 1980 (the ruling class desperately wanting to be a go-between and doing everything to remain such a link), obscured much of the situation in 1956, when all those concessions won by local ruling classes meant tangible and, in comparison to the Stalinist period, considerable victories from the point of view of the daily life of working individuals.

The next generation of theoreticians of state socialism was already maturing by the mid-sixties, and the open letter by Kuron and Modzelewski which was mentioned above was the most important of their statements. Kuron and Modzelewski recognized the basic features of state socialism: the emergence of the new class which they called the CPB (Central Political Bureaucracy), and the mismanagement of the social means of production resulting from pursuit of the interests of this class and from total ignorance of actual social needs—these had to be unknown and unallowable as allowing for their expression would concede that the ruling class does not already know, by definition, the needs of those it was supposed to represent—and the repressiveness of the state police system.

However, the form their theoretical pursuit assumed was still an "open letter" to the first secretary of the party. They appealed to the supreme bureaucrat to curb bureaucracy in the name of the "common people" whom the ruling class had no intention of listening to. (In view of this attempt in our own time, perhaps it is not so exotic that Bakunin wrote letters to the tsar seriously expecting the latter to aid him in his revolutionary ventures.) It must be said, however, that although in form they still addressed their class enemy (in a sense, Kuron defines himself as an early drop-out from a ruling class), in the actual content of their writings they had already looked forward to the establishment of working class control over the economic system and over the political representation of the whole society. They had been right and their writings, although belatedly from the point of view of immediate success, reached the people.

Kuron and Modzelewski also had much resonance with sectors of the young intelligentsia. After 1968, they became practically the basic reading for the student counterculture and emerging 1968 generation. But it was also clear that Kuron and Modzelewski's proposals, if taken seriously, called for unified action on the part of workers and intellectuals, and that this action should secure a minimum of political institutional manoeuverability for the sake of a general class struggle against stifling state control.

Kuron and Modzelewski also made another very vital social and political discovery: they managed to construct their model of state socialist society and to design a cure for its obvious illnesses without mentioning the taboo themes of the Soviets and the Warsaw pact army. They were thus doubly threatening to the ruling class as the latter counted on being able to label any opposition unsound precisely because of its being a threat to national independence. This lesson was well remembered so that all theoretical pursuits thereafter clearly distinguished between seeking a domestic cure and pacifying the external threat.

Kuron and Modzelewski were theoretically right about the emergence of the new political class, but their paradoxical fate was that at the time of their insights the working class was too unaware of Poland's class structure to respond. The ruling class applied threats and mild prison terms, but clearly considered the project a kind of theological exercise in revisionism, a type of inner-party blasphemy, and a minor doctrinal issue. It seems unbelievable now, but this was the case. It took the ruling class a few years—a 1968, a student revolt, and the publication of the Kuron-Modzelewski theory in practically all anthologies of the radical and democratic left published in the West in the late sixties—to grasp the meaning of their theoretical achievements and to lock them in prison again, this time actually for nothing in particular, just for being around (and out of prison) when the 1968 student riots took place and some enemies of the regime had to be conspicuously sacrificed. But 1970 brought a new ruling class and an amnesty of limited scope, and Kuron and Modzelewski had become a living part of the theoretical developments that had occurred in the sixties and which matured in 1980, when both became prominent political figures again.

Kuron actually reappeared on the political scene as a KOR member, who very often took public stands, not always in tune with other KOR members, who thought him overzealous in the political sphere. At the same time he belonged to a group of a very few KOR members who revealed their true political aspirations and in 1980 he was one of the first to speak up on a TV broadcast (originally stolen by a Polish news team from a Swedish TV interview and intended to smear Kuron's public image) on the reasons why the ruling class did not use tanks and guns against the striking workers. Kuron said that "they were afraid that the very next day the party committee buildings would be burnt and secretaries hung from the trees" which was basically a correct observation, but which a TV speaker tried to present, unsuccessfully, as Kuron's incitement to burning and hanging.

Modzelewski has rapidly risen in the Wroclaw hierarchy of Solidarity and until late spring of 1981 he was the national press spokesman of the National Coordination Commission of Solidarity (KKP NSZZ Solidarnosc) thus completing, with Kuron, their theoretical activity of the mid-sixties with practical policy making in the late seventies.

More recent and numerous theoretical attempts to analyze state socialism, stemming from many quarters, have not always been associated with names—the more so because they emerged from group discussions, and team work. A typical instance is provided by an anonymous analysis "Harnessing the Crisis" published in 1979 in a clandestine quarterly "Res Publica" which was an intermediate form of underground publishing activity— halfway between an oppositional KOR paper and an inner-party opposition paper. "Res Publica" was very well written, very theoretically sophisticated, and differed from the KOR-published "Zapis" ("Note") and "Puls" ("Pulse") only in that all the essays were anonymous.

Before I quote it, a word of caution: Kuron and Modzelewski did not emerge in 1980 as universally recognized national heroes, whose theoretical relevance and validity had been recognized. Not only was there a more complex and somehow indirect process of the assimilation of their findings in popular class awareness, not only was there a more spontaneous re-discovery on the part of the working class as a whole, but it was also true that their theory could not be defended intact. For instance, they expressed too much trust in following the Yugoslavian pattern, they were partly under the influence of the 1956 tradition and viewed workers' councils as a possible future vehicle for workers' democracy, and they advocated a new, more radically leftist communist party.

No theoretician can claim that he or she has it all figured out.

So the fragment below should provide an instance of how indirectly but rapidly the new class awareness spread and also how it stopped short of what could only be accomplished with the help of extra-theoretical events. It should also be noted that a degree of perceptiveness about the political structure of both the Polish state socialist system and the state socialist world system dependent on the Soviet Union had already become (by 1979) standard knowledge and a usual point of reference—not a very obvious situation only nine years earlier.

Harnessing the Crisis.

Apparently random changes in the rate of growth of the Polish economy and apparently summary and inconsistent decisions of the ruling group can be ordered in two dynamic orders of activities with a distinctive inner logic and structure. I mean on the one hand economic-political cycles, on the other, simultaneous (and stemming from the same source—from the ruling group) ambiguous, contradictory striving—both towards totalitarianism and detotalization. Successive phases of economico-political crises somehow produce one after another their successors, and each has beginnings of the next one within itself... Likewise the sequences of totalitarian and detotalizing actions; the latter are attempts on the part of the ruling elite to avoid the traps it has created itself in the process of the making of totalitarianism.

The elite had come to believe that its striving to control, i.e. to subordinate all manifestations of social life, and thus the necessary abolition of all self-regulation mechanisms which are independent of the authorities, resulted in quite contrary effects than desired. The process of the construction of totalitarianism not only failed to enlarge the possibilities to steer the system according to a pre-established task, but directly increased the amount of uncontrolled phenomena. On the other hand the present, very limited policy of de-totalitarianization, i.e. the self-limiting of power, gives rise to tensions and bears the seed of renewed enforcement of totalitarianism... The method of enforcing this latter de-totalizing policy by the ruling group gives rise to the insecurity of the executive level of the functionaries who are less certain of their status, and the latter, thus motivated, favor the return of totalitarian tendencies.

Keeping the endogenic nature of both above mentioned processes in mind one should at the same time remember that they are intertwined. For instance the cyclic nature of economic growth is to a large extent an unintended effect of institutional mechanisms and solutions created in the name of a totalitarian utopia. On the other hand the culmination of the cycle (economic crisis) makes the ruling groups sharply aware of the traps of totalitarianism it created and of the disadvantages of their system of control. In other words a crisis can, although it does not have to, become an impulse to undertake de-totalitarianizing activities....

Political crises which accompany successive economic crises are characterized by progressive ritualization in both possible variants of the ritual, i.e. "October-like" (from October 1956) and "December-like" (from December 1970). Moreover, each successive crisis is for the elite an additional chance to settle their inner accounts; for instance the March crisis of 1968 and to a lesser extent the cultural crisis of 1964 provided a chance for a peculiar revenge by a fraction which was forced to play the "bad guys" in the screenplay of the 7th Plenum of the Central Committee in October 1956....

The rejection of economic policy by the Polish economy meant each time that a tendency to produce a non-balanced, self-suffocating economic structure, which would not be verified by objective economic mechanisms (for instance a market) abolished in the process of totalitarianization, had not overcome obstacles in its way.

In multiple crisis situations the ruling group undertook extra-ordinary actions and made non-routine decisions in contrast to the overall tendency for non-crisis situations to produce a self-suffocating structure. These decisions meant most often revision and cutback of investments and shift of capital between sectors of the economy (a transitory unblocking of bottlenecks in the economy). The price paid for serial "unblocking" was heavy material financial losses due to the stopping of already started investments and the freezing of capital. The present crisis (1978) increases this price with the loss of the chance to diminish the distance from the technology of the capitalist countries. Mechanical and administrative cutbacks in imports and investments often make previous capital investments of the period 1971-1975 senseless.

The above mentioned pulsating type of growth with an economic crisis as its turning point also has a side effect, i.e.

increases of gross national product are lower than increases which could have been achieved with the same level of investment if a more balanced type of growth had been selected. Moreover the present low outputs in consumption and real salary levels as opposed to possible consumption and salary levels shows an even greater contrast than the deviations in increase of gross national product. This indicates that the present type of growth prefers "production for production's sake" i.e. excessive growth of the branches which produce the means of production—and subsequently consume most of their products. In other words, this is a situation when the economy works in idle gear, and devours what it produces (machinery, energy, raw materials), and in spite of the growth of its potential the degree of satisfaction of social needs does not grow.

The above facts illustrate very well the intensity of contradictions between the interests of the elite, which is interested in preservation of the present method of decision-making, and the rest of society. In other words, it is a contradiction between stateization and socialization of the means of production....

In the course of subsequent crises the ruling group certainly learned how to perform the ritual of change in public. Successive crisis situations also became an occasion for greater awareness on the part of this group of the practical consequence of the double status of social phenomena. They became increasingly aware of the fact that the very public naming of events or labelling of some people does not only change their functioning in society but also determines to a large extent the inner dynamic of a phenomenon or of an attitude. This crisis-learned knowledge resulted in more cautious operations with language (for fear of undesired consequences) and in more sophisticated manipulative techniques. It may certainly be claimed that this group learned how to divide the crises, i.e. how to stabilize in between in spite of tensions and unsolved conflicts. Among the techniques employed are a depoliticization of the party and a consistent obedience to the rule that party members are not allowed to make use of non-party opinions. Likewise animosities and social aggressions are played upon (e.g. the "old" vs. "new" intelligentsia) and the emotions thus created are channelled within the polarized systems of accessible directions of identification and activity. Among the methods which help separate successive crises (economic methods—if management is frustrated, or political—if broader social forces come to the fore) there is also a permitted persistence of a low level of workers' protest. With this model the lowering of the level of social tensions is usually won in the course of political crisis at the expense of prestige and status for middle levels of management.

This is a frustrating experience for those who occupy these levels, but at the same time their social authority declines and they are forced to rely on the ruling group. The latter becomes the only guarantee of the status of the executive managers....

It is hard for a society to defend itself—because of the lack of information, profound frustration and the difficulty of identifying the enemy, while the psychological need for such an identification is immense. Under such circumstances the very participation in the ritual of change gives rise to the illusion of true democratic participation and makes society wake up for a minute. Society suffers a chronic lack of motivational energies—when structures petrify themselves, possibilities for upward mobility decrease, while entrepreneurial ambitions do not arise.

It is also worth asking what the ruling group failed to learn in the course of successive crises. It failed to learn how to avoid socially costly economic cycles of growth, in spite of the fact that the disadvantages of this pulsation of the economy had been often stressed by theoreticians and had also been expressed in the growth of social tensions.

It seems one of the main reasons why changes fail to occur is—paradoxically—an immense adaptability on the part of the participants in the system on all of its levels. These adaptational possibilities permit the system to function at all, albeit with little efficiency and socially in a costly manner. The main costs of low efficiency are paid by those who find it hard to defend themselves apart from occasional acts of despair, and who depend totally on the state as sole employer. These adaptive mechanisms are for instance various semiformal systems which replace horizontal bonds which are nonexistent in the socio-economic system. They are local shock-absorbers."

Considerations

The above text is interesting for two reasons: a) it demonstrates that there was a growing social awareness of the fact that no amount of political camouflage on the part of the ruling class could prevent society from recognizing a mistaken class-determined state-ization. And b) it demonstrates that there was a growing sense of uneasiness about the adaptational abilities of almost all social strata that are essential to the working of the state and to the coordination of social activities which in fact could act as obstacles to the final overcoming of an impossible situation—but that the working class was still underestimated (which is another effect of the divide and rule policy of the ruling class demonstrated by the author of the above text).

Two years later, in 1980, the crisis assumed another form. All of a sudden there were not only no obstacles to intellectual and theoretical analysis, there was an urgent social need for such an analysis. It turned out that no manoeuver on the part of the ruling class could serve its purpose. No amount of ritualization, no matter how well staged, could help. Ritualization lost relevance. The above passage, in which the analysis of ritualization has been made, also indicates what the workers already felt in 1970 and 1971—that nobody can be fooled by it. This was decisive. It meant that the working class caught up with the ruling class and started its arduous way towards class consciousness and the increasing liberation of zones of social life from the reign of the ruling class. In Polish TV the following speech of Maryla Plonska for KOR (also stolen from a Swedish TV interview) appeared: "What matters is that increasing zones free of the totalitarian state emerge, as islands, in our society." Plonska's speech, a hesitant announcement produced during a shaky interview conducted in the conference room of the Gdansk shipyard, where the strikers' committee met with the deputy prime minister, was the final word in the long list of clandestine, official and semi-official publications and theoretical preparations. It was also a comment voiced from the seat of the working class's largest and best organized movement in the politics of state socialist societies.

It should also be mentioned that many theoretical writings which appeared after August 1980 reflect efforts to cope with the situation and to come up with some ingenious solutions. For instance, there was a tendency to stress the meaning of the political sphere of social praxis, to account for it in the marxian structure of explanation of social growth, and to explain the Polish workers' activites as a politicization and an instance of meaningfulness of the political sphere in general.

In the seventies the most successful attempt of this kind was started by Habermas with his excellent analysis of historical materialism reconstructed with respect to a certain vital political discovery, namely that of the state. Habermas' idea was followed by some Polish thinkers, for instance by L. Nowak, who wrote an analysis of Russian political tradition, in which he claimed that it was always state-centered and state-dominated and that the Soviet revolution meant a reinforcement of this tradition (crowning an already accelerated state-ization arrived at as a result of WWI). Nowak's analysis, albeit not very original nor sophisticated, also indicated, in a very militant fashion, that the ruling class is a threefold ruling class and that it enjoys what had previously been enjoyed only in one third by all previously known ruling classes—it had become a political dictator, an economic owner of the means of production and a spiritual monopolist of the ideological education of the whole society. Nowak had also attempted to come up with an idea of a "folk class" as the opponent of the ruling one in the historical process.

All these theoretical explanations of what went on in Poland after WWII also stemmed from the fact that there developed a number of marxian paradigms in the seventies, which offered new possibilities of "squeezing" useful methodologies from a body of vague doctrine. This scholarly activity, albeit an apparently pious and loyal undertaking at the time, turned out to reveal the illusory nature of the ruling class's legitimacy. As has been pointed out:

"The rulers of Poland, as of other East European countries, do not for the most part believe in the ideals of socialism or in the marxist theory: there is no evidence that they are even aware of Marx's methodology. Furthermore, this progaganda of theirs resembles marxism only in its phraseology. Not only are truncated versions of once-powerful revolutionary slogans arranged in a shameless pastiche alongside chauvinist sentiments and medieval superstitions, but the very meaning of the fundamental terms has been transformed beyond recognition. Thus, for example, the Polish words for "socialism," "socialization" and "internationalism" today designate respectively the existing social order, state ownership, and subordination to the interests of the Soviet Union. The term "anti-socialist force" is used to denote any form of political opposition, while the word "anarchist" is reserved for those oppositionists who belong to some current of the European

socialist tradition. These examples form part of a general phenomenon of conceptual embezzlement, which reaches deep into the
vernacular. It is an Orwellian process, which fundamentally limits
people's conceptual framework, rendering inexpressible a whole
range of ideas. In consequence, these ideas vanish deep into the
collective subconscious, from which they struggle to appear in
periods of social crisis, often in the strangest of new clothes."

The above paragraph should, contrary to the author's intentions, be read in the past tense. It is true that many strange
political ideas re-emerged, some of them directly referring to
political doctrines of the period between the wars as the period
when a democratic interplay of forces was in being. But it is also true
that the presently prevailing theoretical alternatives focus on three
broad aims:

a) to preserve the present social structure and secure the lasting
class rule of the present ruling class while totally reconstructing the
actual workings of the communist party so that it becomes a
political party and actually acquires a political inner life; the ruling
class is preserved only in a form sufficient to maintain a continuity
and international facade, and it reigns, but does not rule;

b) to deconstruct the present political order, especially of those
points of the class power structure which have never yielded so far
and which only after the appearance of independent trade unions
can be openly questioned: the police force run in a terrorist, secret
manner and the political facade of a truncated parliament;

c) to bring about a reconstruction of a broad coalition of all
representatives of the class of employees and especially of the
working class—both within and outside of the political party and
the present political system in Poland; and to get rid of the ruling
class in order to de-state-ize and socialize.

It is, of course, very hard to say which tendency will assume the
leading role in further developments of the huge social movement
which has Solidarity as its organizational framework. However, it
can be said that the class analysis of the following theoretical picture
of the present situation is a decisive step forward as opposed to the
vaguely non-class analyses of the economy as run by "imbeciles"
(Kisielewski, whose book was entitled "Poland—or the Reign of
Half-wits") or to the still patiently loyal vernacular of "truncated
marxism."

The class situation as viewed by many of the youngest Polish marxists, who do not necessarily call themselves marxists, as they want to be independent of any qualification that might link them to the ruling party and its theoretical representatives, is that of a fairly sharp struggle, with both classes locked in a basic combat and slightly uneasy about the new and unexpected means they are employing.

The "young marxists" definitely reject Ernest Mandel's stand. They disagree that an unstable mode of production in the state socialist societies furnishes proof that the bureaucracy is not a class because in indicates a contradiction between satisfying the private interests of bureaucracy and following the requirements of a socialized and planned economy. There is, of course, a discussion concerning the comparability of the class criteria of, let us say, capitalists, feudal landlords and socialist bureaucrats (state owners). But the newest theoretical tendency is to think of ways to harness the class struggle with the classes that have revealed themselves, rather than pretending that these are not classes at all.

These analysts have thus agreed that the very existence of state socialism is a class-generating occurrence: that the appearance of social classes results in a class struggle of growing intensity and institutionalization, that the two extreme possible solutions are a reformist guarantee of a minimun of class privileges in return for practical concessions, and a revolutionary (violent or not) upheaval and abolition of the ruling class, though it is unclear what is to replace this class.

Three main theoretical arguments voiced by the young theoreticians from Warsaw, Torun (A. Zybertowicz), Poznan (S. Magala) and Wroclaw concern the mechanism of class generation, the explanation of the conflict of antagonistic social classes in state socialism, the process of the acquisition of awareness of this conflict, and predictions about possible ways of solving these social conflicts in the future, presuming that social classes are here to stay.

On the subject of the closure of political decision-makers into a class-in-itself the young authors stress the following factors:

a) the manner in which general social property is defined as state property resulting in legal sanctioning of an identification between the state and society, thus hampering the "handing over" of state prerogatives (control, coordination, etc.) to associations of independent employees;

b) the manner in which the members of the political decision-making class are found, co-opted, and maintained in the ruling class. Neither their efficiency from the perspective of general social interests nor their representativeness of hired labor decide their acceptance into the ruling class. Instead, what is decisive is a mechanism common to clandestine communities and terrorist minorities, as evidenced by the "nomenklatura," i.e., the list of persons who have been accepted as potential decision-making staffers in all walks of life;

c) the manner in which society is politically organized within the framework of the institutions of the socialist state to primarily maintain the state's monopoly of political power and turn this monopolistic political power into the sole generator of all economic and ideological decisions and into the repression-coordinator against all activities which threaten the interest of the ruling class. Within that the continuity of repression is much more vital—as reflected in state budgets—than the satisfaction of the biological, social and cultural needs of hired laborers: education, health services and culture get less money from the ruling elite than do the police, secret police and censors."

The authors definitely reject the view that it was the material benefits enjoyed by the members of the ruling class which mattered most to the development of new class consciousness on the part of workers, although nobody can deny that the immense increase in the degree of liberty with which members of the ruling class privately distributed social wealth among themselves in the seventies contributed to a growth in the class awareness of the employee class. This is evidenced by daily reports in the Polish press. The Silesian dailies for example ran a story called "Silesia makes the impudent pay," in which the following revelations could be found:

"In the Voivodship Office in Katowice the following principle had been assumed: all those who acquired flats or houses because of their functions or because of other reasons, should presently be given apartments on generally accepted principles of cooperative sharing. Practically this means that they have either to buy their former houses or flats—the price being determined by the Supreme Chamber of Control—or to leave them.

...The Gierek family news is that a part of a two-family house occupied by Stanislawa and Edward Gierek has been bought off on

May 10, 1976. The other part of this house (122 sq.m.) inhabited by Jerzy Gierek either has to be bought off or the family will have to move to an apartment. Likewise in the case of Adam Gierek, who inhabits a house in the vicinity (137 sq.m.) and has announced that he wants to buy off this house. However, he claims that the proper cost of this house construction is yet to be established. The Supreme Chamber of Control has estimated that the joint cost of the two-house construction (Adam Gierek, Zdzislaw Grudzien—the former first secretary of the party in Katowice) was 27,273,000 zlotys, while in the state treasury evidence the costs had been given as 2,026,000 each. The trememdous difference had been hidden by silently adding it to the cost of the road construction of the so called Murckow highway. Likewise there is the problem of the houses of Tadeusz Pyka (the first representative of the party bosses sent to Gdansk) and Zdzislaw Legomski, where treasury evidence shows a joint value of 3,747,000 zlotys, while the Supreme Chamber of Control estimated the cost at 17,254,000. Both citizens declared a willingness to leave their houses. The house of Wlodzimierz Lejczak was already vacated last year. Its value was estimated at 5,560,000 zlotys, of which more than 4 million had been paid by the Wujek coalmine, while the rest of the cost was covered by the producer, i.e. the Construction Enterprise of the Coal Industry (hence arose the permanent successes of Wujek mine in all sorts of contests of labor). Lejczak's house was to become a center of teaching activities for the community's retarded children."

But the theme of corruption is ambiguous. If on the one hand it is an element in raising popular sentiments to the level required to start actions, it is also true on the other hand that the ruling class is trying to sacrifice as many Gierek people as possible, without at the same time losing any of its actual structural power.

Coming back to the newest theoretical interpretations of the younger Polish Marxists (who are definitely not the only ones to think of Poland nowadays, as will be mentioned in the next chapter): they point out that all "socialist" societies known so far, i.e. all state socialist societies, have a basic contradiction between the vast majority of state employees, and the owners of the state or ruling class. This contradiction of state ownership and socialization gives rise to two basic antagonistic classes whose formation takes a fairly long time, mainly due to the relatively slower rate of growth of the class awareness of the workers.

There is a very limited truth in the marxian definition of "class"—indeed, it is a common denominator of all state employees that they are hired laborers of the state as a single monopolistic employer. But at the same time it is also true that one does not become a member of this vast class of state employees because one has no capital, but only his/her own labor power to sell—but because one is deprived of the possibility of exercising political power and of having a share in public policy decision making.

There is much discussion by these new theorists of the relative importance of the economic vs. the political sphere of activity. A general view is that a) the political sphere is more important in the political constellation and social construction of ordered relationships under state socialism, where a decisive argument in favor of this is that the economic status of an individual is a derivative of his or her political function and place in a general political hierarchy, while b) the economic sphere has been the one to allow a perception and aggravation of class inequalities and conflicts. Although the economic sphere has been very basic in leading people to perceive social relations and designing the movement of opposition, it is also quite clear that non-economic struggles, demands, and activities have justly been chosen as the effective ones.

The making of the independent, self-governed, autonomous trade unions is a new phenomenon in the history of class conflicts in Poland; it means that a class struggle has been reluctantly institutionalized and that heretofore "wild" forms for waging this struggle have been abandoned on both sides. For example, there has been no general lowering of productivity on the part of the labor force but also no political repression and terror on the part of the ruling class.

The first question the young marxists ask is: what chances are there to enhance the prospects of survival of state socialism by harnessing the class struggle and making it yield considerable social, political and economic gains for the working class? The next question is: how are class conflicts decided? It is clear that negotiation within existing institutions is different from a revolutionary overthrow of the whole institutional framework. The prevailing answer is that the emerging organized class struggle provides a "missing link" in the transition to a new form of postcapitalist society which would be free of the undesirable features of state socialism. State-ization of the means of production is but the first step in the direction of socialization and insufficient and wrong if taken only in and for itself. There is an urgent need to elaborate new forms of political life and to gradually neutralize the negative aspects of the institutional shape of the state as an organization of social life.

The relative loss of power on the part of the ruling class does not bring about negative results for the whole society—quite the contrary. However, it may become radically impossible to defend the ruling class's tenets if their monopoly of power becomes their only prerogative with no censorship and terrorist secret police to support it. Further observations will be furnished in the chapter on the nine months (August 1980-May 1981) of the changed political scenery in Poland.

The young marxists have also noticed that marxism itself did not play any direct and simple role in raising class awareness in Poland. Marxism was instrumental in bringing about the class awareness of the ruling class, for it became a useful instrument in manipulating the state machinery. But the working class did not use marxism at all since it has been totally monopolized and appropriated by the ruling class's ideologists. At the same time, due to a particular ironic twist and turn of history, marxism as inspiration, as a non-doctrinaire encouragement to apply economic struggle to articulate political demands and as a school of political thinking with a positive vision of society, did pave the way for the advanced political insights of the striking workers. It may thus be said metaphorically (following Magala in "Philosophy and Social Action" Jan-March 1980) that the ruling class used marxism without Marx to ideologically obscure the actual aims and means of class struggle. The working class used a marxian inspiration without marxist rhetoric in order to articulate demands and execute their fulfillment. The slogan on Gate No. 2 of the Gdansk shipyard "Proletarians of all enterprises unite" is a creative concretization of the slogan "Proletarians of the world unite," which in the case of Poland would be inappropriate, since there internationalism means Soviet supremacy. The slogan invented by the unorthodox Polish workers' approach towards marxism can thus be considered the Polish workers' contribution to the development of a truly socialized socialist society.

Chapter Nine

Unrepeatable Constellations
Or Regular Patterns?

Almost all theoreticians of state socialism, whether Bahro or Konrad, Amalrik or Mandel, Gramsci or Althusser, stress the particular importance of an unrepeatable constellation of events which resulted in Russia's long tradition of undemocratic rule and imperialist policies in Europe. The basic question is, however, whether it was an unrepeatable constellation or a regular pattern of development which produced state socialism. This question is very important as it leads us to next ask about the inevitability of much of what happened after Marx wrote his studies, and after his followers influenced the working masses' movements, even as we see now more clearly than ever that those movements were much more shaped by local national and cultural traditions of political life than by theories—the British context shaping the trade unions, the French shaping the anarcho-syndicalist movements, the German, social democracy, the Polish, a craving for independence and national unity, etc.

The questions are hard to answer in a general sense, but we will try in the specific, namely with respect to what happened in Poland in August 1980, and to show how inevitable this outbreak and its later development were. This is both a question of the validity of historical materialism as a theoretical framework of explanation in matters of social history and a question of the current political evaluation of what is actually going on in the present.

189

The theoretical problem has always been the problem of the scientificity of historical materialism—whether it is, for instance, possible to predict developments of social structure, to design the course of social revolutions, and the like. There is no evidence that any such prediction or design is possible, or so a number of criticisms of historical materialism have argued, of which Popper's in the "Poverty of Historicism" may be the most often quoted. What Popper claims is that in social life as in technical engineering what is to be preferred as a foundation and premise of efficient action and change is "piecemeal social engineering" and not "wholesale metaphysical prophecy." In the introduction to "The Poverty of Historicism" the following objection to the scientific validity of historical materialism and to any possibility of a critically appraisable historical science is made: "The course of human history is strongly influenced by the growth of human knowledge. The truth of this premise must be admitted even by those who see in our ideas, including our scientific ideas, merely byproducts of material developments of some kind or other." But since future growth of scientific knowledge by definition cannot be predicted with the help of current scientific methods and knowledge, and there is therefore no rational method by which to prophesy the course of future scientific pursuits, it follows that one cannot predict the future course of human history. Since the above holds, any science which aims at historicity is bound to go astray—historicism does not make sense in science.

Popper is right on most counts in his criticism of what has been developing as historical materialism. However, his own proceedings are open to similar criticisms—e.g. his reliance on evolutionary image and model, or his suprahistorical idea of rationality which conveniently reveals itself in definite historical embodiments in each stage of the historical drama. More important, his argument has many flaws which stem from a simplified, artificially sharpened distinction between metaphysical social and historical sciences on the one hand, and faultless, rational, natural ones on the other.

Let us take the distinction between historical prophecy and social engineering, for instance. Using Popper's example, if we claim that a tornado is coming we can attach a practical value to this statement, which is nevertheless a prophecy, while if we claim that a certain shelter is able to withstand tornadoes, provided it is constructed in a certain manner, we can indulge in social engineering. What makes one wonder whether Popper really means what he says is that this distinction is external and not totally relevant with respect to the issue in question: in the very construction of a shelter we include our decision about the possible arrival of tornadoes, which is exactly what we are forbidden to do if we do not want to deal with prophecies. But Popper needs this distinction to demonstrate the fact that sciences which are able to design and carry on experiments, are also able to employ a "piecemeal engineering" approach to reality, while sciences which rely on non-observational techniques and a non-experimental approach usually produce prophecies. Thus Popper concludes that "historicists, quite consistently with their belief that sociological experiments are useless and impossible, argue for historical prophecy, the prophecy of social, political and institutional developments—and against social engineering, as the practical aim of social sciences. The idea of social engineering, the planning and construction of institutions, with the aim, perhaps, of arresting, controlling, or of quickening impending social developments, appears to some historicists as possible. To others this could seem an almost impossible undertaking or one which overlooks the fact that political planning, like all social activity, must stand under the superior sway of historical forces."

The full impact of Popperian criticism has become felt in the Polish marxist debates of the late sixties and early seventies. It was in this period that on the one hand there arose a gap in the Polish humanities due to the fact that a number of scholars (most notably Kolakowski, Pomian, Baczko, Baumann, Hirszowicz) were forced to leave the academic life and/or the country. On the other hand there was a tendency to value very highly the Polish logical tradition, the Lvov-Warsaw school which produced the mathematicians and logicians of the order of Tarski, Banach, Mazur, Kurnatowski and Ajdukiewicz. As a result of the simultaneous vacancy in marxist humanities and the the influence of the prestigious logical-positivist legacy a new school has been created, the so-called Poznan School of Methodology. The main representatives were Jerzy Kmita, Jerzy Topolski and Leszek Nowak.

They started with the Popperian approach and then set out within the limited academic freedom of the period to outline a methodological program for a marxist humanist science which could overcome dogmatism and also answer Popperian doubts. All three of these philosophers came up with different answers. Topolski, who is a historian, and works especially on questions of early capitalist development in Eastern Europe, developed his own analysis in which the specificity of marxian historical science consists of a simultaneous application of two methodological approaches which should be balanced in historical explanation. One aims at the discovery of macrostructural processes and historical tendencies to provide a framework for individual decisions and actions. Another seeks to investigate and explain individual events, decisions and occurences. Without the former macro approach the concrete explanations would be atomized; without the micro explanation the global judgements would be too vague and general.

Kmita criticized Popper's absolutization of the criteria of demarcation in the natural sciences, and especially the absolutization of a criterion of correspondence as the sole possible rule governing the development of knowledge and deciding the acceptablity of successive theories, theorems or paradigms. According to Kmita there are at least two possible criteria or rules of acceptance for successive cultural products (be they scientific theories or works of art) namely correspondence and adaptation. In the case of natural sciences we do, indeed, have to employ the rule of correspondence (although the rule itself can be understood in a number of ways), while in the case of the humanities (which resemble art in this respect) we have to apply the principle and the rule of adaptation.

Nowak lifted the marxian methodological framework out of reach of any earthly criticism by inventing an interpretation according to which Marx discovered idealizations and produced advanced and true logical laws within his theoretical framework. If anybody proved that a theorem was wrong, it simply meant that it was misunderstood, that it was not "concretized" enough—and that once a premise or two had been accounted for, theoretical coherence would be back with a victorious smile. This may sound thin, but at the time (late sixties, early seventies) it was all there was in Polish marxism, and Leszek Nowak managed to attract much attention. By the late seventies Nowak dropped his whole idealization theme and started writing on political domination, on the history of statism in Russian social development and on what went wrong in the Russian revolution (its excessive stress on the state as the supreme coordinating institution) and in marxian doctrine (the lack of recognition of the meaning of the political sphere).

None of the representatives of the Poznan methodological school managed to provide a broad enough rebuttal of Popper to be able to claim that the problem of a clearcut answer to the question whether history is a science investigating regularities or collecting unrepeatable constellations was finally solved.

It should be added that not much has been done in other Polish humanist centers to answer this question either, in spite of the fact that the problem had been raised, especially in view of the structuralist wave in the European humanities, very eagerly received in Poland by all kinds of the so-called "traditional humanists" who saw structuralism as a relief from dogmatized marxism and paid lip service to Marx as the first structuralist, proceeding with their own specialized and generally pretty useful research. The growing role of an esoteric bi-monthly *Teksty* ("Texts") should be mentioned, for it rallied excellent minds under a sophisticated aegis which no censorship could follow. However the structuralist discussion of methodology was a typical retreat from reality when it becomes impossible to bear for the average scholar and scientist.

The paradox of a decline of marxism under the sway of a dominant marxist ideology is evident. The younger generation found marxism totally dead and a butt of jokes at best, except insofar as it could be instrumental in shaping one's rhetoric on the way to power. It was clear that linking holistic planning and scientific method was impossible. Herbert Marcuse's *Soviet Marxism* was read and the metaphoric statement, that the bags of concrete carried on human backs during the construction of electric power plants in Siberia had crushed young revolutionary morality, was fully agreed with. The liberal tradition was strong enough to provide a criticism of centralizied state planning which was also reminiscent of the Popperian observation that a centralized planner who has to rely on unreliable knowledge—for all knowledge is individual and can never be fully centralized—has to simplify calculations by eliminating individual differences and forcing stereotyped categories on all kinds of varied interests, pursuits, and beliefs. As Popper himself said: "...this attempt to exercise power over minds must destroy the last possibility of finding out what people really think, for it is clearly inconsistent with the free expression of thought, especially of critical thought.

Ultimately, it must destroy knowledge, and the greater the gain in power, the greater will be the loss in knowledge—political power and social knowledge may thus be discovered to be "complementary" in Bohr's sense of the term."

It would be interesting to ask Popper about the methodological status of the above statement, but for practical reasons it is absolutely paralleled by the stunning development of censorship in Polish intellectual life—a development which produced such an astonishing array of independent, clandestine publishing in the late seventies.

It is profoundly disturbing for a marxist to discover that Popper was right, and that honest efforts to criticize him meet with only partial success. However, one has to be aware of this if an effective criticism is to emerge. Thus let us quote the announcement of KOR which prefaced a Swedish, Polish underground and British edition of the "Black Book of Censorship" based on instructions for censors smuggled out of Poland to Sweden by a former censor from Krakow. KOR issued the following statement, having enumerated the areas in which the ruling class decided to limit information to a ridiculous degree.

"We are dealing with one of the greatest revelations of the postwar period comparable only to the memories of Swiatlo of the October period. While the latter revealed the criminal activities of security forces against citizens and their lives, the documents we are reading reveal another anti-social and anti-national activity of censorship guided by party-state authorities of the Polish People's Republic. It is planned overkill of the national culture and injury to individual personality and social forms by a systematic and methodical stifling of the freedom of speech and information.

The thesis that in our life lies and disinformation play the foremost role is confirmed again. Not only historical tradition, the ideological sphere and national culture are falsified. Elementary facts are also suppressed or distorted, even those whose neglect is a crime against citizens—for instance, the information has been suppressed that a popular floor plate commonly used by construction companies causes cancer and that chemicals employed in agriculture directly threaten human health. This suppression is performed apparently for the sake of social peace and order, in order to pacify society. But at the same time society has reason to feel anxiety and keeping silent or lying will not remove the reasons for this anxiety.

Documents of censorship also reveal another mystification. The censors have assumed the function of guardians and custodians of state secrets. According to periodical reports on censors' activities the "state secrets" rubric is very full, but there is no definite indication as to what secrets these were. In about 700 pages of reports on censors' interventions one could possibly find about 6 truly linked to some state secret. But all other documents clearly demonstrate that censors justify their existence with the need to keep state secrets and that they continue to create those secrets. It is impermissible to consider information on thousands of parasites which attack cattle, perils linked to labor in the chemical industry, social and religious activities of the church, names of artists and scientists and the titles of their works, of books and films, of historical events which took place, of orders which are not allowed, even in obituaries—it is impermissible to consider all these data as state secrets.

We understand the social and national function of state secrets and we know what it means to keep the nation safe and defensible. But documents of censorship prove that principles of state secrets are abused by censors who disarm society and deprive it of a chance to defend itself.

Convinced that the superior social interest requires this decision we publish the following materials which reveal the precision of this anti-human machinery, this anti-citizen, anti-national device. Activities of censorship in People's Poland have to be revealed as much as possible. We shall do everything to fulfill this duty. Therefore a copy of the same text shall be immediately dispatched to all clubs and societies: Polish Academy of Sciences, PEN Club, Union of the Artists and Cultural Workers, Polish Writers' Union, Polish Filmakers' Association, Association of the Polish Theatre and Film Artists, Union of Polish Composers, Association of Polish Musical Artists, Union of Polish Visual Artists, Polish Historical Society, Polish Economic Society, Pricipal Technical Organization, Polish Sociological Society, Polish Philosophical Society, Social Anti-Alcohol Committee, Association of the Polish Journalists, etc.

Further agreement to have the above practices performed by censorship means agreement to a gradual self-destruction of our society. Thus we would like to announce our appeal to notify us of all new censorship interventions."

The above introduction was signed by thirty-one members of KOR: Jerzy Andrzejewski, Stanislaw Baranczak, Konrad Bielinski, Seweryn Blumsztajn, Bogdan Borusewicz, Andrzej Gelinski, Miroslaw Chojecki, Ludwik Cohen, the Rev. Zbigniew Kaminski, Jan Kielanowski, Leszek Kolakowski, Anka Kowalska, Jacek Kuron, Edward Lipinski, Halina Mikolajska, Piotr Naimski, Wojciech Onyszkiewicz, Antoni Pajdak, Zbigniew Romaszewski, Jozef Rybicki, Jozef Sreniowski, Aniela Steinsbergowa, Adam Szczypiorski, Maria Wosiek, Henryk Wujec, Waclaw Zawadzki, Rev. Jan Zieja.

The question of the present chapter title has remained unanswered—it has lost its theoretical urgency with the appearance of a number of practical issues. It may still be that there are some marxists who want to interpret whatever happens in the course of the class struggle in Poland as a confirmation of an iron law of contradictory social forces clashing in class determined patterns and that there are others who claim that the definite historical form of such clashes is a random constellation to which only a descriptive approach can be successfuly applicable. But this distinction should cease to play a significant role. The question has become a truly practical question of a politically committed theory: to support Solidarity and the working class or to stick to the state and the ruling class. The shifting sands of social change and thousands of factors in and out of Poland make individual decisions in this respect vital for further developments in Poland.

PART THREE

SOLIDARITY AND POLISH SOCIETY

Chapter Ten

No Precedent
What Solidarity Is Not

In spite of an almost universal recognition of the novelty of the political forms of organization of the Polish working class under the system of state socialism, there has been from time to time a very understandable tendency to express a certain reservation about the whole affair. "It is hard to become elated because somebody has just reinvented the steam engine" was a frequent comment. The comment was beside the point.

It is true that trade unions in their 19th century forms (not to mention other forms of protection of labor under different circumstances and national traditions) have long been the political organization of the labor force meant to exert economic pressure and win political leverage. The economic definition of trade union members as "the labor force" was recognized as a prerequisite to efficient organization and victorious struggle against the bourgeoisie. It is also true that the trade union Solidarity is based on a recognition that the economic definition of its members as the labor force for the huge monopolist—the state—is primary and basic to recognizing their actual sphere of influence and thus forms a precondition of an efficient struggle in the political sphere.

However, there is a huge difference between 19th century trade unions in the capitalist state and the 20th century Solidarity trade union in state socialist society. The former enhanced actual struggle in the economy as a precondition to a real influence upon economic decision making—political decision making was not at issue as much as the structure of the mode of production. In state socialist societies political decision-making is at issue and at the very outset all the party propaganda wizards started crying out that "Solidarity should never crave political power"—because in state socialist societies political decision making determines the mode of production.

The difference is that whereas in the case of 19th century trade unions the economic organization of the labor force assumed political proportions by involving labor in bargaining which then backfired to become the foundation of a new mode of economic production, in the case of Solidarity the awareness of political helplessness and slavery assumed the economic form of a trade union organization independent of the sole monopolist entrepreneur and political leader, which then backfired into a political reorganization of society depriving the state of its monopoly of organized representation of all sectors of population. This throws the ruling class into a situation where it has to start ruling and stop reigning, a clear loss for those members of the class who think in terms of an absolute monopoly of power.

A quotation from a ruling class propagandist illustrates what Solidarity is not. The following passage has been taken from a letter of the first secretary of a factory party organization addressed to all those who threw their party ID cards away. I also quote the reply of the local Solidarity organization:

"To the comrades who gave their party ID cards away!
The question arises whether Solidarity fought so fiercely to eliminate the guiding role of the party from the statute only in order to establish the guiding role of KOR with respect to the union?
I distinguish a number of tendencies in Solidarity:
1. The tendency of the inspired to go forward. They push Solidarity beyond the agreements signed in Gdansk, Szcecin and Jastrzebie and determined by the statute.
2. Advisory bodies: a) the anti-socialist advisors who want to pull Poland out of the socialist commonwealth and to institute a

capitalist system (activists of Moczulski's Confederation of Independent Poland); b) the advisers of KOR who do not want to pull Poland out of socialism, who want to reform it, and who are led by former members of the party—Kuron, Michnik and Modzelewski. They do not attack socialism as such but they do want to destroy the party and to take over power in the state; c) the advisers of Cardinal Wyszynski, with Mazowiecki, who exert a pacifying influence, and who have won a considerable influence upon Walesa; d) the group of leaders within Solidarity who want to take over power, and who see their own interest as a priority. They want to remove Lech Walesa.

3. There are also trade unionist activists and masses of members— but there is a process of removing from Solidarity committees, the honest workers, the true trade unionist activists, a process of removing those who want Solidarity to be a trade union which cares for social conditions in the factories and for turning industrial potential to the advantage of the working people."

The above litany is obvious: a party mouthpiece, and not a very subtle one at that, wants to have a new trade union shaped and patterned after the old state-owned trade unions and what he means by "true activists" is the cadre of old trade unions—while "honest worker" means simply somebody who believes in everything that the party secretaries deem worth pronouncing.

It is very interesting that this party halfwit cannot imagine that workers can have any ideas of their own, and thus divides the tendencies according to whether the ruling group is the group of outsiders from the ruling party (as was certainly the case with older trade unions), the oppositional groupings, or the Catholic Church.

The "group of leaders" under point (d) was added after a split in the Gdansk Solidarity headquarters over the decision about a general strike in late March (after the secret police massacred Solidarity leaders and the authorities and local prosecutors' office blamed the Solidarity members themselves) and suggests that this letter was written in central party headquarters and spiced with some secret police data on the latest developments within the new trade union...

It is a very revealing letter because it spells out what Solidarity is not—it is not run by the ruling party, but neither is it run by KOR, Moczulski's people, or Cardinal Wykszynski's advisors.

Therefore the workers of "Pomet" were right when they answered their local party boss in the following manner:

"It is obvious that party members respond more quickly to reality than does the organization to which they belong, as was clearly demonstrated by numerous rejections of party ID cards. We are certain that this rejection was a typical response for honest individuals who are able to admit that they have committed mistakes.

Those people work in Pomet, too. Comrade Zywica, formerly a functionary and presently boss of a local party chapter wrote a letter to them but did not acknowledge these rejections. Thus he addressed his letter to "Those comrades who gave their party ID cards away"—they should be a pretty numerous group as comrade Zywica had to mimeograph his letter in a considerable number of copies. What fiction does he live in if he divides his sheep into those who had and those who had not rejected party ID cards?

We do not have these problems in Solidarity: we do not divide our members into religious and non-religious, non-party, party and party-without-ID-cards members.

We do not care about inner party problems. We do not care if and when a special party commission in which Mr. Zywica can be found will finally investigate Zasada's and Gierek's sins. All we care about is when will they face a prosecutor and a judge.

...Let us focus on those fragments of the letter of Mister Secretary in which he discusses our trade union. He accounts for us as much as he does for his own party—but equally with lies. According to Mr. Secretary only the third strongest group in Solidarity is composed of true trade union activists and the broad masses of members. But there are stronger fractions—so claims the secretary—who push us towards the West, who are anti-socialist, who follow Maczulski or Rev. Primar, and finally a group of leaders who want to bring Walesa down.

This is the world according to Mr. Zywica. All we need in Solidarity now are Zionists and anarchists. Does Mr. Zywica hide them under the table to use in better times to come?

We are not astonished to hear these lies, gossip and muck-raking. Mr Zwyca has not thought them up alone. We have heard them from much bigger secretaries! There are still forces in the party which want to base their authority on a quarreling nation in which groups are baited or set on other groups, on a nation of terrified people who are afraid of their neighbors, children, and work conrades. They know that only such subordinates can be guided by truncheons, fear, and a bowl of "regenerative meal" and can contribute to a stabilization of their power and impudence. Those bestial individuals Mr. Zywica would gladly see in a "proper trade union." For a party functionary in our factory, for a person who personally investigates somebody, Solidarity is just one label more to mention with respect to some neutral illusion of some activity."

There is no precedent for Solidarity—never so far has any state socialist society organized by a ruling class of considerable coherence within the iron grasp of the Soviet military threat managed to find a way out without causing a major confrontation. Yet this confrontation was avoided in August, even if barely, due to the very skilful policies of Solidarity—determined, interestingly enough, by spontaneous clashes of opinion in all parts of Poland—and due to a lack of vigilant unity in the ruling class, at least three times afterwards: in November, in late January and in late March.

The very fact that there is no precedent means that the effects and consequences of the the very existence of Solidarity for all spheres of social life are hard to calculate, though some can already be mentioned.

First of all, there is an immense liberation of social energies, which had previously been mercilessly starved by the state organization. For example, within a few weeks after Solidarity won its August victory the Krakow ecological movement (a local "green" party) managed to reveal the squalor of Poland's largest historical treasure, the aluminum mill in Skawina, and in a number of weeks to close the works completely because of obvious threats to the local ecology and to the individuals employed there. In 1980 remuneration and special health allowances and pensions paid to former workers who suffered cancer exceeded the profits earned by the mills.

The liberation of ecological consciousness came just in time: one of the largest scandals of state socialism is a dissipation of responsibility and total disregard of the social costs of production including questions of energy, the well-being of the workers and of course the preservation of the natural environment.

The Solidarity affiliated ecological clubs (most importantly in Krakow, but also in practically all other Polish city centers) stressed the disastrous situation of the natural environment caused by the ruling class's carelessly antisocial policy. Many instances have been quoted of secret police rest houses in the middle of nature parks, of central committee summer residences in the midst of the most beautiful mountain spots, of impudent thefts of land from peasants to build hunting lodges, of the appropriation of local parks in the vicinity of large cities to make secluded summer "paradise centers," and so on. The excessive state sponsorship of alcohol production has also been quoted as an instance of an anti-social policy which results in the death and suffering of thousands of people each year.

These typically ecological concerns are linked to observations of growing soil, water, air and food pollution and Solidarity periodicals paint the following sordid picture:

"For about 20 years, and particularly since 1970, we observe a rapid degeneration of the Polish natural environment, a growing susceptibility to disease (especially in children and infants) particularly in the vicinity of cement, aluminum and copper works where the mortality rate of infants is three times higher than the Polish average. The slogan that technique will make up for technical losses is untrue. If it were so, then why does it fail to do so? Why have the Skawina works below Krakow had to be closed down after taking a heavy toll of up to a thousand victims among the young crew and local population? ...Poland has broken the world record in cancer of the stomach among the rural population as a result of the pollution of river water and soil. The air we breathe is deteriorating as a result of the planned construction of factories without or with illusory antipollution securities. The carelessness and stupidity of the state as investor is clear. The state is not practically accountable, for who can call the state into court. Fiscal punishment is usually calculable for an investor, but for the state this just means that money is sent from one state organ to another.

But this is not all: the tragic ecological situation in Poland as manifested by the low quality of foodstuffs, increasing susceptibility to illnesses especially in cases of children, women and people of fragile health, the destruction of cultural goods (Krakow is falling apart because of the air pollution) which express our national identity, the destruction of the landscape which is significant in

awakening local patriotism, and the increasing shortage of re-
creational areas necessary for the normal work of each society, are
subjects we have to discuss and which merit particular attention."

Ecological awareness was definitely there before Solidarity, but
with Solidarity it became a significant fragment of political
awareness and a significant ideology in its own right. It has also
given a powerful impetus to a consumer protection movement
which has immediately become a huge organization of national
significance, and to local democracy. Both developments are very
important—but neither is itself the same as Solidarity. Thus
Solidarity cannot be identified with consumer defence or with local
democracy in every facet of life, but its existence furnished an
impetus and provided a protection for the growth of such
initiatives.

The Warsaw based national weekly of Solidarity, also named
"Solidarity" and headed by Tadeusz Mazowiecki, presented in its
first issue of April 5, 1981, an interview with Krzysztof Skierkowski, the head of an Association of Foodstuffs Experts which is
an advisory body to the Consumers' Federation, which works for
Solidarity and which aims at parliamentary interventions and
public opinion mobilization in cases of a particular threat to the
consumer.

Skierkowski says, in part:

"Our most vital weapon will be the immediate publicity
granted to our independent findings. We have to be quick and
uncompromising, for consumers are very threatened nowadays.
Take novelties: how many are there?... According to the present law
it is ok to sell a worse commodity under the novelty label at a higher
price. It is thus vital to fight for a law which will protect the
consumer from such manipulation. As an association we intend to
furnish the federation with expertise.

The harmful effects of eating poultry have become an
emotional issue. This meat is more available than other kinds, and
we shall be forced to eat it more now that rationing of other meats is
prevalent. Therefore we are collecting data from endocrinologists,
geneticians and food technologists. Everyone knows that poultry is
raised with the help of hormones added to the fodder. Minister
Zaleski was correct in saying so on TV. But he was only partly
correct. For poultry can, after all, be dangerous. This is a

consequence of the method of raising. It has been suggested that chickens are fed too much high calorie fodder (imported) and that since they are unable to metabolize it properly, too much fat is produced which is stored in enlarged hormone glands. As a result humans eat too many hormones which are concentrated and stored by the organism and can contribute to faulty growth. This is especially true with respect to children. The same thing happens with poultry in the West, where the fodder is made. But a child there eats poultry less frequently because there are other foods to choose from. Our children will eat poultry too frequently out of necessity. The conclusion is that children should not eat poultry more frequently than twice a month."

Another vital development which is not Solidarity as such, but to whose existence Solidarity has contributed more than anything else is the appearance of an immense vitality in local democracy in the regional and daily organizations of all communities. The appearance of an immense wave of interest in the daily running of small community clubs, gatherings, apartment renters' associations, etc. does not however mean that all is totally orderly, and that Solidarity is the towering crown of this spontaneous freely developing life.

The growth of direct democracy is not very uniform, nor is it unhampered, nor understood by all. Sometimes it is hard to see that local democracy which enables the citizens to make daily decisions (and these local decisions rarely have a political appearance) has very much the same meaning as the central state method of making society's decisions. But people have started to perceive that in order to take themselves seriously as citizens they have to decide where to build a school, how to fix faulty installations in a factory, and what to do about the quality of food in a student cafeteria. They have also started to understand that they have to have a right to say what they think of these matters—that the delegation of such a right to others is part and parcel of a huge process of robbing themselves of their dignity and turning them into slaves.

It is no coincidence that people who have been performing sophisticated analyses of the political options of historical figures in Poland's independent political life between the wars are presently passionately discussing these basics of direct democracy. Nobody believes in the paradise of a social system totally based on the principles of direct democracy—but nobody gives up the idea that it is a desirable form of piecemeal social engineering to reinforce and create this element in the social landscape of socialist society. Thus in a "Vocabulary of Democracy" which ran in the most popular Catholic weekly ("Tygodnik Powszechny," with a circulation of 80,000, though ten times more could be sold if this would not make it clear that the party's equivalent,"Polityka," commands less attention) one of the nation's finest young political sociologists, who had previously only published historical comments on non-political topics, Macin Krol, says:

"Local democracy can only function well if the functions of superior authorities and of the authorities chosen democratically at the lowest level are clearly distinguished. It should be perfectly clear what rights local authorities have. Their budget, their manner of election and type of dependence on superior authority has to be quite clear. Experience demonstrates that local democracy functions best when direct democratic principles are increasingly employed. Thus it is vital that the administrative structure of the state, of the trade union, and of large social organizations of any kind, includes a spot for the lowest level to run by direct democracy...

Local democracy is also one of the best securities against two dangers which constantly threaten each democratic structure, bureaucratization and oligarchization. Bureaucratization consists of all functionaries' structures (which are indispensable in all organizations) becoming autonomous and acting not within the people's mandate and for their sake, but for themselves. Oligarchization consists of the tendency of representatives elected by society to exercise their power without respect to society's attitudes. Tendencies towards bureaucracy and oligarchy exist in every democratic system, thus each democratic system requires some securities. The largest endowment of the lowest levels with local democracy and direct democracy is the best possible guard against these tendencies.

It is sometimes said that because of the need for efficiency and rapidity of action it is only very few situations that may be considered suitable for direct democracy. I think this is wrong and results from a mechanical repetition of schemes which exist in a capitalist economic system transferred unreflectively into the economic system of a planned society. These schemes are based on an assumption that a centralization of decision-making favours progress. At present both this belief and the very idea of progress are being questioned. It should also be said that even in the economy itself one can abandon the centralist ideas, as demonstrated by a successful experiment in the Volvo works in Sweden, where the crews have been divided into small brigades which work on some tasks from the beginning to the very end and achieve better efficiency rates than workers on long assembly lines.

There is thus no reason to prevent the parents of the children who attend some school from deciding about the school's program, about which teachers they want to employ, and about the plan of daily lessons in the school. The ministry could design a minimum, while the rest could be decided by the parents' association. There is no reason for local food shops not to be directed by a committee of the inhabitants of that part of town, no reason to prevent those same inhabitants from organizing their own network of services, social services, and elementary medical care. Architecture and construction decisions can also be subject to this basic level of direct decision making. The above list can easily be made longer. Of course, once these rights are granted the costs may increase—but the costs would probably be immediately offset by the savings resulting from the diminished bureaucratic structure. Moreover the variety so produced would feed color into social life.

But the most important gains from the increased range of direct democracy cannot even be measured. They consist of stimulating those active social attitudes and beliefs which result from self-conscious participation in decision-making. Only local democracy guarantees the preservation of spontaneity and of the authenticity of social attitudes. Finally, participation in local democracy is the best possible school of citizen education. For democracy is hardly learned in a theoretical way and passive participation in state democracy is a meagre education. How to organize a meeting, how to vote, how to make compromises, how to fight with dignity, how to be coherent and responsible—the individual has no better chance to learn this than in participation in decision making at the lowest level of all these grand structures, at the level I call local democracy."

We may sum up the above remarks with the statement that Solidarity is a trade union in that it recognizes that the basic common denominator of the members of the class of state employees is the fact that they sell their labor to the state. However, it is also clear that by doing so Solidarity is recognizing and revealing the basic structure of state socialist society which is political domination by the ruling class from which all other kinds of domination follow. By showing this, even indirectly, not necessarily recognizing it in statutes and ideology, Solidarity provides a huge stimulus to all those spontaneous social energies and forces which aim at the de-state-ization of society and the dismantling of the absolute domination of the ruling class over the working masses. The forms of social life to emerge from this will definitely not be capitalist, and neither will they consist of the substitution of one ruling class by another. The constant control exercised over the workings of Solidarity by its ten million members is obviously an instance of a democratic check against such a possibility.

One of the tactics of the ruling class was to invite a few prominent leaders of Solidarity into their own ranks, and thus to design a strategy of dissolving the August 1980 hopes and victories, the base of the movement. That this is, indeed, a threat and that it is clearly recognized as such can be seen from the following exchange of letters which preceded Gwiazda's resignation from the National Coordination Committee of Solidarity. The trade unionist press printed the letter together with Walesa's answer and local comments—I quote the local Poznan comment voiced by the editor in chief of Poznan's Solidarity periodical.

"Open letter of Andrezej Gwiazda to Lech Walesa: Lechu, I address you with an open letter as I am motivated by cares for the most essential matters of Solidarity. Three years ago, on April 3, the Founding Committee for Free Trade Unions was made on the coast. For many years we had observed the egoism and arbitrariness of the administration and the workers' helplessness. The main source of evil I have seen is the degradation of a society paralyzed with fear. Breaking through the fear barrier, the ability to formulate and defend our own views and to organize in order to defend them—these were the main features of free trade unions in which we were both active.

The achievement of these aims called for cooperation of the intelligentsia and workers. From the time of the rise of KOR, the period of isolation of these social strata was over. The period of isolated protests by these social strata—like the intelligentsia's in

1968 and the workers' in 1970—was over. Our activity was parallel to KOR's, for we thought it our duty to defend each individual prosecuted for his/her views. This was an elementary condition of our activity.

I was always in favor of telling people the whole truth. Everybody who wanted to work for us had to know what he risked and what our aims were. We had a profoundly religious Anna Walentynowicz and an atheist party member Bogdan Lis, and a KOR member Bogdan Borusewicz. We talked to everybody. We have never promised people too much. We said that they would achieve as much as they could win themselves. We had also said that nobody can give democracy to somebody else, that democracy lies in everybody's hand. Maybe this is why people believed us. They believed us in the August strike period and this is why Solidarity came about. How distant it seems now, this period of leaflet distribution, from the point of a huge official mass organization with activists, funds, government negotiations. It is clear that Solidarity realizes the values of free trade unions and that it is Poland's historical chance and hope—a trade union and a movement of moral revolution which has become the foundation of all social transformation. Each shadow cast upon the union aims painfully against the hearts of the Poles. Inner democracy is the need of our union. An antidemocratic environment, external threats, constant struggles and tension—all this makes one inclined, on all levels of union activity, to reject or leave democratic principles. But if our union fights with the methods taken over from our enemies—we have to lose.

It is my duty to speak of it, for my name apart from yours, for the name of Anna Walentynowicz and some others became the symbol for those who fought for a new union in the August struggle. It was a coincidence—our merits are not larger than the merits of others, but we are endowed with a grater responsibility in view of tolerating a situation in which admiration for symbols has allowed us to replace the democratic rules of union activity with our own personal arbitrary decisions.

Let us face it: the message of March 31 on delaying the strike meant practically its calling off. Without evaluating your decision on objective grounds, let me notice that we were not entitled to make it. If negotiations with the government continued to crawl, we should have called a session of the National Coordinating Commission. I am co-responsible for what happened next. Let us bypass the subjective reasons for what happened—the truth is that the two of us broke union democracy. We did not prevent the autocratic decision from being made without asking for the advice of a statutory organ of the union. I know that both of us can find thousands of explanations for what happened and why. But I also know that inner-union democracy is necessary. It is conditioned by a complete openness of everything and a multisided flow of information, and it is buried with a stifling of criticism and censoring of union periodicals. Each member of a union has to preserve the right to criticize even after a decision has been made by the union. Union discipline calls for subordination to decisions made by the union, but leaves one the right to a separate opinion on the subject. This is what makes us different from totalitarian organizations.

However, criticism of a decision we made as a result of the meager results of negotiations with the government provides a starting point for an action by enemies of Solidarity or by naive ones. We are being defended against illusory enemies from KOR. The meaning of this action is obvious—they want to make us quarrel among ourselves and to make us split. We are to agree to repress our activists and experts who stem from KOR. We are, of course, the next ones in turn. On my part I would like to say that I do not want such a defense. I do not need letters and telegrams which support the negotiating group. I read those with distaste. I hope you do, too. I say that criticism of a chairman or deputy chairman is a normal phenomenon. Otherwise the union will be autocratically ruled. Elected statutory bodies will lose their meaning. Decisive influence will be exercised by officials and advisers who are not controlled and not burdened with responsibility, thus being free to manipulate. In order to protect our union from running into a dead end street, from losing those values which we had fought for, it has to be said aloud.

As a deputy chairman of the National Coordinating Commission I feel co-responsible. Therefore I resigned on April 1. This was not a desertion—I am taking it back under the influence of the decision made by the National Coordinating Committee. I will act as long as the same NCC wills me to do so. I will resign when democratic values, in the name of which I had created this union, are betrayed. I count on the same declaration from you, Lechu.—Andrzej Gwiazda."

To which Walesa replied:

"You have written an open letter to me and reminded me of a joint struggle, the free trade unions, the August strike and Solidarity. I do not have to be reminded—I remember it well. I want the same I wanted then—I want Poland to be Poland and I want life to be bearable in our country. Solidarity should help in achieving that.

You are sore that our last talks with the government did not succeed and that the aftermath was mixed. I could point out that you are at least co-responsible and I could remind you what you thought and said in Warsaw. But I do not reject responsibility myself. I am convinced that the agreement signed with the government on March 30 was the best solution for the country and that we won what we could have won then. More important is that we lost nothing.

We made a decision to call NCC on Monday, not Tuesday. I think still that it was the only decision possible under the circumstances and I do not understand why you changed your mind about it. The decision did not destroy the conditions for union democracy, but created them.

Democracy is vital for our union. Therefore I insist that all elections are always performed in the foreseen date-lines. Only thus can our union secure leadership trusted by workers and feeling a responsibility to those who elected them. I am not very good in theoretical thinking, but this seems to me the most important thing in democracy.

I think that the people who care for the future of our country and the strength of our union should work in order to increase the share of the union's activities in the life of the country and to increase the union's unity. Open letters we can write when we retire. By the way, I wanted to retire already, to leave the leading post in the union. But I came to the conclusion that I am not allowed to do it as long as there is a possibility that the union can fall victim to adventurism or irresponsibility. I think that I can still do something for the country and for the union with courage and reason. I wish you the same. Lech Walesa."

The Poznan regional periodical of Solidarity added the following comment of its own:

"Gwiazda, apart from Lech Walesa and Anna Walentynowicz, is the outstanding figure in our union. His signatures are placed under the documents which founded Solidarity, his face is visible in all photographs, in all films which registered the most important events of the recent history of Poland. Everybody who listened to the talks between the striking commission and government commission in August 1980 knows how much we owe to the knowledge, courage, uncompromising attitude, and openess of Andrzej Gwiazda.

Everybody who follows the successive contacts of Solidarity with the authorities knows that these features of Gwiazda have often helped us and that successive stormy sessions of the National Coordination Committee confirmed that the exceptionality of Gwiazda is an exceptionality of his personality and not of any rights nor privileges that he might acquire. In the period of preparedness for the general strike many individuals expressed doubts about the share of some leaders in the political decision making. We conveyed a few days ago decisions made by shipyard workers with respect to Anna Walentynowicz. We reminded our readers about Anna's history. One of the regional leaders charged us with tendentious propaganda. I think that he objected to our criticism of the shipyard's decision about Anna Walentynowicz. Well, the comparison of her life story and of this decision, the very comparison of facts, does not mean that we object to the decision—all we want is to make people think and reflect. Hiding facts, distorting them, and being willing to promote one's own "uniquely proper" interpretation is the standing property of government mass media.

...Lech Walesa is a man whose activities and authority have gone beyond inner union matters and have to be assessed in terms of the state, nation and society.

However, he is also our colleague, a living, creative human individual and any attempts to put him beyond the rules of union activity are as a matter of fact attempts to close him out of union life. Solidarity cannot allow for such a careless loss of individuals who are vital for its organization."

The letter exchange between Walesa and Gwiazda was indicative of the fact that there were huge differences of opinion between various groups within Solidarity with respect to the general strike.

I think that Walesa was right, and that much more was won with the threat of the strike than could possibly have been won with the strike itself, where the major victory, the most vital one since August 1980, was the registration of the trade union Solidarity for individual peasants. But I can also admire the attitude of the other leaders who stuck to democracy and did not allow Walesa to become a symbol and idol.

The political situation in Poland after this last confrontation became very complex—there was a withdrawal from terror on the part of the ruling class, but there was also a growing uneasiness as to the possible controllability of the spontaneous events.

The tactic, probably suggested by Kania after the provocation of Bydgoszcz misfired, was to stage a "renewal of the party." Leaders visited large factories and pretended that they took what workers had to say seriously, and that the coming congress of the party could still be prepared successfully by the working-bodies of the ruling class members, by coordinators, functionaries, managers, etc. The plan looked promising.

Prime minister and minister of defense Jaruzelski's pleas for a moratorium on strikes could have been taken seriously had it turned out that the police were not free to terrorize, but there could be no guarantee that Solidarity would stick to a moratorium which would mean failure to defend its members. Kania was still manipulating the ruling class which was split into fractions and deprived of any coherence except for the inner party loyalties of lobbies and gene-ration groups. But the problem was that investigation showed that if truly democratic congress elections were held, not more than a tiny fraction of the elite would survive the new spirit of the citizens. To hold a communist party congress immediately, which was what all workers demanded, meant to throw more that 80% of the ruling class members out of the government. On the other hand, not to call the congress would mean that nobody but the ruling class would be left in the communist party, which would thus collapse into a marginal tourist attraction deprived of any real significance.

The decision to hold the congress in late July was the compromise agreed upon, and an attempt to win gains during the delay and to prevent such huge sacrifices of the ruling class by a showcase sacrifice of some top former leaders. From this point of view it is interesting to consider the following discussion in the

Central Committee—75 days before the special party congress scheduled for late July, and a month after Torun party members spontaneously elected "horizontal structures of the party" and their own secretary, disregarding the official one, and a few days after another demonstration of Solidarity's strength occurred during the May 3rd celebrations.

The fragments quoted are taken from speeches made, among others, by: Mieczyslaw Rakowski—the Deputy Prime Minister, who, since 1957, was the editor-in-chief of the weekly "Polityka," which is read by liberal managers, medium party echelons, and some intellectuals. Rakowski was always very loyal to the ruling class, but had to wait until 1980 to become eligible for top posts—partly due to his international contacts (for example, he went to Davos to negotiate with Poland's creditors) and to a general belief that he could talk to Solidarity. Kazimierz Kakol—a former minister of religion famous for heading the 1968 Gomulka propaganda campaign bi-weekly, the ultra-conservative "Law and Life," and a dean of the journalist faculty of Warsaw University; virulently anti-Jewish and linked to secret police fractions, he was always eager to call for law and order. Absent from public life in the seventies, especially in the second part of the decade, he reemerged on TV as a promising warrior for the cause of the ruling class. Andrzej Werblan—a member of the Political Bureau, educated and considered to be one of the stoutest stalinists, albeit an intelligent one—definitely on the outs now, but formerly a head of Polish sciences and a prestigious sponsor of the party school of the humanities. Stefan Olszowski—a member of the Political Bureau, formerly exiled by Gierek to an embassy in East Berlin, in alliance with Tadeusz Grabski, spectacularly punished by Gierek for open criticism in 1978. A stalinist, but also an intelligent one.

Rakowski: The members of party headquarters have finally visited the factories, where the heart of the party strikes. They have heard many bitter words and evaluations of their activities. Obviously they deserved it, for it is hard to imagine that a few hundred thousand party members were incited by some sordid forces to indulge in malicious criticism. However, this way of rationalizing is dear to many comrades...(It is clear that Rakowski is performing the expiation ritual, but it is also clear that he is too much of a follower of the former political rhetoric of the ruling class, and far from clear that the factories will allow the ritual to be effective.)

Kakol: Torun should be viewed in a principled manner. The party organs there are headed by a man who has been exiled from the party. Discussions have accompanied this exile, but the decision has been made. The presence of famous party functionaries on this "fractional conventicle" will certainly not serve the cause of stimulating the reflection, will certainly not prevent the activity which should, I feel, be called openly with its name. (Kakol refers, of course, to the famous Leninist refusal to acknowledge the right of party members to have differing views, to defend them and to form fractions within the party)

Werblan: Most of the people who sit with us in this room will definitely finish their political activity on this top level at the ninth congress. I am convinced that it is a duty of every member of the Central Committee, also of the members who have to leave, to contribute according to his knowledge and experiences to the progress in the process of renewal. If we all had this attitude, our party way would be much simpler. (Apart from the note of resignation there is probably a plea that former ruling class members should not be forgotten.)

Kruk: Our selective approach to history, our tradition bound manner of talking about partnership with the Soviet Union, all this has added to the hundreds of years of distrust among our nations. True presentation and explanation of various problems, political and economic cooperation are not favored by our propaganda. (Although the speech is still cloaked in doublespeak, there is an admission that there is bad propaganda and a fresh distrust in relations with the Soviets.)

Olszowski: Along with the crisis background there is a renewal of the rightist, anarchist, nationalist and anti-Soviet tendencies. Their followers attempt to write their counterrevolutionary interests and demands into the working class demands and interests. They disseminate information whose only aim is to make society unstable and anxious and to turn social energies against socialist order. (This is a straightforward threat: a promise that all that is "truly working class interest" will be recognized by Olszowski, while all that is not will be punished especially those who oppose the secret police—"socialist order"—and those who oppose censorship thus "making society anxious and turning it against socialist order.")

Jerzy Wiatr: The danger of revisionism is constant and it usually occurs at historically decisive points. But one should speak equally strongly about another danger—on abusing the slogan of re-visionism, on abusing this weapon with which so many concepts in theory, politics, economy—even very useful concepts—have been shot down.

Jerzy Urbanski: The political enemy has brought the charge that all people of top posts have dirty hands. It is true that in that climate there were many individuals starting to get rich at any cost. But there is too much stress on a single punishment—exiling from the party and delegating to the prosecutors' office. We do it, too, but only when there is enough reason...

Josef Blajet: In the ninth plenum announcement there is a mention of a necessity to talk within the party. This is correct, but who will talk to the central authorities of our party and to the regional authorities in local committees?

I think that it would be fair to say that the ruling class is split with respect to the degree of liberty it should grant to inner-party democracy (mostly being afraid to allow it), but it is never split with respect to the necessity of fighting Solidarity and maintaining the whole institutional framework of their class rule. The problem they see is the probability of successful ritualization—Rakowski seems to believe in it, Olszowski does not.

Chapter Eleven

The Church of the Oppressed

The standard image of religion as an opiate of the people does not hold in Poland. Opiates of the people have been produced by media wizards and coordinated by party propaganda bosses—the opiates produced were obviously improbable, nobody believed in them, but they did function.

However, because they functioned in a primitive manner, backed by the readiness to employ terror and state violence, they did strange things to the materialist world outlook they allegedly incorporated. Since the growing awareness of class divisions in Poland's state socialist society rendered the ideological appeal of the (propaganda disseminated) materialist world outlook invalid— what attraction can there be in an ideology which boils down to the powerful getting richer?—the need grew for another ideology which would at least leave spiritual values intact, if not actively promote them.

The ruling class's ideology was invalid for at least two reasons. One was that it was perfectly clear that the only rationale behind the "world forces of socialism" was the pursuing of statist policies by Soviet Russia and that everything else must yield to that. It is quite possible, for instance, that the Soviets are disappointed that the Polish communists have not been hung by the masses as this would be a negligible sacrifice for them and a perfect reason to intervene. The second was that the making of the ruling class's position required a reduction of general upward mobility and living standards and, most of all, of any feeling of autonomy and part-icipation in decision making by most working people. Thus statist ideology was backed by no real promise, and therefore sounded quite empty. This was not, in itself, dangerous for the ruling class—ideology does not have to be believed to be functional; it can simply monopolise and distort discourse. But it meant that if the working class did arrange some mass action and coordinated it according to some new values—then the ideology fostered by the ruling class would be on the refuse heap, completely unusable.

And this was indeed the case. The ideology of Solidarity is in the making and it is very hard to say what the precise outcome will be. However, in the hot days of the August confrontation it was catholic Christian phraseology and catholic church liturgy and iconography which dominated the scene. Why?

One obvious answer is that Poland has been predominantly catholic since the 18th century and has remained so until now. But there is also another, more recent reason for this massive employment of religious symbols and for the feeling of national mobilization and spiritual strength issuing from celebrations of Holy Masses by the striking workers. I want to make this perfectly clear: the religious symbolism has had no magical function—the workers did not present ostentatious celebrations to ensure their protection by Holy Forces. The witnesses describe it in the following way:

"In the religious practices of the workers there is nothing ostentatious. There is dignity and a self-control of emotions—although in difficult moments the theme of prayer and religious song recurs constantly. In the press and in media releases the world saw people kneeling on both sides of Gate No. 2 during the Holy Mass. International public opinion was already used to the fact that it is not the communist authorities who tolerate the believers, but

Christians who tolerated the authorities and construct socialism together."

There was, of course, no historical necessity for the catholic church to provide an ideology and reinforcement for the emerging class of state employees, the workers. It might have been very much the same as it is nowadays in most West European countries, where workers are not primarily Christian in their world outlook. But on top of the ideological attractiveness of Christianity as a value system which stresses an individuality so often trodden down by the emerging ruling class, there came a very palpable and lasting impression that the church itself was being repressed and per-secuted—the catholic university of Lublin was systematically crippled in its international contacts and national publicity, catholic publications were limited in scope and heavily censored in spite of the fact that 90% of the country was catholic—and this helped create an immense support for the church by the whole population.

When the ruling class, following the policy of atheization demanded by Moscow, refused to allow the church to construct new buildings, the population started illegal construction sites and defended them. Peasants started converting regular household buildings, ostensibly erected for domestic purposes, into churches. Can you imagine a better symbol of national support for Chris-tianity than private homes becoming churches and priests along with people defending their rites against the secret police, ad-ministrators and party bosses? The lines of class division coincided with the lines of ideological religious division. Whoever was in the ruling class had to pretend total devotion to a materialist world outlook—pretend is a good description, as most of those people visited churches or priests if they felt ill or threatened. Whoever was in the exploited class clung to the catholic faith. The neglect of the catholic life became a precondition for successful upward political mobility which in turn made the church a real church of the oppressed.

Thus August 1980 observers were right in noting:

"The strikers made their choice of a moral guarantor of the truth and right of their demands—they chose somebody who could not be subordinated by "historical reasons," "class interests" or hard arguments of military alliances. They chose God... This was visibly repeated in all the images and crosses which accompanied the strike, in the daily Holy Mass close to Gate No. 2, and in the rosary that Walesa had around his neck when signing the final agreement. The religious terms in which the workers' protest was couched made outsiders wonder. This was clear from the number of pictures in the foreign press showing workers who kneeled on the street during the strikers' Mass. This religiosity made the rebellion manifest and endowed it with peace and dignity. There was nothing of a revengeful striving for fanatical confrontation. One can say today, carrying under one's eyelids the image of these days and grasping their most significant features, that John Paul II had left his imprint on the August days. These had followed his suggested poetics: of confronting the most difficult matters while at the same time linking decisiveness and openess, as manifested in his words and deeds, in his striving for a profound ethicization of the human world."

The church of the oppressed was the frame of reference when a huge mass mobilization was needed and it was truly the backbone of mass symbolism. It has to be said, at the same time, that the church of the oppressed has also won another label which it owes to the repressions of the ruling class, namely, that it is not a political force, i.e. it does not attempt to formulate earthly policy and to shape social attitudes in the political sphere. This has left the church pure of any charges that it pursues its own policy of church self-interest or religious propaganda. It is indeed purely moral, providing spiritual support for the working masses—and that is something else that the catholic church owes to the Polish ruling class.

The further development of the church and church ideology in the ongoing class struggle in People's Poland is uncertain. It is quite possible that the ruling class will try to profit from the relative interest of the church in stablity in order to curb a possible development of the left radical political parties or semi-party groups by sponsoring the growth of Christian-based political organizations, thus trying to buy the working class off with concessions to the church and to prevent the development of radical class awareness.

However, this is by no means certain, as the decomposition within the ruling class may be too advanced to allow for any coherent policy. On the other hand the church itself is not anxious to become a political factor, aware that this would immediately ruin much of its appeal. The papal speech to the delegation of Solidarity in Rome was a masterpiece of this profound conviction that the role of the Polish catholic church must be support of a moral and indirect kind:

"The making of Solidarity is a very important development. It demonstrates that all the working people in Poland, in various professions, the intelligentsia, and also rural workers—are ready to assume a responsibility for the dignity and value of their work performed in various places in our homeland...

The common good of society can be reduced ultimately to what each man in a given society is and how he works and lives.

Hence your self-governing activity has—and should always have—clear reference to the whole social morality. It refers primarily to the morality linked to a sphere of labor, to a relation between an employer and an employee, but also to many other spheres of morality—personal, environmental, professional, and political. I think that at the roots of your huge initiative which has been born in the weeks of the August struggle in the coast and in other great centers of Polish labor, there is some mass attempt to lift the moral level of society. Without this lifting there can be no true progress. And Poland has a right to true progress—the same right as any other nation, and somehow a particular one—since it was paid for by huge historical experiences and directly with vast suffering in WWII..."

To put it in other words: the Pope realized that the reason for Poland's unparalleled lack of decline of religiosity with the growth of urbanization and industrialization was associated with the fact of the independence of the church from the state and superiority of its untainted ideology (untainted, that is, by services rendered to the ruling class). The language of religious symbolism, expressed so clearly by the kneeling strikers in Gdansk, is the only language left in which the whole nation can express its emancipatory ideals. As Michael Szkolny put it, while noticing that due to the role of church ideology Poland's catholics could find the religious faith attractive even though in most social matters they reject the Episcopate's stand (contraception, for instance, and abortion):

"Whatever the actual politics of the Episcopate, the church's privileged "independence" from the state has meant that religious symbolism is now the only language capable of expressing the ideas of social emancipation: a language symbolizing at once the continuity of the Polish cultural heritage, the ancient struggle for national independence, and the identity of the individual...

In the wake of the profound economic changes in post-war Poland there developed a real change in the social content of religion. This was accompanied by the rise among the new urban masses of a strong current of subconscious protestantism. The failure of the church hierarchy to adapt its rigid orthodoxy to the radically changed social conditions led urban catholics of all classes to reject those aspects of religious dogma which they found intolerable, while in no way allowing this rejection to weaken their religious faith.

This phenomenon is reflected in contemporary attitudes towards such questions as divorce, contraception and sexual mores, which are similar to those prevailing in most protestant countries of Northern Europe. At the same time, the decline of episcopal authority, combined with the continuing power of religious symbolism, led to a proliferation of small groups of radical catholic intellectuals espousing various beliefs, often imported from other cultures. The emergence of this catholic underground in the sixties and seventies, and its interaction with the left intelligentsia, has been one of the crucial factors in the development of an intellectual opposition since 1968. This collaboration has been more fruitful at a practical than an ideological level. In practical politics it has been conducted according to the principle of absolute solidarity in the face of a totalitarian power."

The above remarks are an accurate reflection of the situation of the church and religion in Poland. It should also be added that Cardinal Wyszynski's speech, broadcast by Polish TV in order to pacify the strikers in August 1980, (which also criticized government, but those parts were censored, resulting in the workers' disbelieving his TV appearance) has had no effect. Holy Mass was duly celebrated, but a breakdown of the strike because of the urgent appeal of the church was not in sight.

This is the limit of the church's influence upon the workers.

Chapter Twelve

Nation, Class and State

It has rarely been discussed in the marxist literature of either the past or the present why the history of labor movements is replete with acts of inexplicable working class loyalty to national symbols and causes. Early in this century, for example, labor movements in many countries voted for war credits and armaments for their national armies thus enabling their governments to wage WWI.

Theoretically speaking a standard marxian analysis cannot explain national allegiances interfering with "proletarian internationalism" and even class struggle within each state without resorting to convenient schemes of "betrayal of internationalist class interests," and this parallels its inability to explain Stalinism apart from a description of a particularly vicious personality grabbing unexpected opportunities. However, leaving behind standard marxist preconceptions about the dominance of economic relations, it is sufficient to reflect on the pattern of socialization in modern societies to notice that one's "national community" is by far the most important locus of control in the coordination of overall socialization. Education, the army, the penal system, and "culture" in general, are all organized on a national level and national reference is their broadest common denominator.

Of course this phenomenon is by no means new: as early as the beginning of the 18th century, when Poland was still a vast Commonwealth and "democracy" of the nobility, it was not uncommon for the nobility, burgers and peasants alike to start joint "confederate" actions in order to prevent blatant violation of domestic political processes by foreign powers. From a class-focused point of view such cooperation was definitely an aberration, for the oppressed peasants were uniting with their exploiters and demanding restoration of a domestic political order under which they were the most exploited victims!

Yet, this is reality, and no degree of sympathy for marxian theory should prevent us from trying to understand it. Some contemporary authors do suggest that matters of culture, nationalism, and religion belong to the sphere of the "community" and that this sphere should be distinguished as relatively autonomous from both economic and political distinctions and struggles, and hence from the prerogatives enjoyed by various classes and political strata with respect to the economy and state.

Although interesting, even this suggestion seems not to take things far enough. The stability and endurance of a national community and the willingness to adhere to national values far surpass any loyalty felt for state organizations and—as has already been mentioned—for class generated political programs. Indeed the special and extreme stability of nationalism merits a special explanation. Perhaps this explanation can be found in the existence of an everpresent national element in a majority of the socializing influences encountered by the individual in the course of his or her development.

Joseph Stalin, who wrote an occasional theoretical pamphlet (or ordered its writing on his behalf) commented upon the national question and came up with a semi-definition of a nation as a community bound by common language, territory, historical continuity, and shared traditions. This definition does not hold water—languages shift and change, sometimes they are extinguished or kept "inactive" in social life; territorial transformations are always an element of historical process and shared traditions are subscribed to by groups which do not necessarily share them in a national sense—or they are invented sometimes even for ideological purposes. Yet Stalin's common sense definition does reveal two vital features of every nationalism: a) a set of demarcation criteria for the "in-group" which are vast enough to include most of the people an individual may interact with in the course of his or her life (provided that international contacts are not the daily bread of the average citizen—which they seldom are, and which was especially true before the advent of mass cultural pilgrimages under the banner of "tourism"); and b) a set of demarcation criteria for the "out-group" which are narrow enough to identify most neighboring populations organized within different political state organizations and competing with one's own nation-state in various respects.

The socialization programs that go beyond national bounds are few and far between. Christianity and socialism, the most famous instances of such attempts, went—after a period of struggle and uncertainty—national. The appearance of national churches and the birth of Protestantism have their analogues in the appearance of a diversity of socialist movements and their adaptation to the national political, economic, and social processes proper for each country. Socialization patterns have a compelling force which historically trims every universal design to national frameworks.

The whole period of the Cold War may be considered a period of extensive nationalization of problems which appeared as a result of the coexistence of two socio-economic systems. It is also interesting that the two superpowers which trimmed their activities to the requirements of their national frameworks are not even nations in the traditional meaning of the word. Both are conglomerates of various ethnic groups, but this does not prevent them from behaving in a typically "nationalistic" manner. Does this mean that nation focused socialization brings about inherent restraints which nobody—so far—has been able to supersede? Or that coordination of socializing influences on a national scale must feed the excessive "power" of one's national reference, a power which is taken for granted, rarely analyzed, and almost never counteracted? Indeed, why should one counteract habits, customs, and innocent patterns of thinking and acting which are so dear to one's memory? These questions are very complex and no sound theoretical answer has been provided for them.

In the case of Poland it seems that the loss of an independent Polish state, which did not survive the end of the 18th Century and did not reappear on the map of Europe until 1918, has caused a profound intensification of the national frame of reference. The fact that Polish Romantic poets had to replace society's lawyers, teachers, and politicians shifted the whole burden of socialization to national culture and away from practical activities of administration. The durability of this national pattern has been proven in the years since World War II. Sociological research carried on by Stefan Nowak since 1957 has confirmed a vague feeling on the part of Polish intellectuals that the majority of Poles view the state and the "state-leading groups" as historically coincidental, much as Americans view the successive groups of victorious politicians arriving with every new president. Devotion and loyalty go to the nation, the national community and tradition, which are felt to be definitely superior to the political organization of society. Thus what may appear as a purely demagogical slogan—"We have signed the agreement, as a Pole does with a Pole"—which appeared after the Gdansk, Szczecin and Jastrzebie agreements had been signed, was actually an expression of loyalty to Poland on both sides of the class barricades. This loyalty to the national heritage which surpasses differences of class and politics is by no means an unmixed blessing. Certainly patriotism is very often abused for reasons of State propaganda. However, history also demonstrates that patriotism is not always an easy target for state propaganda, and that manipulations are sometimes clearly detectible.

In actual historical process, classes, nations and states are interacting organisms with individuals shifting their loyalty and membership between classes and states, but rarely so between nations. This, I think, is the basic factor responsible for the durability of nationalism. One may change his or her class loyalty, or one may think one has to change it—and the same holds true for states, which are by no means always loved by their citizens and occasionally left or betrayed. However it is very rarely that one changes one's nation: it is hard to rewrite the process by which one learned to speak, read and write, the process by which one underwent socialization in the most primary groups with which one ever makes acquaintance. One of the most important factors in the development of the USA as a strong industrial society was its ability to incorporate new citizens and new members of all social classes without depriving them of all their national bonds, which, however, were politically and socially neutralized—at least in the vast majority of cases.

Thus, unless new means of socialization appear or new necessities press us to de-individualize upbringing—and all attempts so far have been disastrous—the nation is here to stay, for better or worse.

The abolition of classes is already a well established political, social and economic program however difficult it may have proved to be to carry this program through. The abolition of states is a dream which is certainly perceived with some sympathy by most people, though there is so far no practical alternative to the state. On the other hand, the abolition of nations, attempted at present mainly by "existing socialist" imperialism is a project that promises to provoke resistance on an unforeseen scale.

Chapter Thirteen

Women's Liberation

There is no Women's Liberation movement as such in People's Poland, nor has there ever been any organization which tried to achieve political aims by organizing women as a separate group.

A general impression of sexual injustice prevailing in the broad left coalitions of the European "people's fronts" of the thirties prompted the ruling class to make a "Woman's League" after the war, but it has vegetated until today, almost totally forgotten by now. Indeed, it turned out that this "Women's League" was only another lever in the state's machinery of control, this time via propaganda about sexual liberation. But the only liberation there was consisted of token women who were prominently displayed in some political decision making bodies, but always as tokens only, without any coherent women-centered policy, nor any coherent personal policy at all.

However, there was true liberation of women as independent social agents of change, as individuals. It occurred in two ways: first, there was an immense participation of women in the general upward mobility due to industrialization, and some traditionally male dominated professions had their sexual exclusiveness broken down under the pressure of a labor supply which was partly female and by some side-effects of state propaganda, which boasted of a total lack of sexual discrimination. This boasting did result in an increased labor participation by women even though it didn't in any significant way reduce the household patterns of women's work nor provide a more comprehensive program of relieving household maintenance people from their duties; and, second, there was an immense urbanization which contributed to a more independent, less community and tradition bound world outlook, leading to changes in personal plans, including sexual mores. New legislation was basically favorable for women but the fact that it was introduced just before a popular movement to obtain it might have started helped disarm potential rallying points for women's political movements.

However, the injustice of sexually determined social divisions of labor is preserved in the structure of household duties in most family types in Poland, and aggravated by market shortages. In view of this, most of the ideological formulations resembling women's liberation slogans stem from professional women, predominantly in the arts, journalism and science. The injustice comes, of course, from family role patterns. However, this is not an easy question to address. On the one hand it is still true in most Polish families that one expects the mother to be more active in household duties and child care than the father—although there is a growing tendency in the younger generation not to allow this pattern to set in. But on the other hand, one also has to realize that what is true about the church developments is also true about family transformations.

The transformation from a male-centered, male-dominated family household as the basic production unit of society towards a family as a small unit of partners of both sexes plus children who are jointly taken care of (while money is also earned by both sides, often with the woman earning more) has already occurred for many, and is well advanced in most city families. However, this development has been kept almost totally at the grass roots level, and found little external expression. The reason is clear: facing the threat of a totalitarian state, the family must become a solidarity outpost, a very compact and mutually loyal group, and must deal with other families in the same spirit of solidarity in the face of the totalitarian threat.

The family has thus acquired an identification function which could not be delegated to any larger agency because of their being controlled universally by the ruling class. In a questionnaire fed to samples of Polish students of both sexes in the late seventies most of the respondents answered that social life and political loyalties either were of no interest to them or could be dealt with with the help of a few propaganda formulae nobody believed in anyway. On the other hand all respondents praised highly the value of family and friendship relations, and of intensive interactions within family and friendship circles.

This leads us to the following conclusions: even if the early attempts at state propaganda backed an ostentatious liberation of women only to the extent of freeing them to become part of the labor force in the nation (though a very considerable part), it was not totally useless, for it formed a precondition of actual liberation in their personal lives due to the new partner-like status they might claim in family relations. On the other hand, when the structure and pattern of family life began to change and women became partners, this phenomenon was not reflected in any new ideological formation or any new suggestion of what a women's movement might fight for, because the family became an oasis in society, where a refuge against the claims of the totalitarian monster could be found.

This is a very inexact comment. Let us try to probe more deeply into: a) the daily situation of women in Poland and b) the ideologies of feminism as developed by professionally active and "ideologically" aware Polish women. The daily life of most Polish women has not been a very happy one over the past few years (1978-81), partly due to food shortages, and rationing has only partly alleviated this burden. One may say that the difficult situation with market supplies partly threw Polish families back into the traditional male-centered pattern. Not because families went back to a male-centered model, but because women had to devote more time to daily chores and routines, so that women resumed their previous household-centered position. So it was not a male-domination backlash per se, but a "more labor from the wife" phenomenon which occurred.

The overwhelming support of women for Solidarity—both by their direct participation as workers and by their indirect support expressed in public, stemmed from the fact that women recognized a number of postulates voiced by Solidarity as postulates of their own. The demand for increased legal protection of mothers who were employed before pregnancy occurred was an instance of this bond. One should understand that a demand that working women should be given a chance to obtain full salary for a year after childbirth and then given an option of either a return to their previous post or another period of leave, up to two additional years, also partly compensated by the employer, is not an extravagant demand, and neither does it mean that a woman is being driven away from the labor force to household activities. It means that the importance of the family is being recognized and that an option is given for a woman to work, paid, in her family home if she so chooses. This is vital. Neither unqualified support for a family-oriented model of woman, nor for a labor-profession-oriented woman can be totally justified on feminist grounds in the Polish context.

Meanwhile, the fourth issue of the national weekly of Solidarity brought the following report "24 hours from a woman's life" filed from Lodz, the largest textile center in the county, where female labor prevails:

"When her older daughter was three, and the younger, one, she started working because they could not make ends meet from a single salary. She worked in the three-shift system, her husband in the two-shift one, and that was convenient, for it would always leave one of them with the kids. For instance, she left for second shift at one p.m., and her husband returned at half past two, so that the girls were only alone for an hour and a half. Even then, in spite of her putting the girls to sleep before leaving, her husband had once seen the girls on a window sill and barely managed to catch them (they live on the fourth floor)....Almost all of the women working in the weaving section (ironically called the "finishing off" section) have varicose veins, some become deaf, some are allergic, and some display all of these.... She is presently working on a "malivat" type of machine which is ok compared to the weaving section and she would not complain was it not for night shifts....

Last week she had night shifts.

She leaves the plant at six a.m., and sometimes before she reaches home she buys bread and cottage cheese, so it is seven when she gets back. She wakes the children up, prepares breakfast, sees the youngest one, a boy, to school. Then she sleeps for a little while on the couch. She does not even undress—at ten twenty she has to run to school again to see him back home. After he returns sleep is out of the question: mummy this, mummy that, give me some bread and jam. "God, where can I find jam?"—but then she relaxes, the boy is small and falls ill very easily, has just come back from the hospital after jaundice, he should eat well. "Go play with the kids outside, dinner will be ready in a minute."

She cooks soup or a main course for dinner, either this or that. Two courses she prepares only on Sundays, for a day of feast is a day of feast.

After dinner she does some washing, some sewing, or shopping, for sometimes food appears before the shops close. Detergents, shampoo, rarely meat—but the day before yesterday she got some beef and a pound of sausages. Her younger girl laughed and kissed the sausages.

As far as shopping goes she does not use her kids. Other women send their kids to stand in shopping lines, but she has never done it. She buys almost everything, for her husband says that he has no patience to do it and would rather not eat than wait in lines.

Before evening she gets some rest but the kids go to and fro and switch the TV on, while her husband noisily prepares supper. "We almost cease to talk normally, just arguments and shouts."

She dreams of a sanatorium. A doctor whom she had even consulted privately, advised her to cease worrying, to sleep a lot, to take long walks, to think of pleasant things.

That is good. She could not bring herself to tell him how much she really sleeps, to tell him that whenever she sits down her head falls on her shoulder, that when she napped one day, the kids started a fire in the kitchen and the cupboard burnt, and that when she napped a few minutes before Christmas somebody stole her carpet left in front of the apartment door, which made her unhappy the whole Christmas through.

Yes, but she would like to visit a sanitorium apart from her leave. All her leaves she spends with her mother in Mazurian lake district. Her mother is old and ill and she says that she will start taking holiday tours when her mother dies. Every year they visit her mother's village, but this is not a proper rest. She does what she always does at home—cooks, washes, sweeps, but does not have to hurry to work and she can sleep as much as she wants to.

She has not been to the cinema for years, she does not care much for TV—till August 1980 she just watched family programs and American movies, to see what others live like. But now she is an avid TV viewer to follow the news about Solidarity.

"I am interested in everything, in what went on in Bielsko, Radom, Suwalki, whether they strike agreements with the authorities or not. And I pray that they win. Also films of the "Workers' Cases" series, and by the way, do you know why they did not show "Man of Marble" on TV Sunday?"

She even went to see the film on workers from Gdansk in the cinema on Sunday. A truly beautiful movie, this is what they said in her factory and in her husband's factory, too. "I like the way they stood fast by this lady that was fired from the shipyards, and Walesa who talked real hard to the prime minister, and was not afraid, and this Holy Mass under the gate was very moving, too. Jesus, I never dreamed to see something like that. When I was coming back home someone stole 500 zlotys from my purse but I did not regret this crowded streetcar ride back home."

She joined Solidarity for she is for justice and she would like the workers to have it better.

"People talk in our factory and in shop lines on making those people who ruined the country responsible, and on punishing them. I am for it, too, but I think that even if Solidarity succeeded only in getting free Saturdays, abolishment of the third shift, and paid maternity leaves for us it would already be very much. For women it would be a salvation. We would start living a human life."

The above story tells us about the daily toil of an average woman who enjoys the benefits of an independent job but at the same time looks to Solidarity to have her work ameliorated and her life made more easy and bearable. It shows how the development of a new family with its duties divided between the sexes has been obscured by the common front the family unit has to present vs. the state. It shows how female support for Solidarity arises from energies which under different circumstances could have gone into an independent female political movement.

The female story would be incomplete if one did not mention the life story of Anna Walentynowicz, whose firing became a direct signal to start the August 1980 strike in Gdansk, and whose life story was then—for professional women, especially in the media—a symbolic story of women's role in postwar Poland, and of the exploitation of their double labor. The story, as written by Hanna Krall, a famous journalist of "Polityka," was censored by the latter and appeared first in a clandestine publication in late 1980, and then, on January 11, 1981, in the catholic weekly, "Tygodnik Powszechny," which was not afraid to run the story, as opposed to "Polityka."

The story summarizes women's fate as a subplot of general social development since 1945. Stemming from the village poor, Walentynowicz became a shipyard worker in the early fifties, and for her excellent work she was sent over as one of the delegates to a Berlin youth festival where she disliked much of the propaganda. Then, also in the fifties, she took part in a session of state trade unions, where the sum of 3,000 zlotys was to be given away in prizes for the best workers. Because the trade union officials—the top three—decided that they had to repay themselves their losses in the lottery, they divided it all between themselves. Walentynowicz protested and was promptly interrogated by the secret police which accused her of listening to Radio Free Europe. She says it might have been the beginning of her present attitudes and her role in the making of independent trade unions. She was very active in December 1970. By October 1971 she was alone again—her son went to the army as a draftee and her husband died.

Sometime in 1978 she heard about independent trade unions from Western radio. The founders of coastal free trade unions were Krzysztof Wyszkowski who subsequently went to Warsaw, Andrzej Gwiazda, who is still in Solidarity, and Edwin Myszk, who turned out to be an agent of the security service, as was discovered later due to some minor case of petty theft from some shop.... This is how her daily work started, how she discussed her problems with new trade union people, how they tried to fight for even the smallest details, how they opposed inhuman treatment by management, how they were enraged by the way the privileged party and government owners of People's Poland behaved.

She had been refused entrance to her section of the shipyards, and then had been allowed back when the strike was already on. And in her description of what happened after the first tentative agreement with management, in the crucial moment of the whole strike, she tells about another woman, fragile Alina Piendowska, who is probably the major figure of the breakthrough decision to carry on:

"After long talks we compromised a little. But everything started getting vague again. Then we asked quite simply: will you hire us again or not? Leszek, too....In half an hour the personnel boss brought our employment papers in, the head manager had given us 1500 zlotys more per month. All the demands of the shipyard striking committee were met, others would be met in future. We thought it was a victory. We were leaving the building when Alinka Pienkowska, a small woman, very fragile and so courageous, started shouting "And what about those other people?! How shall we now look in the eyes of those who supported us in the city?!!!"

Alinka is a nurse in the shipyard hospital. She had always taken care of everything. So we rushed to the microphone to stop the people, while Leszek had already called the strike off. The microphones were switched off and only management broadcasts that the strike was over were heard. I started crying. People were leaving for home. Everything was falling to pieces. Then Alinka started running among the people asking the same questions. They stopped. Listened to her. Those, who had not left the shipyards yet, stayed. By Monday almost all came back. Today, two months since August, we all feel very tired. We work from nine in the morning till ten in the evening. We talk to people. We meet. Discuss. Difficulties that the government makes are also a pain—they disinform society, they talk to us in one way, in another to old trade unions, in another with their "mutants," the trustees of government. The national council of old trade unions disturbs us a lot, because they would like to rule the people but do not know what to stick too..."

The world symbolized the Polish August in images of Walesa and the Pope's portrait on the shipyard gate. However, it would be more appropriate to symbolize it with Anna Walentynowicz and Alina Pienkowska—the woman who sparked the fire and the woman who prevented it from going out too soon.

Chapter Fourteen

Class Compromise: How To Turn Nationalization Into Socialization

Nine months have elapsed since August 1980 and Poland, although still in a very grave economic situation, is no longer rocked by open conflict. The peasant Solidarity has been officially registered as a result of a nation-wide protest and there are preparations for a general strike following the ruling class's last attempt to stop Solidarity by naked police violence. Concentrated efforts of the ruling class, police provocateurs, and Soviet military exercises have failed to break the working class. Police brutality has been confronted by quiet but determined efforts to punish the policemen and to reform the judicial system. Political pressures have been countered by persistent and successful efforts to allow farmers to associate freely in their own version of Solidarity. The Soviet threat has been equally stubbornly yet peacefully countered by a nation-wide preparation for invasion—special handbooks, leaflets and instructions have been disseminated with instructions on what to do in case of military invasion, and Solidarity has switched its centers into the largest factories in the country, under the determined shield of the working class.

The retardation of social reconstruction—unavoidable in the face of the new political activity of the Polish working class—has produced only disasters for the ruling class. Even in the heart of the communist party the movement toward reform assumed the form of a demand for an extraordinary congress of the party (due in late July 1981—the longest officialdom could postpone it), and an open demand that the whole functionary body be changed, and that the new functionaries should be more controllable and stay in office no more than two terms.

What is the most urgent problem in the near future? It is the huge social reconstruction project which is slowly emerging from the turmoil of political struggle—the project to socialize the nationalized state socialist system. The reform required is twofold: first, it must be based on an effort to work out a mechanism for efficient social control of a centralized economic structure by making this structure subservient to the interests of the working class and making it impossible for the ruling class to reassert its power; and second, it requires a socialization of the nation, a process so far used only as an ideological excuse by the ruling class, but one which will presently be viewed as opening new alternatives and not just manipulating a closed number of old symbols by old rulers.

The socialization of the national state of Poland is the project which would have been called revolution, had not its political formula been so peaceful and so quietly enacted by very rational activities. It consists of:

a) dismantling the state's repressive machinery and subjecting it to regular democratic control to prevent a gradual renewal of the ruling class's ability to manipulate all social strata with threats of terror;

b) reconstructing democracy and especially directly democratic forms of control and coordination of all spheres of social life, to prevent a new ruling class gaining a monopoly of decision-making power;

c) working out a democratic means of running the state (understood to be the sole political framework of all political processes) which cannot be discarded at present for both internal and external reasons.

The above process has to take place in a very complex international setting. Poland has so far prudently avoided all forms of open conflict with allies and especially with the Soviet Union—all appearances of conflict came only from propaganda efforts of the Soviets to threaten political opponents of the ruling class, but have no other background. However, there is every possibility that a slow march of the Polish working class toward freedom and democracy will become a stimulating factor for reform movements in other state socialist countries—it is both a hope and a danger of the future developments in class struggle in state socialist societies.

The most hopeful scenario is that Poland will truly be left to decide its further course and that this will eventually lead to elaboration of a transitory form leading to a socialized national economy and national form of political organization.

A more somber scenario reflects the fears of the Polish working class that the international situation which brought us some breathing space in 1980 and continues to do so in 1981 can bring about a new threat in the near future. This new threat can only come from a new unlikely (and unholy) alliance on the part of the ruling class of the Soviet Union and the ruling classes of the Western countries which are Poland's creditors. The Polish developments could become the provocation for an unholy co-operation between power elites in different social systems and a reminder that a kind of warmed up cold war tactics can work for the ruling classes on both sides with the losers in the long run being the world's working people.

The ruling class of Poland has played upon national senti-ments in the course of the struggle by projecting an image of a new partition of Poland, a loss of our national independence if we displease the Soviets. This shameful and sorry argument, pitifully testifying to the true ideology of the ruling class, had one ominous possible meaning. It may very well be imagined that a new partition of Poland caused by an alliance of the world's ruling classes could occur without an open act of military-political aggression against the Polish state. In Yalta and afterwards Poland was sold over to Stalin as a result of many accidental factors—and it may well happen that new life could be breathed into this spirit of Yalta (1943) by deciding that Poland has to be effectively controlled by two centers if the world relation of spheres of influence is to be maintained. It may, for instance, be decided, that the Polish economy, the labor force and raw materials, have to be supervised by the capitalists who have been creditors of Poland in the 1970-1980 period, while this is secured by granting the Soviets a right to pacify the political structure and to run the country according to the Soviet idea of what political-military shape Poland should assume and stick to.

Ironically enough, this would turn the Polish working class once again into the avant-garde of the world working class. Needless to say, nobody is eager for this heroic role to become a reality. Historians may wonder whether Poland has not already fulfilled its historical role by indicating a new way towards socialization of our state systems—and whether this is not, after all, the basic argument in all theoretical disputes on the future of the socialist idea in the modern world.

The Polish working class has definitely demonstrated that the future of socialism—if by socialism we understand the reconstruction of society in a way which allows the labor providing masses, the working class, to achieve political, economic and cultural emancipation and to coordinate more directly the development of macrostructural organizations—is in the struggle to overcome the legacy of the state as the political superorganization of modern societies.

Ownership of the means of production, and rejection of "opiates of the people" are not enough to have a liberated working class and a socialist society. The element which matters most now in this world of nation-states and power blocks is the patient and bloodless reconstruction of political systems. I do not claim that the Polish experience is the only one possible but I think that this is an experience which cannot be mistaken for a partial cosmetic rearrangement of the pieces of the state jigsaw puzzle.

All liberation tactics of the present period—be it the cultural revolution of the students and the young, be it a women's liberation movement or a leftist political struggle against establishment vested interests—all these appear within Solidarity, and all of them rightly recognized the state owned by the ruling class as the major enemy of social development and the increase of social justice, political freedom, and economic democracy. The world is not the same after 1980—and the courage and perseverance of the Polish working class is a hopeful sign for the future. The future depends on us—and if it does not, it should. This was the spirit of the Polish workers, students, peasants, of all strata of the Polish society which understood that they form a class of state employees exploited by the class of state owners.

Thanks to them Poland does belong nowadays to the—none too numerous—group of nations which decide their fate by majority action. The author is proud of this position which does not blind him to the fact that this is not to be taken for granted and does not belong to any nation forever. Only daily struggle can secure it. It is this "normality" of which a worker spoke in the documentary "Workers 80" from Gdansk, where, asked what he thought Poland would be like, after the agreements have been signed, answered:

"I do not know...maybe it will be better...it will be a little more free...a little more just..." So be it.

Publisher's Postscript

Martial Law and Beyond

Starski's account of Solidarity's achievements and prospects hardly prepare the reader for the efficiency and apparent ease of the crackdown which the Polish government carried out in December 1981. However, rather than reflecting a unique naivete, Starski's refusal to be alarmed at the prospect of government action and his accompanying stress on the confusion, inefficiency, and imminent disintegration of the ruling class, seem to have been shared by the large majority of Poles.

The Heritage of Repression and Solidarity's Optimism

The history of Solidarity's predecessors, clearly recounted by Starski and certainly familiar to all Poles, shows that historically the government was repeatedly willing and able to crush resistance rather than allowing meaningful reforms, much less the revolutionary reorganization Solidarity's rank-and-file desired. Starski was clearly aware that the state employed delaying tactics to undermine Solidarity's legitimacy and defuse its militance through promises of negotiated concessions, all the while watching for a chance to reassert its own power.

Note: This postscript has been added to Starski's manuscript by the South End Press collective in lieu of his own conclusion. It is based on media reports and analyses, and especially on interviews with Starski and other Solidarity members, conducted in Poland in late 1981.

For example, he documents government responses to earlier instances of Polish resistance and uprising. In each case he shows the unwillingness of the authorities to bend, save under the most extreme pressure. At the same time, he shows that given the opportunity, they are quick to employ force to roll back reforms and destroy movements. He reports "strike, riot, heavy loss of life and damage to public buildings," with what result? A shuffling of executives holding official posts and some phoney promises of future consultations. The 1970-71 strikes were followed by a new level of "technocratic-party" alliances and nothing more. He describes how the government has attempted to undermine Solidarity's legitimacy through its control of the media, and to foist the blame for its own mismanagement of the economy on the actions of the workers. He argues that "the ruling class is never split with respect to the necessity of fighting Solidarity and maintaining the whole institutional framework of their class rule." The lesson the leaders took from the 1970 uprising was that "every committee building in every city must be provided with a reinforced helicopter landing on the roof. Another was the need for an exorbitant pay raise for the secret police and special anti-mob police, and a very considerable growth in size and equipment of these units as well." These are not lessons learned by people interested in social reform or hesitant to employ military force.

In the same vein, Starski describes how, in the early days of the Solidarity upsurge, "when Oszowski demanded a military takeover in the country and suppression of unrest, Jaruzelski replied that there were over 500 factories on strike at the moment and that the army would have to storm 500 fortified castles—and that no Polish officers would easily command fire in front of the Polish workers in those factories." This reply did not imply a willingness to alter the society to end the turmoil. Instead it suggested, even if only implicitly, a strategy of delay, of trying to get the workers out of the factories and to a lower level of readiness and organization, and of trying to solidify the allegiance of the army, until the moment when repression would be possible.

And indeed evidence suggests that the government followed just such policies even while Solidarity leaders hoped for successful negotiations and tempered the militance of their movement in part to achieve such successes, perhaps the exact reverse of what was necessary. This, at least, seems one reasonable interpretation of

Starski's evidence and as he himself explains: "although this [ruling class] monopoly [on political power] had been questioned and had been practically denied by the daily spontaneous activity of millions of workers, the ruling class hoped to sit this through and wait until the day when all the mechanisms of subjection and terror could be switched on again.... Therefore the ruling class was desperately trying to both prevent the police and secret police from any activity which might bring about another confrontation, and to preserve these forces for a better opportunity." Why then did Starski and Solidarity choose to minimize this obvious danger? Did their strategies expose them more than was necessary?

Solidarity's mass base had its roots in the mines and factories of Poland, and this base of workers desired, from the beginning, the removal of the Communist Party from its controlling position in Polish social life. But there was an immense impediment to pursuing its removal directly. The threat of Soviet invasion was real and keenly felt by almost everyone. Short of a revolution, precluded by this threat, the movement had to chart a course which would sustain its members' commitment, win a steady evolution of society in a desirable direction, and not provoke a Soviet intervention or, for that matter, a Polish confrontation. These needs converged to encourage the Polish workers to belittle the government. It seems likely that ridiculing the state was a way of enhancing Solidarity's prestige and morale, of encouraging themselves while their movement gained momentum, and of assuring themselves that they could make steady gains without provoking a military confrontation.

Solidarity's Factions

Within Solidarity's leadership there appear to have been a number of factions with different ideas of how to attain the above-mentioned aims. One of these groups expressed the desire of the mass base for immediate victory. Its spokespeople were always the recipients of the loudest cheers—reflecting the emotions of their audiences—and the fewest votes—reflecting the common sense of the same audiences.

There were two other factions actually vying for electoral leadership within Solidarity. The first, led by Walesa, focused on political democracy first and economic democracy second. It was disposed to negotiate with the party in good faith with the hope that meeting their demands for order would be rewarded by genuine efforts to reach viable agreements. The second, with Gwiazda as one of its leaders, thought economic reform had to be pursued in advance of political change. More important, it had less faith in the government's sincerity, feeling instead that it was the strength of the movement, not its willingness to discipline itself, that could win concessions from party negotiators. This faction mistrusted the negotiating dynamic fearing that it undermined democracy in the movement, and thus the base's activity and its morale.

These debates existed in the context of the universal awareness that the Soviets must not be provoked to enter in force. Almost all leaders felt that "not crossing the line" of the tolerance of the Soviet militarists was the key to avoiding intervention. Only a tiny minority felt that the Poles had already long since crossed such lines and that the really critical factor was the level of preparedness and strength of the likely opposition, and therefore the cost of such intervention: the same factors which might prevent the Polish leadership from attempting a crackdown.

Why December?

The movement was therefore wedged by a mass base eager for results and by a Soviet threat that tempered demands. Moderate leaders in Walesa's camp had the day, and their policies were often geared to appeasing the government and soliciting concessions, rather than building the movement and forcing concessions. For example, as far as we know there was no effort to organize within the military or police. As time and the government strategy of blaming Solidarity for economic dislocation began to take their toll, as morale began to drop in the face of the seeming impossibility of negotiated advance and the absence of on-going coordinated activism, and as the government finalized its preparations, the moment for repression came. The workers were no longer occupying five hundred factories, but in their last meetings before the crackdown they had exhibited a new desire to take the offensive again, especially with active strikes in which workers would seize and operate factories, and this could be expected to raise morale rapidly. The government could easily calculate that its chances for a successful crackdown might never again be as high.

Reports of what actually transpired in those days of struggle are still far from clear, reliable, or complete. There is no way to know the scale of the resistance, nor whether its limits were a function of workers giving in to despair or strategically waiting to fight on better terms. We don't know whether workers are now resigned, a new conformity having replaced the recent mood of rebellion, or militarily disorganized but still committed and eager to revive their movement at the first real opportunity.

Which Way Poland?

Partly because of this unavoidable ignorance it is far from clear what the future holds for Poland, but two basic scenarios suggest themselves. Retrenchment, if the workers are resigned, or renewal, if the movement is only temporarily stalled.

In the first case the government will eventually relax its grip somewhat, there will be purges within the party, a restructuring of the trade union apparatus and, of course, efforts to resurrect the failing economy. Beyond these, however, there may be more significant transformations. On numerous occasions Starski alludes to the fact that the various factions of the ruling elite in Poland have long since learned that workers' upsurges provide a dangerous but opportune moment for pushing their own agendas against those of other more entrenched factions. It is the resolution of such intra-elite struggles that may bring interesting reforms, even in the retrenchment scenario.

In Stalinist bureaucracies, a narrow politically identified elite benefits while everyone else suffers under a blanket of stultifying conformity and repressive intolerance. Though the most extreme forms of Stalinism passed with their creator, many leading bureaucrats in Eastern bloc countries still see society through a political prism which reveals themselves, and only themselves, as the rightful rulers of their society. In Western media parlance, these are the "hardliners." But in fact there is usually a split in this elite, some being partial to outright coercion and police repression, and others preferring more subtle methods of cooptation and "restrained repression." Beyond these groups, however, there is another faction which often takes a non-Stalinist view of things that allows for broader representation in elite decision-making. The primary roots of this faction probably lie outside the party, though there are certainly representatives within as well. These managers, local planners, and intellectual workers of various kinds would like a greater share of society's governing responsibilities and prerogatives for themselves. They favor a liberalization that would allow them greater access to culture, intellectual freedom, and decison-making power. One of the most remarkable facets of Starski's account is the light it sheds on the tactical commonalities and strategic differences between representatives of these factions. Most important, neither the Stalinist nor anti-Stalinist factions are interested in workers' claims to manage their own lives at work and in their communities, though they are quite happy to exploit the chaotic circumstances sometimes produced by workers' movements for their own narrow benefit.

In the Polish retrenchment scenario—should it occur—we would likely find three factions struggling for power. The more repressive Stalinists, of whom Oszowski seems to be a representative, will seek a return to a tight reign of political supervision of all sides of Polish life. Their main strength will lie in the inner core of the Communist Party itself. Another faction, perhaps associated with Jaruzelski, and also having its roots largely within the party, will be a bit more liberal, offering clemency to many Solidarity activists, and seeking more enlightened means to restore party dominance. The last and perhaps most interesting faction, for which Rakowski seems to be the chief party spokesperson, may have its primary roots among academics, professionals, managers, engineers, scholars, and the like: people whose identities are not a function of their party affiliation so much as their economic role. It will seek to restore the party, but primarily it will be concerned to decentralize economic decision-making in the service of local managers and technocrats, and to liberalize censorship and the arts and culture to the benefit of all intellectuals. This is the faction which will propose creative reforms designed to create a kind of pluralism after the darkness of martial law. They may, for example, propose a reestablishment of Solidarity, perhaps even with the right to strike, though other limits to its overall organizing capacity and independence will be imposed. Thus, if this last faction does carry the day, some trickle down effects will benefit workers as well. But no faction will worry about self-management in the workplace or the econommy as a whole, or about the democratization of political and social life—Solidarity's principal concerns.

Retrenchment assumes that the workers have surrendered and accepted the impossibility of their dreams, that fatalism and the hegemony of the ruling class have reasserted themselves, and that it will take considerable time before the coercive and depressing conditions the workers are forced to endure impel them to try again. This may not be the case: the Polish workers may have been caught unprepared, and their movement may be temporarily derailed. For the moment, the workers may be demoralized. But perhaps the stories of dockers divided into two teams such that the first loads cargos and the second simultaneously unloads them; of workers in tractor factories who in two weeks manage to produce only two tractors; or of tool workers who make parts which don't fit one another, are indicative of an underlying confidence and will to resist. What then?

The main short-term problem of the Polish economy is not that workers are not or were not working, but that the Poles have a huge debt, little credit for international trade, and thus a serious shortage of supplies and spare parts which they need to get from outside. Naturally this situation is aggravated by strikes, but strikes also have the potential to lead to structural economic changes that might address the difficult problem of shortages. If Polish workers have been caught off guard but have not lost sight of their aims or confidence in their ultimate ability to create a new kind of democratic socialist society—however vague and as yet incompletely formed their image of that new society might be—"retrenchment" will not be the label to apply to the process that will unfold in coming months and years. Rather, the movement will be born anew, to again apply pressure, this time with fewer misconceptions about the motives and aims of state leaders.

In the retrenchment scenario it will be some years before the workers' grievances and militance resurface, just as they did some years after each of the other historic "defeats." But in the "left scenario" that resurfacing must already be underway. In this case, the slogan, "The winter was yours, the spring shall be ours," may prove prophetic and not merely dramatic.

When we wonder what kind of victory the Polish or other workers' movements in Eastern bloc countries could possibly have, we come up against a difficult problem. When Poles are free to express their feelings about their situation openly, that is, when daily habits and party hegemony are effectively challenged, the result is an outpouring of militant indignation at their plight. They view their society as a "huge asylum" in which a moribund and intellectually defunct party administers by guile, deceit, and coercion. They decry their society's "monotony" and "lack of freedom," and especially the corruption of their leaders. Though Solidarity was never able to clearly enunciate or even evolve all its goals, some emerged with great force and popular support. The Polish people wanted real democracy in political life: an end to censorship, free elections, a decentralization of political power, and an end to police repression. They wanted economic self-management as well as an improved standard of living. During the months leading up to the Polish crackdown, there were meetings and discussions throughout Poland to try and develop a clear picture of exactly what "self-management" might look like in schools, factories, and all of society's other institutions. Solidarity leaders had begun to discuss the kinds of social ties that would have to prevail between economic units if planning was to be truly social and democratic.

The fullest expression of the Polish people's desires can only be accomplished by the creation of a truly democratic socialist framework of decision-making in the polity and economy of their society. Short of this, however, one could imagine a sequence of reforms which might be won by a continually assertive workers' movement like Solidarity—provided such a movement was strong enough to ward off repression and prevent major crackdowns, and yet disciplined enough to settle for a process of steady improvement rather than a no-win showdown with Soviet power. This would not be an easy task, to keep the cost of repression high enough to discourage state action, and yet to continue to win reforms and advances sufficiently important to elicit high morale and commitment from the base of activists—all while keeping democracy in the movement intact. Yet this hopeful scenario could presumably still occur in Poland—a scenario with historic implications for other countries of Eastern Europe, for the Soviet Union, and for the West as well—in spite of its present derailment by martial law. Whether the revolutionary movement will get back on track or not, we can only guess.

Conclusions

By enacting martial law the Polish regime sought to deflate the movement of workers' opposition that threatened its prerogatives and ultimately even its existence. Of course Polish party leaders preferred to succeed without Russian intervention, partially out of a desire to save lives, primarily out of a desire to maintain their own control over the situation. As Starski recounts, the Polish regime has employed violence again and again in response to worker activism. The December martial law crackdown was well planned; while it stalled at the bargaining table to demoralize Solidarity's mass base, the state was preparing the ultimate arrest of its negotiating partners. This "socialist" government, which rules in the name of the workers, could not allow their representatives to remain at liberty, much less to participate in the direction of society.

"Existing socialism," whatever else it may be, is obviously not a system where workers rule the economy with the purpose of advancing social fulfillment. If socialism means workers controlling their own lives and the distribution of the fruits of their labors, and it must at least mean that, then Starski's account shows that Poland is not a socialist country and never has been. The recent imposition of martial law makes clear (once again) that even in the most liberal of the "existing socialist" societies there is a ruling elite that is more than willing to defend its position, power, and advantages, by force when necessary. The claim of these people to be "socialists" is obviously pure propaganda.

The real socialists in Poland are in jail and hiding out; they are not in the Politbureau. It is possible for Western leftists to be responsible to their values and to combat the real evils of "anti-communism" while simultaneously stating the truth about the communist regimes of the East. Indeed, one can't ignore the truth about these regimes and simultaneously combat anti-communism effectively. For if the only thing that leftists have to offer is more of what the Polish workers are fighting against, anti-leftism under any label is a reasonable response of clear-thinking people. To really combat anti-communism and anti-leftism, it is essential that leftists are not only honest about the realities of "existing socialism" but that they distinguish it clearly from any socialist vision which they propose as an alternative.

Starski's book is a major contribution to our understanding of Solidarity, Polish society, and "existing socialism" as a general system. Hopefully readers will study it to learn not only about the East, but also about dynamics of social change and political stuggle as they might be relevant to our own societies. Hopefully too the processes at the fulcrum of change in Poland will prove resilient and the movement for workers' self-management will reemerge stronger and more coherent than ever.